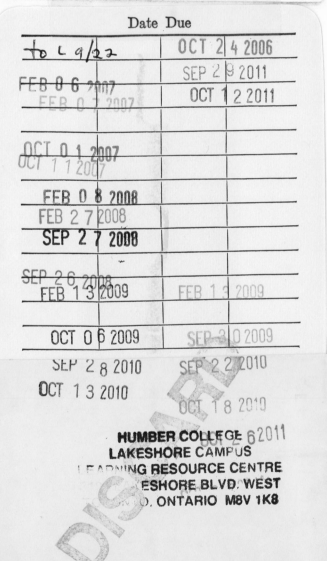

Date Due

to L 9/22	OCT 2 4 2006
FEB 0 6 2007	SEP 2 9 2011
FEB 0 7 2007	OCT 1 2 2011
OCT 0 1 2007	
OCT 1 1 2007	
FEB 0 8 2008	
FEB 2 7 2008	
SEP 2 7 2008	
SEP 2 6 2008	
FEB 1 3 2009	FEB 1 3 2009
OCT 0 6 2009	SEP 3 0 2009
SEP 2 8 2010	SEP 2 2 2010
OCT 1 3 2010	OCT 1 8 2010

Fac-simile of the twenty-eighth page of the *Biblia Pauperum*, representing, with the text from the Old Testament, David prevailing over Goliath, and Christ delivering the souls of the patriarchs and prophets from limbo. [*Frontispiece*.

THE BOOK:

ITS

𝔓rinters, 𝔍llustrators, and 𝔅inders,

FROM

GUTENBERG TO THE PRESENT TIME.

BY

HENRI BOUCHOT,

Of the National Library, Paris.

WITH A TREATISE ON THE

𝔄rt of 𝔆ollecting and 𝔇escribing 𝔆arly 𝔓rinted 𝔅ooks,

AND A

LATIN-ENGLISH AND ENGLISH-LATIN TOPOGRAPHICAL INDEX OF THE
EARLIEST PRINTING PLACES.

EDITED BY H. GREVEL.

CONTAINING ONE HUNDRED AND SEVENTY-TWO FAC-SIMILES
OF EARLY TYPOGRAPHY, BOOK-ILLUSTRATIONS, PRINTERS' MARKS, BINDINGS, NUMEROUS BORDERS,
INITIALS, HEAD AND TAIL PIECES, AND A FRONTISPIECE.

𝔏ondon :

H. GREVEL & CO.,

33, KING STREET, COVENT GARDEN, W.C.

1890.

Republished by Gale Research Company, Book Tower, Detroit, 1971

Library of Congress Catalog Card Number 77-155741

PREFACE.

HE first edition of M. Henri Bouchot's fascinating volume, *Le Livre*, translated and enlarged by Mr. E. C. Bigmore, under the title of *The Printed Book*, having become exhausted, I have availed myself of the opportunity to subject the work to a careful revision.

The extensive additions, which include sixty-five new illustrations, and the entirely fresh matters treated of in this edition, make it practically a new work, while under the process it has grown to nearly double its original size.

Considering the wide range of the subject, this work can claim to be no more than a summary and condensed survey of the history of *The Book*, and of the arts involved in its production. At the same time, it may be found to prove a useful compendium of the thousands of unknown and forgotten essays that have been published on the history of *The Book*, and which M. Bouchot has so skilfully contrived to condense into a single volume.

The technical aspect of the subject has not been forgotten either, and is dealt with in separate chapters, which have had the advantage of being revised by specialists in the several subjects. This has been particularly the case with the chapters on Types and on Binding, which have received a careful treatment; although, considering the importance of each subject, a whole volume might hardly have been sufficient to treat these topics exhaustively. A special chapter, based on a treatise by M. A. Einsle, of Vienna, has also been added, on the art of collecting and describing early printed books. This will doubtless be welcomed by many students who have no access to such recondite information. For the same reason the bibliographer will be glad to have the appended Topographical Index, by which he will be enabled at once to discover the English names of the towns on the early Latin titles.

H. G.

CONTENTS.

CHAPTER I

14 . . TO 1462.

PAGE

Origin of the Book—Engravers in relief—The St. Christopher of 1423—Origin of the Xylographs—The Xylographs, *Donatus* and *Speculum*—The Laurent Coster legend—From block books to movable characters—John Gensfleisch, called Gutenberg—The Strasburg trial—Gutenberg at Mayence—Fust and Schoeffer—The letters of indulgence—The Bible—The Catholicon—The Mayence Bible—Causes of the dispersion of the first Mayence printers—General considerations . I

CHAPTER II.

1462 TO 1500.

The Book and the printers of the second generation—The German workmen dispersed through Europe—Caxton and the introduction of printing into England—Nicholas Jensen and his supposed mission to Mayence—The first printing in Paris; William Fichet and John Heinlein—The first French printers; their installation at the Sorbonne and their publications—The movement in France—The illustration of the Book commenced in Italy—The Book in Italy; engraving in relief and metal plates—The Book in Germany: Cologne, Nuremberg, Basle—The Book in the Low Countries—French schools of ornament of the Book; Books of Hours; booksellers at the end of the fifteenth century—Literary taste in titles in France at the end of the fifteenth century—Printers' and booksellers' marks—The appearance of the portrait in the Book 42

CHAPTER III.

1500 TO 1600.

French epics and the Renaissance—Venice and Aldus Manutius—Italian illustrators —The Germans: *Theuerdanck*, Schäufelein—The Book in other countries—

PAGE

French books at the beginning of the century, before the accession of Francis I. —English printers and their work—Engraved plates in English books—Geoffroy Tory and his works—Francis I. and the Book—Robert Estienne—Lyons a centre of bookselling: Holbein's *Dances of Death*—School of Basle—Alciati's emblems and the illustrated books of the middle of the century—The school of Fontainebleau and its influence—Solomon Bernard—Cornelis de la Haye and the *Promptuaire* —Jean Cousin—Copperplate engraving and metal plates—Woériot—The portrait in the book of the sixteenth century—How a book was illustrated on wood at the end of the century—Influence of Plantin on the Book; his school of engravers— General considerations—Progress in England—Coverdale's Bible 107

CHAPTER IV.

1600 TO 1700.

Tendencies of the regency of Marie de Medici—Thomas de Leu and Leonard Gaultier —J. Picart and Claude Mellan—Lyons and J. de Fornazeris—The Book at the beginning of the seventeenth century in Germany, Italy, England, and Holland— Crispin Pass in France—The Elzevirs and Enschedé and their work in Holland— Sebastian Cramoisy and the Imprimerie Royale—Illustration under Callot, Della Bella, and Abraham Bosse—The publishers and the Hotel de Rambouillet—The reign of Louis XIV., Antoine Vitré syndic at his accession—His works and mortifications; the Polyglot Bible of Le Jay—Art and illustrators of the grand century—Sébastien Leclerc, Lepautre, and Chauveau—Leclerc preparing the illustration and decoration of the Book for the eighteenth century . . . 161

CHAPTER V.

THE BOOK IN THE EIGHTEENTH CENTURY.

The Regency—Publishers at the beginning of the eighteenth century—Illustrators in France ; Gillot—The school of Watteau and Boucher—Cars—The younger Cochin; his principal works in vignettes—French art in England; Gravelot— Eisen—Choffard—The *Baisers* of Dorat ; the *Contes* of Lafontaine—The publisher Cazin and the special literature of the eighteenth century—The younger Moreau and his illustrations—The Revolution—The school of David—Duplessi- Bertaux — The Book in Germany; Chodowiecki — In England; Boydell and French artists—Caslon and Baskerville—English books with illustrations—Wood engraving in the eighteenth century ; the Papillons—Printing offices in the eighteenth century 194

CONTENTS.

CHAPTER VI.

THE BOOK IN THE NINETEENTH CENTURY.

PAGE

The Didots and their improvements—The folio Racine—The school of Didot—Fine
publications in England and Germany—Literature and art of the Restoration—
Romanticism—Wood engraving—Bewick's pupils, Clennell, etc.—The illustrators
of romances—The generation of 1840—The Book in our days in Europe and
America 230

TYPE, PRESSES, AND PAPER 250

BOOKBINDING.

Early bindings; superiority of English work—Panel-stamps invented in the Low
Countries—The binding of the first printed books—French binding in the time
of Louis XII.—Influence of German and Netherlandish binders on the art in other
countries—Italian bindings—Aldus—Maioli—Grolier—Francis I.—Henry II. and
Diana of Poitiers—Catherine de Medici—Henry III.—The Eves—The "fanfares"
—Louis XIII.—Le Gascon—Florimond Badier—Louis XIV.—Morocco leathers—
Cramoisy—The bindings of the time of Louis XIV.—The Regency—Pasdeloup—
The Deromes—Dubuisson—Thouvenin—Lesné—The nineteenth century—English
binders—Roger Payne—Francis Bedford—Blocking 262

LIBRARIES 307

THE ART OF DESCRIBING AND CATALOGUING INCUNABULA 322

THE METHOD OF COLLECTING THEM 352

LATIN-ENGLISH AND ENGLISH-LATIN TOPOGRAPHICAL INDEX 367

GENERAL INDEX 375

LIST OF ILLUSTRATIONS.

PAGE

1. The Fool; Playing Card of Taroc (fifteenth century) 3
2. St. Christopher (1423) 4
3. Xylographic Plate, cut in Flanders (1440), representing Jesus after the flagellation . 5
4. Xylographic Plate, representing St. John. *Ca.* 1440. With a text of the commandments of the Church 6
5. Part of a *Donatus* taken from a xylograph, the original of which is preserved in the Bibliotheque Nationale 7
6. Fac-simile of page 5 of the first edition of the *Ars Moriendi* 11
7. Xylographic figure from the *Ars Moriendi*, copied in reverse in the *Art au Morier* . 12
8. Figure of the school of Martin Schongauer, taken from the *Rationarium Evangelistarum* of 1505, and copied from the corresponding plate of the *Ars Memorandi* . . 13
9. Portrait of Gutenberg, from an engraving of the sixteenth century 15
10. Letters of indulgence, from the so-called edition of thirty-one lines, printed at Mayence in the course of 1454 21
11. Fragment of the Gutenberg Bible, printed in two columns. Beginning of the text in the second column; original size 23
12. Fac-simile of the Psalter, 1459 31
13. Colophon of the *Catholicon*, supposed to have been printed by Gutenberg in 1460 . 33
14. Colophon of the Bible printed in 1462 by Fust and Schoeffer, which is the first dated Bible 35
15. Imprint of Arnold Ther Hoernen, printer, of Mayence 45
16. Mark of Colard Mansion 46
17. Specimen of Caxton's type, from the *Canterbury Tales*, 1476 46
18. Woodcut from Caxton's *Game and Playe of the Chesse* 47
19. The Knight, a woodcut from Caxton's *Game and Playe of the Chesse* . . . 48
20. Music, a woodcut from Caxton's *Mirrour of the World* 49
21. William Caxton, from Rev. J. Lewis's *Life* 50
22. Fyshing with an Angle 51
23. Mark of Wynkyn de Worde 52
24. Mark of Richard Pynson 53
25. Imprint of Nicholas Jenson to a *Justinian*, printed in 1470 at Venice . . . 55
26. *Letters* of Gasparin of Bergamo. First page of the first book printed at Paris, in 1470 58
27. Colophon in distichs in the *Letters* of Gasparin of Bergamo, first book printed at Paris, at the office of the Sorbonne 59

PAGE

28. *Rhetorique* of Fichet, printed at Paris in 1471 60
29. Mark of Guerbin, printer at Geneva, 1482 63
30. Wood engraving in Matteo Pasti, for Valturius' *De Re Militari* (Verona : 1472) . . 64
31. Title-page of the *Calendario*, first ornamental title known 66
32. Engraving on metal by Baccio Baldini for *El Monte Santo di Dio*, in 1477 . . . 68
33. Metal engraving by Baccio Baldini from the *Dante* of 1481 69
34. Plate from the *Hypnerotomachia Poliphili*, printed by Aldus Manutius, in 1499 . . 71
35. The planet Mercury and the City of Rome, engraving from the *Divina Comedia* (Venice, 1491) 72
36. Plate from Bonino de Bonini's *Dante*, at Brescia, in 1487 . · 73
37. The creation of woman, plate from the *Schatzbehalter*, engraved after Michael Wohlgemuth 74
38. The daughter of Jephthah, plate taken from the *Schatzbehalter*, engraved after Michael Wohlgemuth 76
39. Title of the *Nuremberg Chronicle*, printed by A. Koberger, 1493. Fol. . . . 77
40. Title of the *Apocalypse*, by Albert Dürer, printed in 1498 78
41. Title of Sebastian Brandt's *Ship of Fools*, printed in 1497 at Basle, by Bergman de Olpe 79
42. The Bibliomaniac. Engraving from the *Ship of Fools* 80
43. A medical man of the fifteenth century, from *La Mer des Histoires* 84
44. Mark of Philip Pigouchet, French printer and wood engraver of the fifteenth century 85
45. Mark of Jean Dupré, printer at Lyons 86
46. Mark of Simon Vostre, printer at Paris, 1501 87
47-49. Ornaments of Simon Vostre 87
50. Border in four separate blocks in the *Heures à l'Usaige de Rome*, by Pigouchet, for Simon Vostre, in 1488 88
51. Plate copied from Schongauer's *Carrying of the Cross*, taken from the *Heures* of Simon Vostre 89
52. The Death of the Virgin, plate taken from the *Heures* of Simon Vostre, printed in 1488 90
53. Mark of Antoine Vérard, printer at Paris, 1498 91
54. Border of the *Grandes Heures* of Antony Vérard 93
55. Plate from the *Tristan* published by Antoine Vérard 94
56. Page of the *Grandes Heures* of Antoine Vérard : Paris, fifteenth century . . . 95
57. Typographical mark of Thielman Kerver 97
58. Plate from a *Book of Hours* of Simon Vostre, representing the Massacre of the Innocents 98
59. *Dance of Death*, said to be by Vérard. The Pope and the Emperor 99
60. *Dance of Death* of Guyot Marchant in 1486. The Pope and the Emperor . . . 101·
61. Mark of Guy Marchant, printer at Paris, 1485 102
62. Frontispiece to Terence, published by Treschel at Lyons in 1493. The author writing his book 104
63. Mark of Treschel, printer at Lyons, 1489 105
64. The anchor and dolphin, mark of Aldus Manutius, after the original in the *Terze Rime* of 1520 109
65. Aldus Manutius 111
66. Mark of Lucantonio Giunta, of Venice 112
67. Title of the *Theuerdanck* 114

PAGE

68. Plate taken from the *Theuerdanck*, representing Maximilian and Mary of Burgundy . 115

69. Portrait of Queen Elizabeth from the *Book of Christian Praiers*, printed by John Day, 1578 117

70. Woodcut from Coverdale's Bible, 1535. Cain killing Abel 118

71. Woodcut by Hans Holbein from Cranmer's *Catechism*, 1548 120

72. Mark of Philippe le Noir, printer at Paris, 1536 123

73. Vignette taken from the *Illustrations de la Gaule et Singularitez de Troye*. Queen Anne of Brittany as Juno 124

74. Mark of François Juste, printer at Lyons, 1526 125

75. Mark of Guillaume Eustace, 1517, binder and bookseller at Paris . . . 126

76. Title of the *Entrée d'Eléonore d'Autriche à Paris*, by Guillaume Bochetel . . . 127

77. Mark of Geoffroy Tory, printer at Paris, 1529 128

78. Full page of the *Heures* of Simon de Colines, by Tory 129

79. *Heures* of Geoffroy Tory. The Circumcision 130

80. Mark of Simon de Colines, printer at Paris, 1527 131

81. *Heures* of Simon de Colines, with the mark of the Cross of Lorraine . . . 132

82. Emblematical letter Y, taken from the *Champfleury* of Geoffroy Tory . . . 133

83. Macault reading to Francis I. his translation of Diodorus Siculus. Wood engraving attributed to Tory 135

84. Robert Estienne, after the engraving in the *Chronologie Collée* 137

85. Mark of Robert Estienne, printer at Paris, 1541 138

86. Mark of François Estienne, printer at Paris, 1538 139

87. Printing office of Josse Badius of the commencement of the sixteenth century . . 140

88. Portrait of Nicholas Bourbon. Wood engraving of the commencement of the sixteenth century 141

89. King and Death. Vignette from the *Dance of Death* by Holbein 142

90. Page of the *Metamorphoses* of Ovid, by Petit Bernard. Edition of 1564 . . 144

91. Portraits of Madeleine, Queen of Scotland, and of Marguerite, Duchess of Savoy, after the originals of Cornelius of Lyons 146

92. Portraits of Francis, Dauphin, and of Charles, Duke of Angoulême, after the originals of Cornelius of Lyons 146

93. Captain of foot, from the *Entrée de Henri II. à Lyon*, 1549 147

94. Title of Jean Cousin's *Livre de Portraiture*, published in 1593 by Le Clerc . . 149

95. Engraving by P. Woériot for Georgette de Montenay's *Emblèmes* . . . 152

96. Portrait of Christopher Plantin, printer of Antwerp 155

97. Plantin's Mark 156

98. Frontispiece of a book from Plantin's printing office 159

99. Mark of Etienne Dolet, printer at Lyons, 1542 160

100. Letter engraved by A. Bosse 161

101. Title of the *Métanéalogie*, engraved by Leonard Gaultier . . . , . 163

102. Title engraved by Claude Mellan for Urban VIII.'s *Poesies*, printed at the Royal Printing House, in 1642 167

103. Title of Pluvinel's *Manège Royal*, engraved by Crispin Pass in 1624 . . . 171

104. Title of the *Imitation* of the Elzevirs 172

105. Mark of Bonaventure and Abraham Elzevir, printers at Leyden, 1620 . . . 173

106. Plate taken from the *Lumière du Cloistre*. Copperplate by Callot . . . 176

PAGE

107. Title of the *Manière Universelle*, by Desargues, in 1643, by Abraham Bosse. . . 178
108. Print by Abraham Bosse, representing the booksellers of the Palace under Louis XIII. 179
109. Frontispiece of the Dictionnaire de l'Academie, 1st edition 1694 183
110. Antoine Vitré, printer to the King, by Ph. de Champagne 184
111. Tailpiece of Sébastien Leclerc for the *Promenade de St. Germain* . . . 186
112. Small figure of Sébastien Leclerc for Richesource's pamphlet 188
113. Frontispiece by C. Le Brun, for the first edition of Racine, 1676 189
114. Letter by Cochin for the *Mémoires d'Artillerie* of Suvirey de St. Remy . . . 194
115. Vignette by Gillot for the *Chien et le Chat*, fable by Houdart de la Motte, in 1719 . 197
116. Vignette for *Daphnis et Chloe* by Cochin, for Coustelier's edition 201
117. Title-page engraved by Fessard after Cochin for the works of Madame Deshoulières, 1747 203
118. Vignette taken from P. Corneille's *Théâtre*, by Gravelot 204
119. Border designed by Choffard, in 1758 205
120. Frontispiece by Eisen for the *Voyage* by l'Abbé de la Porte, 1751 206
121. Vignette by Eisen for the *Quiproquo* in the *Contes* of Lafontaine, in the edition of the *Fermiers Généraux* 208
122. Card of the publisher Prault, uncle by marriage of Moreau le Jeune 210
123. Tailpiece from the *Médecin malgré Lui*, by Moreau le Jeune 211
124. Vignette of the *Pardon Obtenu*, designed by Moreau le Jeune, for Laborde's *Chansons*, in 1773 213
125. Title designed by Moreau le Jeune in 1769 for the publisher Prault 215
126. Frontispiece of the *Glossarium* of Du Dange, Paris, Osmont, 1733 217
127. Illustration by Stothard, from one of the *Keepsakes* 220
128. Illustration by Blake, from Blair's *Grave* 221
129. Tailpiece engraved on wood by Jean Baptiste Papillon (before 1766) 222
130. Experiment in engraving in relief by Moreau le Jeune for Renouard's edition of La Fontaine's *Fables* 224
131. Portrait of Thomas Bewick 225
132. Wood block by Bewick, from his *Fables*, 1818. The fox and the goat . . . 226
133. Wood block from Bewick's *British Birds*. The common duck 227
134. Benjamin Franklin, by C. N. Cochin 228
135. M. Ambroise Firmin Didot 233
136. Wood engraving by Clennell after West, for the diploma of the Highland Society . 235
137. Vignette by Devéria for the *Fiancé de la Tombe* 237
138. Vignette by Jean Gigoux for *Gil Blas* 239
139. Vignette by Daumier for the *Cholera à Paris* 241
140. Vignette by Gavarni for *Paris Marié* 242
141. Balzac writing his *Contes Drôlatiques*. Vignette by Gustave Doré . . . 243
142. Illustration by Cruikshank, from *Three Courses and a Dessert*, by Clarke . . 244
143. Wood engraving by Clennell after Stothard, for Rogers's *Poems*, 1812 . . . 245
144. Illustration by Ludwig Richter, from Bechstein's *Märchenbuch* 247
145. Type-founder in the middle of the sixteenth century. Engraving by Jost Amman . 252
146. Mark of Jodocus Badius of Asch. Engraving *à la croix de Lorraine* . . . 258
147. Workman engaged on the vat with the wire frame. Engraving by Jost Amman . 259
148. Balance used by Jenson, at Venice 261

PAGE

149. Bookbinder's shop in the sixteenth century. Engraving by Jost Amman . . . 264

150. Cover of the *Evangeliarium* of Noyon, made of skin, copper, and horn, with reliquaries 265

151. Cover of a book in enamelled goldsmith work of Limoges, fifteenth century, representing Merlin l'Enchanteur transformed into a scholar 266

152. Bibliomaniac of the *Ship of Fools* 267

153. Binding in gold, ornamented with precious stones, having been used for a cover of an *Evangeliarium* of the eleventh century (Louvre) 269

154. Binding for Louis XII. Collection of M. Dutuit, of Rouen 271

155. Arms of the University of Oxford, in which a bound book appears 273

156. Cover of an old Koran 275

157. The fourth part of a binding for Thomas Maioli (sixteenth century) 275

158. Binding for Grolier in the collection of M. Dutuit 279

159. Binding for Francis I., with the arms of France and the Salamander 280

160. Mark of Guyot Marchant, printer and bookbinder. He published the *Danse Macabre* of 1485 281

161. Binding for Henry II., with the " H " and crescents 282

162. Binding for Henry II. (Mazarin Library) 283

163. Italian binding for Catherine de Medici, with the initials "C. C." 285

164. Binding with the arms of Mansfeldt, with lined scroll work, from the Didot collection 287

165. Part of a binding having belonged to Jacques de Thou (sixteenth century). . . 289

166. Mark of Nicholas Eve, binder of Henry III. and Henry IV. 290

167. Sixteenth century binding, called *à la fanfare*. In the Dutuit collection . . . 291

168. Le Gascon binding 293

169. Binding executed by Le Gascon for the MS. of Lafontaine's *Adonis*, having belonged to Fouquet (seventeenth century) 295

170. Le Gascon binding for Cardinal Mazarin 297

171. Mosaic binding of the eighteenth century for the *Spaccio de la Bestia Trionfante* . . 299

172. Mosaic binding of the eighteenth century with the arms of the Regent. M. Morgand's collection 301

CHAPTER I.

14 . . TO 1462.

Origin of the Book—Engravers in relief—The St. Christopher of 1423—Origin of the Xylographs — The Xylographs, *Donatus* and *Speculum*—The Laurent Coster legend — From block books to movable characters — John Gensfleisch, called Gutenberg —The Strasburg trial—Gutenberg at Mayence— Fust and Schoeffer—The letters of indulgence— The Bible—The Catholicon—The Mayence Bible — Causes of the dispersion of the first Mayence printers—General considerations.

THE Book has ever been the most faithful reflection of the period in which it was written and illustrated. Simple and genuine from the beginning, embellished

with crude illustrations, it assumed in the sixteenth century the grand airs of the Renaissance, gay or serious according to requirements, decked in what were then called *histoyres*, or wonderful engravings, daintily printed either in Gothic, Roman, or choice Italic characters. At the close of the fifteenth century it had partly abandoned *wood* for *metal* or line engravings, heightening its mysticism or its satire at the whim of passing politics and religious wranglings. Then, under the influence of the painters and courtiers of the *Grand Monarque*, it becomes completely transformed, donning the perruque, so to speak, indulging in allegory and conventionalities, pompous and showy, and continuing the coquetries of the regency, the pastorals and insipidities of the following reigns, until at last it suddenly assumes with the heroes of the Revolution the airs of classic art. Thus the Book, the child of Painting, has always been as closely connected with the manners of our forefathers as that art itself. The artist submits more than he thinks to the tendency of his surroundings ; and if he at times impresses his mark, it is because he has more or less received his first influence from others.

The fashion of emblematic representation in the sixteenth century placed under the portrait of Gaston de Foix a figure of a fast-growing plant, ripe as soon as it was in bud, with the Latin inscription, " Nascendo maturus." The Book deserves the same device ; from its first day up to now it is a marvel of simplicity and harmony. There was hardly any groping in the dark, except with those experiments which preceded the discovery of printing ; it may be said that from the moment Gutenberg conceived the idea of separating the characters, of arranging the words in the form, of inking them, and of taking a proof on paper, the Book was perfect. At best we see in later times some modifications of detail, but the art of printing was mature, mature from its birth.

But before arriving at what appears to us to-day so simple, namely, the movable type placed side by side, forming sentences, many years passed. It is certain that long before Gutenberg

Fig. I.—The Fool: Playing Card of Taroc (fifteenth century).

a means was found of cutting wood and metal in relief, and reproducing by pressure the image traced. Signs-manual and seals were a kind of printing, inasmuch as the relief of their engraving is impressed upon some sheet by the hand. But between this simple fact and the uncritical histories of certain special writers, attributing the invention of engraving to the fourteenth century, there is all the distance of historical facts and legends. Remembering that the numerous guilds of *tailleurs d'images*, or sculptors in relief, had in the Middle Ages the specialty of carving ivories and of placing effigies on tombs, it can be admitted, without much stretch of imagination, that these people one day found a means of multiplying the sketches of a figure often asked for, by modelling its contour in bold lines in relief on ivory or wood, and afterwards taking a reproduction

Fig. 2.—St. Christopher (1423).

on paper or parchment by some kind of pressure. When and where was this discovery produced? We cannot possibly say; but it is certain that playing cards (Fig. 1) were produced by this means, and that from the year 1423 popular figures were cut in wood, as we know from the St. Christopher of that date belonging to Lord Spencer.

It is not our task to discuss this question at length, nor to decide if at first these reliefs were obtained on wood or metal.

One thing is certain, that the single leaf with a figure printed upon it preceded the xylographic book, in which text and illustration were cut in the same block. This latter process did not appear much before the second quarter of the fifteenth

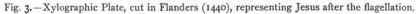

Fig. 3.—Xylographic Plate, cut in Flanders (1440), representing Jesus after the flagellation.

century, and it was employed principally for popular works, the taste for which was then universal. The engraving was probably a kind of imposition, being palmed off as a manuscript; the vignettes were often covered with brilliant colours and glittering gold, and the whole sold for something better.

The first attempts at these little figures in relief, invented
by the image-makers and diffused by the makers of playing

Fig. 4.—Xylographic Plate, representing St. John. *Ca.* 1440. With
a text of the commandments of the Church.

cards, were but indifferent. The drawing and the cutting were
equally unskilful, as we may convince ourselves from the fac-
similes given by M. H. Delaborde in his *Histoire de la Gravure.*

An attempt had, however, been made to put some text at the foot of the St. Christopher of 1423, and the idea of giving more importance to the text must have dawned upon many booksellers. At the mercy of the writers who fleeced them,

Fig. 5.—Part of a *Donatus* taken from a xylograph, the original of which is preserved in the Bibliotheque Nationale.

obliged to recoup themselves by charging exaggerated prices for the most ordinary books, they proposed to take advantage of the engraving in order to obtain on better terms the technical work needed for their trade. At the epoch of the St. Christopher, in 1423, several works were in demand in the universities, the schools, and with the public.   Among the first of these were the Latin Syntax of Ælius Donatus on the eight parts of speech, a kind of grammar for the use of young students, and also the famous *Speculum*, a collection of precepts addressed to the faithful, which were copied and recopied without satisfying the demand.

To find a means of multiplying these treatises at little cost was a fortune to the inventor.   It is to be supposed that many artisans of the time made an attempt ; and without doubt it was less the booksellers themselves, mostly mere dealers as they were, than the image cutters and sculptors who were tempted to the adventure.   But none had yet been so bold as to cut in relief a series of blocks with engravings and text destined to compose a complete work.   That point was reached very quickly when some legend was engraved at the foot of a vignette, and it may be thought that the *Donatus* was the most ancient of books so obtained among the " Incunabula," as we now call them, a word that signifies origin or cradle.

The first books then were formed of sheets of paper or parchment, laboriously printed from xylographic blocks, that is to say, wooden blocks on which a *tailleur d'images* had left the designs and the letters of the text in relief.   He had thus to trace his characters in reverse, so that they could be reproduced as written ; he had also to avoid faults, because a phrase once done, well or ill, was permanent.   It was doubtless this difficulty of correction that gave the idea of movable types.   If the engraver made gross mistakes, it was necessary to cancel the faulty block altogether.   This at least explains the legend of Laurent Coster, of Haarlem, who, according to Hadrian Junius, his compatriot, discovered by accident the secret of separate types while playing with his children. And if the legend of which we speak contains the least truth, it must be found in the sense above indicated, that is in the correction of a mistake, rather than in some innocent game with which the churchwarden of Haarlem was occupied. However, we shall have occasion to return to the subject of these remarks, but in passing we must state that engraving in relief on wood alone gave the idea of making xylographic blocks and of forming them into books. Movable type, the capital point of printing, the pivot of the art of the Book, suggested itself later on, according to necessities that made themselves felt when there was occasion to correct an erroneous inscription ; but, at any rate, it was not known at the outset. Doubtless, to vary the text, means were found to replace entire phrases by other phrases, preserving the original figures ; and thus the light dawned upon these craftsmen, while occupied in the manufacture and sale of their books.

According to Hadrian Junius, Laurent Janszoon Coster had published one of those *Speculums* which were then so popular (the mystic style of which exercised so great an attraction on the people of the fifteenth century), viz., the *Speculum Humanæ Salvationis.* Written before the middle of the fifteenth century, made popular by manuscripts, in spite of its fantastic Latinity and of its false quantities, this ascetic and badly conceived poem from the first tempted the xylographists. Junius, as we see, attributes to Laurent Coster the first impression of the *Speculum*, no longer the purely xylographic impression of the *Donatus* from an engraved block, but that of the more advanced manner in movable types. In point of fact, this book had at least four editions, similar in engravings and size of letters, but of different text. It must then be admitted that the fount was dispersed, and typography dis- covered, because the same unintelligible fount of letters could not be adapted to different languages. On the other hand, the identity of the vignettes indicates sufficiently the mobility of the types. In comparison with what may be seen in later works, the illustrations of the *Speculum* are by no means bad ; they have the appearance, at once naïve and picturesque, of the works of Van Eyck, and not at all of the character of the German miniaturists ; properly illuminated and gilded, they lent themselves to the illusion of being confounded with the *histoyres*, drawn by hand, and this is what the publisher probably endeavoured.

All the xylographic works of the fifteenth century may then be classed in two categories : the xylographs, rightly so called, or the block books, such as the *Donatus* with fixed type, and the books with more or less fixed plates and with movable types, like the *Speculum*, of which we speak. This mystic and simple literature of pious works for the use of people of modest resources acquired in printing the means of more rapid reproduction. Then appeared the *Biblia Pauperum* (see Frontispiece), one of the most celebrated and the most often reproduced of the block-books, and the *Ars Moriendi* (see Fig. 6), a kind of dialogue between an angel and the devil at the bedside of a dying person, which, inspired no doubt by older manuscripts, retained for a long time in successive editions the first tradition of its design. On labels displayed among the figures are found inscribed the dialogue of the demons and angels seeking to attach to themselves the departing soul, the temptations of Satan on the subject of faith, and the responses of the angel on the same subject.

We can see what developments this theme could lend to

Fig. 6.—Fac-simile of page 5 of the first edition of the *Ars Moriendi.*

the mysticism of the fifteenth century. Composed of eleven

designs, the *Ars Moriendi* ran up to eight different editions. From the middle to the end of the fifteenth century the text was in Latin, then in French, under the title *L'Art au Morier* (Fig. 7). In the French edition will be found the blocks that served for the second impression of the work. About 1480, more than fifty years after the first attempt, the *Ars Moriendi* was still

Fig. 7.—Xylographic figure from the *Ars.Moriendi*, copied in reverse in the *Art au Morier*.

so much in demand that an attempt was made to take it up again with all the resources of typography as much as in its earliest days. The original subjects, copied in a very indifferent manner, adorned the text, which was set up in Gothic letters, with a new and more explicit title : *Tractatus brevis ac valde utilis de Arte et Scientia bene moriendi* (4to, s.l. et a.), but the order is inverted, Fig. 5 of the xylographic work becoming No. 3 of the edition of 1480.

The *Ars Memorandi*, another xylographic work, of which the subject, taken from the New Testament, was equally well

Fig. 8.—Figure of the school of Martin Schongauer, taken from the *Rationarium Evangelistarum* of 1505, and copied from the corresponding plate of the *Ars Memorandi.*

adapted to the imagination of the artists, had an equally glorious destiny. The work originally comprised thirty blocks, the fifteen blocks of text facing the fifteen engravings. The designs represented the attributes of each of the Evangelists, with allegories and explanatory legends. Thus, in that which relates to the Apostle Matthew,

No. 1 represents the Birth and Genealogy of Jesus Christ,

No. 2 the Adoration of the Magi,

No. 3 the Baptism of St. John,

No. 4 the Temptation of Christ,

No. 5 the Sermon on the Mount,

No. 6 the Parable of the Birds.

The angel that supports the whole is the emblem of St. Matthew the Evangelist.

This mnemonic treatment of the Gospels proceeded from symbols of which we have no means of finding the origin, but which without doubt went back many centuries earlier. However that may be, their success was as great as that of the already quoted works. In 1505 a German publisher published an imitation of it, under the title of *Rationarium Evangelistarum* (Fig. 8); and this time the copyist of the illustrations, although trying to retain the tradition of the first xylographers, none the less reveals himself as an artist of the first order, at least a pupil of Martin Schongauer. Some of the conceptions of the *Rationarium* recall exactly the engravings of the great German master, among others that of the Child Jesus (plate 12), which nearly approaches the style of the Infant Jesus of Schongauer; besides, the principal figures leave but little doubt on the subject. We find the same wings on the angels and on the eagles, the same head-dresses on the human characters, often the same attitudes.

From the preceding can be judged the extraordinary favour which these productions enjoyed. From their origin they were diffused through the whole of Europe, and attracted the attention of excellent artists. Nevertheless their beginnings were difficult. The movable types used, cut separately in wood, were not constituted to give an ideal impression. We can besides understand the cost that the making of these characters must have occasioned, which were designed to stand one by one without the possibility of ever making them perfectly uniform. Progress was made in substituting for this imperfect process types that were similar, identical, easily produced, and used for a long time without breaking. Following on the essays of Laurent

Fig. 9.—Portrait of Gutenberg, from an engraving of the sixteenth century.

Coster, continuous researches were brought to bear on this point ; but as the invention was said to be his, and as it was of importance to him not to divulge it, so that he should not forego his profit, it so happened that much time was lost in his workshop without much success. Here history is somewhat confused. Hadrian Junius positively accuses one of Laurent Coster's workmen of having stolen the secrets of his master and taken flight to Mayence, where he afterwards founded a printing office.　According to Junius, the metal type had been the discovery of the Dutchman, and the name of the thief who appropriated it was John.　Who was this John?　Was it John Gensfleisch, called Gutenberg, or rather John Fust?　But it is not at all likely that Gutenberg, a gentleman of Mayence, exiled from his country, ever took service with the Dutch inventor.　As to Fust, as we shall see, he only was mixed up with the association of printers of Mayence as a money-lender, from which the unlikelihood of his having been with Coster may be gathered.　We also find Gutenberg retiring to Strasburg, where he pursued his researches.　There he was, a kind of broken-down gentleman, a ruined noble, whose great knowledge was, however, bent entirely on invention. Perhaps, like many others, he may have had in his hands one of the printed works of Laurent Coster, and conceived the idea of appropriating the infant process.　In 1439 he associated himself with two artisans of the city of Strasburg, ostensibly in the fabrication of *Mirrors*, which may be otherwise understood as the printing of *Speculums*, the Latin word signifying the same thing.　These men were obliged to surround themselves with precautions ; printing was as yet only a practical means of multiplying manuscripts, to impose on the unsuspecting ones, and fortune awaited him who, keeping his counsel, made use of this invention.　The following will prove this, as well as bearing on the subject.

A legal document discovered in 1790 by Wencker and Schoepflin in the Pfennigthurm of Strasburg, and afterwards. translated into French by M. Leon de Laborde, makes us at length acquainted with the work of Gutenberg and of his associates Andrew Dritzehen and Andrew Heilmann.　Apparently these three men were, as we have said, *Spiegelmachers*,.

that is 'makers of mirrors. They had jointly entered into a deed by the terms of which, if one of the partners died in the course of their researches, his heirs would have no rights beyond an indemnity corresponding to the amount invested by him. It happened that Andrew Dritzehen did die, and that one of his brothers aspired to occupy his place in the partnership. The dead man left debts behind him; he had squandered his florins by hundreds in his experiments. Gutenberg having offered to pay up the amounts expended, the heirs of Dritzehen, who wanted more, summoned him before the judge to show why he should not make place for them in the work of experiments and making of mirrors. The witnesses in their testimony before the court told what they knew of the inventions of the partnership. One among them deposed that, after the death of Dritzehen, Gutenberg's servant went to the workshop and begged Nicholas Dritzehen, brother of the deceased, to displace and break up four forms placed in a press. A second testified that the works of Andrew had cost him at the least three hundred florins, an enormous sum for those days. Other witnesses painted Gutenberg in a curious light: they made him out to be a savage, a hermit, who concealed from his associates certain arts which the deed did not stipulate. One fact proved that the experiments were directed towards the manufacture of metallic characters. A goldsmith, named Dünne, maintained that he had received more than a hundred florins for work belonging to printing material "*das zu dem trucken gehoret.*" "Trucken!"—"Typography!" Here the word was found, and from that day usage has sanctioned it.

Thus before 1439 John Gensfleisch, or Gutenberg, was devoted to the art of reproduction of texts, and had consecrated his life and feeble resources to it. Three problems

2

presented themselves to him. He wanted types less fragile than wooden types and less costly than engraving. He wanted a press by the aid of which he could obtain a clear impression on parchment or paper. He desired also that the leaves of his books should not be anopistographs, or printed on one side only. There were many unknown things to vex his soul, of which he himself alone could have a presentiment. Until then, and even long after, the xylographs were printed *au frotton*, or with a brush, rubbing the paper upon the form coated with ink thicker than ordinary ink ; but he dreamt of something better.

In the course of his work John Gutenberg returned to Mayence. The idea of publishing a Bible, the Book of books, had taken possession of his heart. The *Spiegelmacher* of Strasburg was on the road to ruin. The cutting of his types had ruined him, and on his arrival in his native town, his stock in trade, which he carried away with him, was of no great weight : some boxes of type, an inconvenient form, and perhaps an ordinary press, like a wine-maker's press, with a wooden screw. The idea of using this unwieldy instrument for the impression of his forms had already occurred to him ; but would not the *frotton* serve still better ? The force of the blow from the bar would break the miserable type, the raised parts of which could not resist the repeated strokes. In this unhappy situation Gutenberg made the acquaintance of a financier of Mayence, named Fust, who was in search of a business, and who put a sum of eleven hundred florins at his disposal to continue his experiments. Unfortunately this money disappeared, it melted away, and the results obtained were it appears, absolutely ludicrous.

It is certain that John Fust did not enter on the engagement without protecting himself. From the first he bound his debtor in a contract for six per cent. interest, besides a share in the profits. In addition he stipulated repayment in case of failure. Gutenberg, incautious, as is the way of inventors, had signed away all that he possessed to procure funds. It is however presumed that, during the continuance of his investigations, he set up in type some current books with the resources at his disposal, that served a little to lighten his debts. But the printing house of the *Zum Jungen* at Mayence was far from shining in the world, because the partnership with Fust was aimed only at the publication of a Bible, and not at all with the *Speculums* and *Donatus* that were so much in vogue at that time. Besides, the money-lender made a point of pressing his debtor, and did not allow him any leisure to labour outside the projected work.

About this time a third actor entered upon the scene. Peter Schoeffer, of Gernsheim, a caligrapher, who was introduced into the workshop of Gutenberg to design letters, benefited by the abortive experiments, and, taking up the invention at its deadlock, carried it forward. John of Tritenheim, called Trithemius, the learned abbot of Spanheim, is the person who relates these facts; but, as he got his information from Schoeffer himself, too much credence must not be given to his statements. Besides, Schoeffer was by no means an ordinary artisan. If we credit a Strasburg manuscript written by his hand in 1449, he had been a student of the "most glorious university of Paris." In the workshop of Gutenberg his industrious and inventive spirit, to use the same expressions as the Abbot of Tritenheim, found natural food and a productive mine, and this caligrapher dreamt of other things than merely drafting his letters for wood blocks, to be cut by the engravers. Gutenberg, arrested in his career by the wants of life, the worries of business, and perhaps also by the fatigues of his labours, may have let the new-comer know something of his expectations. One cannot know, but it is certain that, shortly after, John Fust was so fascinated by Schoeffer, so attracted by his youth and his skill, that he resolved to put new capital into the business. He did more : to permanently attach him, he gave him his granddaughter in marriage—not his daughter, as was thought until M. Auguste Bernard rectified this mistake.

We have now come to 1453, the year preceding the first dated monument of printing in movable types, *The Letters of Indulgence.* It may be acknowledged that this sudden affection of Fust for his workman depended on some interested motive, and not upon any particular kindness of heart, of which the Mayence citizen seemed incapable. Had this former student of the university of Paris found the means of rapidly founding metallic types, the search for which had cost Gutenberg so many sleepless nights ? Did he complete it by applying to the fount the matrix and punch which had then and for centuries served the makers of seals and the money-coiners ? Perhaps, as was most probable, the two associates arrived at the same result, and, putting their experiences together, were enabled to conquer difficulties hitherto insurmountable

The year 1454 witnessed the diffusion throughout Christendom of letters of indulgence, accorded by Pope Nicholas V. to the faithful who wished to aid in funds the King of Cyprus against the Turks. These circular letters, scattered abroad by thousands to every corner of the world, had employed numerous copyists. Arrived at Mayence, the distributers found a workshop ready prepared to furnish copies in the shortest possible time. They set to work and brought together all the available type, cast or cut, to set up these famous letters. Among the impressions was that of which we give a reproduction (Fig. 10), which belongs to the edition called that of thirty-one lines. The original, now in the Bibliothèque Nationale, was delivered for a consideration to Josse Ott von Mospach on the 31st of December, 1454.

It is not without interest, for the history of the Book and

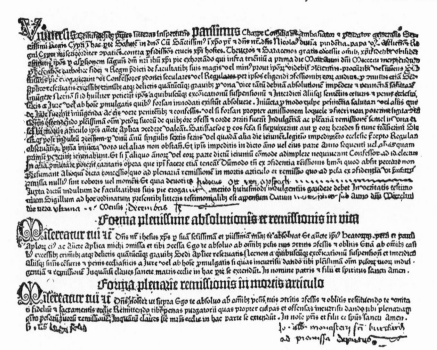

Fig. 10.—Letters of indulgence, from the so-called edition of thirty one lines, printed at Mayence in the course of 1454.

Printing, to note here that these letters of indulgence, the clandestine traffic in which was largely accelerated by the rapidity of production and, it may be said, the small cost of each copy, formed one of the causes of the religious reform of Martin Luther. They afforded a means of raising money, and were so generally resorted to that in the register of the Hôtel de Ville of Paris, preserved in the Archives Nationales

(H 1778), it may be seen that the sheriffs requested the Pope to allow them to employ them in the reconstruction of the bridge at the Hôtel de Ville.

The ice once broken, Fust and Schoeffer found it hard to keep a useless hand. For them Gutenberg was more of a hindrance than a profit, and they sought brutally to rid themselves of him. Fust had a most easy pretext, which was to demand purely and simply from his associate the sums advanced by him, and which had produced so little. Gutenberg had to all appearance commenced his *Bible*, but, in face of the claims of Fust, he had to abandon it altogether, types, forms, and press

In November 1455 he had retired to a little house outside the city, where he tried his best, by the aid of foreign help, to establish a workshop, and to preserve the most perfect secrecy. Relieved of his company, Fust and Schoeffer were able to continue the impression of the Bible and to complete it without him. If matters really came to pass in this way, and Schoeffer had no claim to having previously discovered the casting of type, there is but one word to designate their conduct : robbery, and moral robbery, the worst of all. But what can we think of these people ?

One thing appears to be certain : that the so-called Gutenberg Bible, whether commenced by Gutenberg or not, was issued by Fust and Schoeffer alone about the end of 1455 or at the beginning of 1456, and proves to be the *first completed book*. Having retired to his new quarters, Gutenberg was taking care not to remain too much in the background, but the reconstitution of his workshop must have cost him enormous time. He also missed the caligrapher Schoeffer : his own Gothic letters, engraved on steel with a punch, had not the same elegance. When his work appeared in 1458 it could not sustain comparison. The Bible which Schoeffer issued was more compact, the impression was more perfect, the ink better,

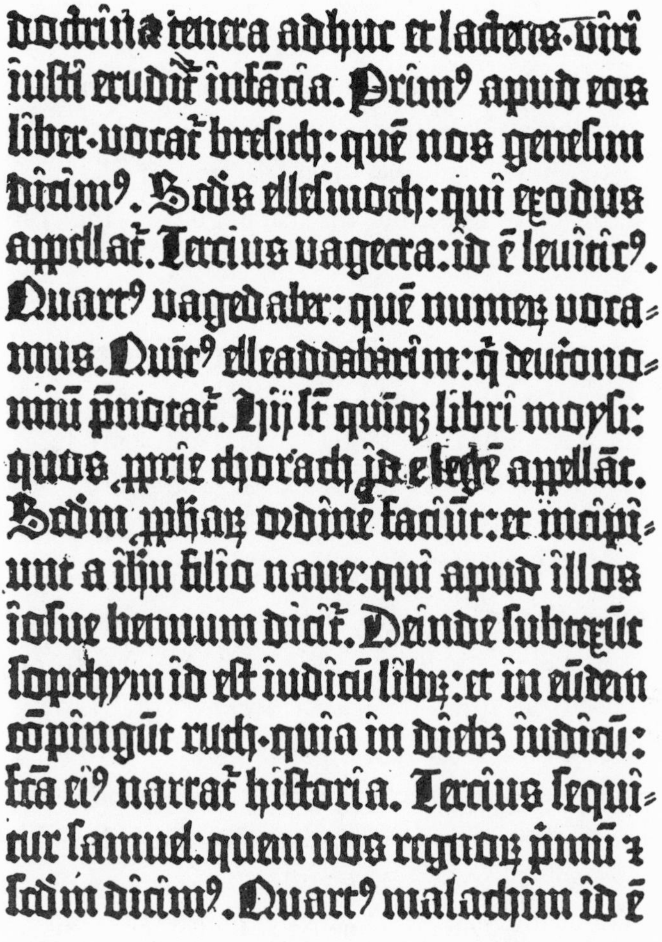
doctrina tenera adhuc et lactens. viri
iusti erudiret infancia. Primus apud eos
liber vocatur bresith: quem nos genesim
dicimus. Secundus hellesmoth: qui exodus
appellatur. Tercius vagecra: id est leviticus.
Quartus vagedaber: quem numeri voca-
mus. Quintus elleaddabarim: qui deutrono-
mium prenotatur. Hii sunt quinque libri moysi:
quos proprie thorath id est legem appellant.
Secundum prophetarum ordinem faciunt: et incipi-
unt ab ihesu filio nave: qui apud illos
iosue bennum dicitur. Deinde subtexunt
sophtim id est iudicum librum: et in eundem
compingunt ruth. quia in diebus iudicum
facta eius narratur historia. Tercius sequi-
tur samuel: quem nos regnorum primum et
secundum dicimus. Quartus malachim id est

Fig. 11.—Fragment of the Gutenberg Bible, printed in two columns. Beginning of the text in the second column; original size.

the type less irregular. Thus the original inventor, in his connexion with Fust, made an unfortunate competition for himself. We give here a fragment of this celebrated book, a kind of mute witness of the science and mortifications of the first printer.

It is also called the Mazarine Bible, from the fact that De Bure discovered the first copy in the Mazarine Library, and was the first to give evidence concerning it. The book was issued at the end of 1455 or beginning of 1456, for a manuscript note of a vicar of St. Stephen at Mayence records that he himself finished the binding and illuminating of the first volume on St. Bartholomew's Day, 1456, and the second on the 15th of August. St. Bartholomew's Day is the 13th of June, and not the 24th of August, as the catalogue of the Bibliothèque Nationale has it.

Mr. Bernhard Quaritch gives a *resumé* of arguments put forth by foreign writers, tending to clear up the claims of Gutenberg to the first Bible, and as the subject is of very high importance we cannot do better than here reproduce, with his permission, the arguments in favour of Gutenberg. He says:—

" A late critic who first believed in the Coster legend, then recanted, then believed again and still believes in it, on the faith of three things, namely (1) the actual existence of undated Donatus fragments evidently early and of Dutch origin ; (2) a phrase used in the *Cologne Chronicle* of 1499 ; (3) the Junius story printed in 1588—has discussed the history of the first press of Mayence in a very acute and able essay on Gutenberg. His conclusion is that no *Book* is known earlier than the above forty-two line Bible, and that it was printed about 1454-55 by Peter Schoeffer ; that there exists no trace of Gutenberg as a printer ; that the thirty-six line Bible printed in types used by Pfister at Bamberg in and after 1461 *may have been* produced at Mayence before 1460. This judgment is unconsciously biassed by a certain patriotic *animus* against the name of the man to whom the invention of Printing is usually ascribed on sufficient evidence. It may not be amiss, therefore, to quote a succession of accessible authorities on the subject for those who are not in immediate possession of the facts.

" 1454. An Indulgence of this *date* is printed in the type of the forty-two line Bible.

" 1456. The rubrication of the Paris copy of the forty-two line Bible proves it anterior to this year.

" 1457. The Psalter of this date bears the names of *John* Fust and *Peter* Schoeffer.

" 1468. *Peter* Schoeffer, surviving *John* Fust, prints the Institutes of Justinian, with a statement that a different *John* had preceded *John* and *Peter* in the practice of printing at Mayence.

" 1465-99. Ulrich Zell, who left Mayence in 1462, declares plainly the absolute priority to all other typographers of *John* Gutenberg, who made experiments in printing from 1440 to 1450, and began to print a Bible in missal-type in 1450.

" 1470. Pierre Fichet, in the Paris edition of Gasparinus of this year, states that John Gutenberg invented typography at Mayence.

" The specific information in the *Cologne Chronicle* is the most valuable of all the early external evidences, for which reason I quote it in full below. Of the printed monuments themselves, all persons on all sides are agreed that no *Book* is now in existence except the forty-two line Bible, to which we can with documentary certitude assign so early a date as 1455-56. A work of such magnitude, as well as earliness, must have occupied some years in its production. With all the practical facilities of our own time, two such volumes, in such type, so carefully worked by means of assiduous revision and rearrangement, could hardly be printed by a London printer now, with less than a year's effort; at the infancy of printing, we may reckon four or five years for the time that was necessary. If Schoeffer printed it, he (who, by his own statement, was the *third* Mayence typographer) must have begun the work in 1450, and must have prepared himself for it by several years' preliminary studies (in the choosing and making of types, the elaboration of the process, the construction of machinery and appurtenances, the gathering of material, etc.). Consequently, if Schoeffer was the printer of the forty-two line Bible, he must have begun his practical career as a typographer not later than 1445. This logical conclusion is a clear *reductio ad absurdum.* We do not know when Schoeffer was born ; most authorities say between 1420 and 1430. We do know that he was alive and still printing at the end of the year 1502, that in 1465 Fust called him 'puer meus,' that in 1449 he was a student and caligrapher at Paris. Men began earlier and finished sooner in those days than now ; old age was considered to have set in at fifty : few persons reached the age of seventy. The probability is that Schoeffer was about eighteen years of age in 1445 ; but it is sufficient for our purpose to know that he could have had nothing to do with typography in 1449 when he wrote and ornamented a manuscript in Paris. It is utterly impossible that a young student in Paris, so engaged in that year, could have produced the two volumes of the forty-two line Bible at Mayence between 1450 and 1456, without any preparation or training—except by a miracle, which does not usually happen in the workaday world.

"We reproduce here, out of the *Cologne Chronicle* (printed in 1499 by Johann Koelhof), the passage referring to the invention of printing :

" 'Of the Art of Bookprinting.

" 'When, where, and by whom was invented the inexpressibly useful art of printing books ?

* * * * * *

" '*Item.* This highly valuable art aforesaid was invented first of all in Germany at Mayence on the Rhine. And it is a great honour to the German nation that such ingenious men are to be found therein. And that happened in the year of our Lord A.D. 1440; and from that time onward until the date of (14)50, the art, and what appertains to it, were investigated and essayed. And in the year of our Lord 1450, it was then a golden year, it was then begun to print, and the first book that was printed was the Bible in Latin, and it was printed with a massive character such as the letter in which Mass-books are now printed. *Item*, whileas the art was invented at Mayence as aforesaid in the mode in which it is now commonly used, the first prefiguration was, however, invented in Holland, in the *Donatuses* which were formerly printed there. And from and out of them the beginning of the aforesaid art was taken, and it was much more masterly and subtilely invested than the same manner was ; and the longer it has been practised the more artistic has it become. *Item*, there is one named Omnebonus who writes in a preface to the book named Quintilianus, and also in many other books, that a foreigner from France named Nicolaus Genson was the first who invented this masterly art, but that is manifestly false, since there are yet alive those who testify that books were printed at Venice before the aforesaid Nicolaus Genson came thither, where he began to cut and prepare letters (types). But the first inventor of Printing was a citizen of Mayence, and was born at Strassburg, and was named *junker* Johan Gudenburch. *Item*, from Mayence the aforesaid art came first to Cologne, next to Strassburg, and then to Venice. The worthy man, Master Ulrich Tzell of Hanau, still a printer at Cologne at the present time in the year 1499, by whom the aforesaid art was brought to Cologne, has related verbally to me the beginning and progress of the aforesaid art. *Item*, there is also a set of wrong-headed men, and they say that books were printed formerly also ; but that is not true, since there are found in no lands any of the books which were printed at those times.'

" If we analyse the above statement—which, though dated 1499, must be regarded as the result of conversations between 1465 and 1472—we find the following points :—

"(1) Johann Gutenberg was the actual inventor of printing, in 1440.

"(2) The first book printed by him, after preliminary essays in 1440-50, was a Bible, in missal-type, printed (or begun) in 1450;

"(3) There had been a foreshadowing or suggestion of printing in the Donatus sheets impressed in Holland before Gutenberg's time;

"(4) There had been no typography anywhere before the time of Gutenberg; notwithstanding the assertions of some wrong-headed and perverse persons;

"(5) A reiteration of the statement concerning Gutenberg.

" If No. (3) could possibly have referred to *typography* at Harlem or elsewhere in Holland, it would have stultified all the rest of the chapter, (1), (2), (4), and (5) being in direct contradiction to such an interpretation. Only a rash man will see in it anything else but an allusion to the printing of engraved blocks or *Xylography*, which was an invention of great utility for multiplying school-books, cheaper and easier than the old way of having copies multiplied by penmen; but not equal to the *masterly and subtle* invention of movable types.

" The Harlem story, beginning with Coornhert and Junius in the fifteen-sixties (just a hundred years after Zell's removal to Cologne), is seen to be pure fable when unassociated with the above paragraph (3). The perverted ingenuity which has frequently torn that paragraph away from its context, and used it as a confirmation for the Coster legend, cannot be too strongly deprecated."

Of the copies of the Gutenberg Bible which turned up during the last forty years the following recapitulation may not be uninteresting :—

" 1847. A copy sold in London; bought by Wiley and Putnam against Sir Thomas Phillipps for Mr. Lennox of New York, for £500. Now in the Lennox library.

" 1858. The duplicate from the Munich library, sold at Augsburg, bought for the Emperor of Russia for 2,336 florins, about £245.

" 1858. The Bishop of Cashel's copy, sold in London; bought by Mr. Quaritch for £595. Passed into Lord Crawford's library, and was bought by him again at Lord Crawford's sale in 1887 for £2,650.

" 1872. An imperfect copy, with seventeen leaves in fac-simile, appeared for sale in Berlin by Mr. Albert Cohn at 4,000 thalers (about £600), and after passing through the hands of two purchasers successively, was bought at about £1,800 for a New York library, in which it now remains.

" 1873. Mr. Henry Perkins' copy, sold at Hanworth Park, near London, in 1873; bought by Mr. Quaritch for £2,690. Now in Mr. Huth's library.

The Perkins' copy on vellum (two or four leaves in fac-simile), bought for Lord Ashburnham for £3,400. Now at Battle.

" 1878. A copy on vellum, with painted initials and miniatures, was found in Spain by M. Bachelin. He had it restored by Pilinski in fac-simile, and sold it (after offering it to Mr. Quaritch for £2,000) to Mr. Albert Cohn, who resold it to the late Mr. H. Klemm of Dresden. It is the most interesting copy now in evidence, being the only one with contemporary miniatures, and is now deposited for exhibition in the new Buchhändler-Börse at Leipzig.

" 1884. In February, the Kamensky copy of the Old Testament portion bought by Mr. Quaritch at Sotheby's for £760. Now in America.

" In May, an odd volume belonging to Lord Gosford fetched £500.

" In December, Sir John Thorold's copy was bought by Mr. Quaritch at Sotheby's for £3,900. It still remains in Great Britain.

" 1887. Mr. Quaritch bought Lord Crawford's copy, as mentioned above, for £2,650.

" 1889. February. Lord Hopetoun's copy bought by Mr. Quaritch at Sotheby's for £2,000."

But so many copies absolutely similar in aspect, and of so regular a style, put in the market from day to day by Fust and Schoeffer, gave rise to protests from the caligraphers. Criticism always attends upon success, but having once obtained the result, the two associates did not hesitate to proclaim themselves as the printers of the Bible. On the publication of the Psalter, which followed the Bible at a year's interval, they gave their names and added a date, 1457, the first instance of a date being recorded in a book. This second work, which preceded the Gutenberg Bible, was of so skilful a typography, that it might have been passed as the work of an expert caligrapher ; the faults remarked in the letters of indulgence are no longer perceptible ; type had attained perfection ; in two years printing had reached its culminating point.

We here reproduce a *facsimile* of the second edition of this celebrated work printed in 1459, two years later.

The Bibles, like the *Durandus* of 1459 and the *Catholicon* of 1460, had an interest for many purchasers, while the Psalter would have concerned only a few wealthy churches. All the existing

Fig. 12.—Fac-simile of the Psalter, 1459.

copies of both Psalters indicate that they were adapted simply to Mayence uses, and until one is found which conforms to the use of some church outside that city, we shall be inclined to consider that the book was *privately printed* in the modern sense, and that the issue was extremely limited. It is not the sort of book which would have been wilfully destroyed, or which could

have perished from decay. Many an honest man might have
been tempted to steal it, but its obvious splendour and value
would have made it safe even in the hands of a plunderer.
The cost of production must have been enormous, and could
only have been paid for by private munificence. The sale of
copies, as ordinary book-ware, could never have reached any
possible figure high enough to cover such an expense. This
explains the extraordinary scarcity and enormous price of the
Psalter, a copy of the second edition of which was sold
at Sir John Thorold's sale for the extraordinary sum of
£4,950.

In spite of his disappointments, Gutenberg did not rest
idle. If he had seen his two enemies rob him of his claim
of priority in the invention, he wanted to show that, reduced
to his own exertions and to the restricted means furnished
him by charitable people, he also could print well. Two years
after the *Bible* another dated book, set up in Gothic letters,
appeared at Mayence; this was the *Catholicon* of John
Balbus, of Genoa. It had not yet occurred to these first
printers to exercise their art otherwise than on religious works.
It is admitted by general opinion that the *Catholicon* issued
from the press of Gutenberg; on the other hand, M. Bernard
believes that it ought to be attributed to a printer of Eltvil,
who published in 1467 a vocabulary called the *Vocabularium
ex quo* with the same types. The former theory may be sustained by the words of the colophon of the book, which is a
sort of hymn to God and a recognition to the city of Mayence
without any mention of the name of the printer. Now in the
situation in which Gutenberg found himself, in the face of his
rivals, would he not have claimed the great discovery as his
own? But if M. Bernard is mistaken, and if our supposition

has no foundation, what a beautiful act of humility, what a noble idea of his character, Gutenberg gives us when he writes : " With the aid of the Most High, Who unlooses the tongues of infants and often reveals to babes that which is sealed to learned men, this admirable book the *Catholicon* was finished in the year of the incarnation of our Saviour MCCCCLX. in the mother-country of Mayence, famous city of Germany, which God, in His clemency, has deigned to render

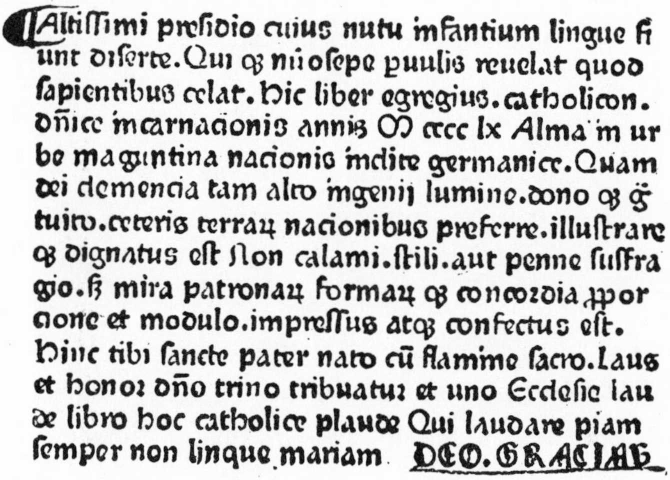

Altissimi presidio cuius nutu infantium lingue si
unt diserte. Qui os nii osepe puulis reuelat quod
sapientibus celat. hic liber egregius. catholicon.
dnice incarnacionis annis M ccc lx Alma in ur
be maguntina nacionis inclite germanice. Quam
dei demencia tam alto ingenii lumine. dono os gra
tuito. ceteris terrau nacionibus preferre. illustrare
os dignatus est slon calami. stili. aut penne suffra
gio. s mira patronau formau os concordia propor
cione et modulo. impressus atos confectus est.
Hinc tibi sancte pater nato cu flamine sacro. Laus
et honor dno trino tribuatur et uno Ecclesie lau
de libro hoc catholice plaude Qui laudare piam
semper non linque mariam. DEO. GRACIAS.

Fig. 13.—Colophon of the *Catholicon*, supposed to have been printed by Gutenberg in 1460.

the most illustrious and the first of cities ; and this book was perfected without the usual help of pen or style, but by the admirable linking of formes and types " !

Its excessive rarity is too well known to require any comment, and its literary merit is so considerable that the London editor of *Stephani Thesaurus Latinus* has pronounced it " the best Dictionary for the Latin Fathers and Schoolmen." Sir John Thorold's copy sold for £400 and Wodhull's for £310.

3

The history of these first printers, it is easy to understand, has to be regarded with caution, for they were of so little consequence in those days that authentic documents relating to them have for ever disappeared. If we except that of the Pfennigthurm of Strasburg, of which we have before spoken, and the deed of claim for money from Fust to Gutenberg dated 1455, we are forced to quote from authors living a long time afterwards, who perpetrated, without knowing better, the errors of oral tradition. It is nearly always the same with men who have occupied a large place in the history of art; posterity only finds out their genius at the time when no one knows anything about them. For Gutenberg the situation was still more terrible; his rival, Peter Schoeffer, survived him, who for his own reputation's sake did not care to preserve his rival's memory; and if, as is believed, Gutenberg left pupils and heirs, Henry Bechtermunze, Ulrich Zell, and Weigand Spiess, he has the additional misfortune that Bechtermunze is now reputed as the printer of the *Catholicon*, of which we have just given the history. We need not here refer to Albert Pfister, one of his workmen, dismissed at the end of his work, who having obtained from his master some rejected types, was presumed later to have invented printing. We find this artisan established at Bamberg about 1460, where he set up Bibles in movable types, the first known being the thirty-six line Bible, a specimen of which is preserved in the Bibliothèque Nationale and the British Museum. But Albert Pfister showed that he was not at all an inventor by the mediocrity of his work, and more so by the old types that he used. If he had known the secret of engraving the punches, he would have cast new letters and have given a better appearance to his work.

In these statements all is supposition and contradiction.

That which is certain—and the dates are there to prove it—
is the enormous progress made and the productions of Peter
Schoeffer. In 1459 he published his third book, Durandus'
Rationale Divinorum Officiorum, in folio. As in the Psalter,
Schoeffer employed initial letters printed in red, which the rival
workshop could not do in the *Catholicon,* the rubrics of which
were to be painted by hand, as in manuscripts. A great
number of types were broken at the beginning, but he was

Fig. 14.—Colophon of the Bible printed in 1462 by Fust and Schoeffer, which is the
first dated Bible. There are two different editions with this signature. The
above is from the second edition.

confident of ultimate success. In 1460 he gave the *Constitutiones*
of Pope Clement V., with a gloss and commentaries by John
André; here was the first example of a process much employed
in manuscripts, but of which the typographical composition was
very difficult. Again, in 1462 *a new Latin Bible* issued from
his workshop *in two folio volumes,* which is the first dated
edition. The first volume has two hundred and forty-two
folios in double columns, the second two hundred and thirty-
nine. It commences with an epistle of St. Jerome, and on

the last leaf of the second volume is the colophon here reproduced.

This book, one of the first worthy of the name, and which is called by preference the *Mayence Bible*, appeared in one of the most troubled epochs that the episcopal city had had to go through. Subject to its archbishops, who were at the head of all the lay lords and fighting men, the city found itself in 1462 the prey of two prelates of equal title, who refused to give way to one another: Diether of Isenburg and Adolph of Nassau. Adolph surprised Mayence on the 27th October, 1462, pursuing his adversary, who scaled the walls with a rope to escape quicker, and the city was sacked and pillaged from its foundations. What became, in the midst of this turmoil, of the obscure persons who were then the printers of the Bible? Doubtless their insignificance saved them from disaster, but as it was long before peace was re-established, and as, on the. other hand, the entire edition of their last volume could not be kept back, we incline to believe that they were for a time going about the country as itinerant booksellers. Paris was their point of travel already indicated —Paris, towards which all their desires were directed. The university where Peter Schoeffer was instructed in letters, and which truly passed for the first in Europe, appeared to them an opening of the first order. If we may believe Walchius (*Decas Fabularum Generis Humani:* Strasburg, 1609, 4to, p. 181), John Fust himself went to that city, where he put books on sale from sixty crowns a copy, then fifty, then forty, according to the prevailing system in matters of discount. Fust was above all things a business man; he caused it to be spread about that he had a marvellous copyist establishment beyond the Rhine, and that he had come to dispose of several copies ; upon which the corporate scribes of the university, becoming aware of the imposition, cried out furiously and declared it a diabolical invention. We may now take this tale of Walchius as a fable, for the registers of Parliament, on being consulted, rest silent on the proceedings instituted against the "magician" of Mayence. At the same time, we must not lose sight of the fact that the booksellers had their masters, their syndicate, if we may use the modern word, charged to prohibit fraudulent publications. They were too much interested in the suppression of printed books to discard the matter coolly. Parliament had nothing to do with it.

The revolution of Mayence had by far greater results than one would have expected from these insignificant changes. The printing workshops, or at least the successors of Gutenberg, began to be dispersed, and Fust and Schoeffer having established a school of printers in the city, their trade was no longer a secret. Deprived of their liberties by the new Archbishop, many of them expatriated themselves. We shall have occasion later to name some of these exiles, through whom the art of printing was spread almost simultaneously throughout the world : at Cologne and at Strasburg, in Italy and Spain, without reckoning Holland, France, Switzerland, and the country around Mayence. We have before named the episcopal city of Bamberg ; it had the singular fortune to be the second city to possess a printing office, but it disappeared as quickly as it was established, with its founder Albert Pfister, without leaving the least trace ; we do not find printing there again till 1480, more than twenty years later.

Gutenberg died early in 1468. He was interred in the Church of the Dominicans at Mayence, by the pious care of a friend, who attributed the invention of printing to him on his tomb.

We may begin to comprehend the influence of this man upon a discovery of which all the world was then talking, but amongst the troubles of the archiepiscopal city the respective merit of the inventors did not receive their proper due. Peter Schoeffer and John Fust were but little affected by the political crisis. After two years' suspension, they, always working and always surpassing themselves, reappeared with a Cicero, *De Officiis*, 1465, quarto. This time they freed themselves from religious publications, and, still more extraordinary, they also employed Greek types.

Such, detached from the incredible contradictions of writers on the history of printing, and sketched solely on its main lines, is the origin of printing as it exists at this day. First came the image engraved in relief, which we need not go so far as China to find, like some of our predecessors. Upon this image were often cut, by the same economical process, legends of explanation that presented the idea of imitation of manuscript; and the xylographs appeared with or without pictures. Then from the correction of errors in these books followed the discovery of movable characters. This wooden type, possible when it was used with a *frotton* for printing, would quickly break under the press, the idea of which was gained from the common press of the wine-makers. Then a kind of type metal had to be found which could be cast in a mould struck by a punch. This punch was not invented for that purpose; it served previously for the makers of coins and seals. The fabrication of type from the matrix was a simple adoption. The lead thrown into the matrix gave the desired type. Thus the first books were made, of which we have briefly related the composition.

As to the proportion of glory due to each one of the first

printers, it is necessary to guard equally against error on one side or the other. We have sought to separate from the heap of publications probable theories or those based on certain documents. That the origin of the *Donatus*, and the *Block-books*, was Dutch it would be puerile to deny, because, on one side, the block engravings are sure ly of the school of Van Eyck, and, on the other hand, Ulrich Zell, who inspired the *Cologne Chronicle* of 1499, assigned positively to Holland the cradle of the *Donatus*. At any rate, it was by a pupil of Gutenberg, a question we have discussed. After this we will trouble ourselves but little about Laurent Coster. The name makes no difference in a matter of this kind.

As to Gutenberg, we have not been able to go as far as M. E. Dutuit, who in his *Manuel d'Estampes* (vol. i., p. 236, etc.) doubts Gutenberg's right to the title of inventor. It is sufficient to state that in a letter of William Fichet, prior of the Sorbonne, of whom we shall have more to say presently, to Robert Gaguin, which Dr. Sieber of Basle found at the beginning of a work entitled *Gasparini Pergamensis orthographiæ liber*, published in 1470, nearly twenty years after the first work at Mayence, Gutenberg is proclaimed the inventor of printing. Without any other, this testimony of a *savant* who was the first to bring the German printers to Paris appears to us well nigh irrefutable.

As to John Fust and his grandson by marriage, Peter Schoeffer, they are so well defended by their works, that there is no more to say here ; doubtless grave presumptions arise as to the propriety of their conduct towards Gutenberg, but we are not so presumptive as to censure them beyond measure. We know nothing precise of the time or of the men either.

Let us now imagine humble workmen, the most simple of *gens de mestiers*, to employ the French expression then in use, shut up in a kind of dim workshop, like a country forge, formed in little groups of two or three persons, one designing and the other cutting the wood, with a table near at hand, on which is held the engraved block after its reliefs have been rubbed with sombre ink, who afterwards, by means of the *frotton*, apply the damped paper to the raised parts of the block ; we shall then have without much stretch of imagination all the appurtenances of the xylographic impression. If we add to this primitive workshop the matrix in which the types are cast, the box in which they are distributed, the form on which they are arranged to compose the pages, and a small hand-press, with blacker ink and paper damped to permit the greasy ink to take better, we have a picture of the printing office at the time of Gutenberg, Fust, and Schoeffer, and of the first printers with movable types.

Thus typography was born of painting, passing in its infancy through wood-cutting, revolutionizing ideas and in some degree the world. But the mighty power of the new art was not confined to itself ; it extended the circle of engraving, which till then had suffered from the enormous difficulties of reproduction. As if the time were ripe for all these things, nearly at the moment when the first printers were distinguishing themselves by serious works, a Florentine goldsmith accidentally discovered the art of line engraving.* What would have become of this new process if the presses of Gutenberg had not brought their powerful assistance to the printing of engravings? It will be found then that printing gave back to engraving a hundredfold that which it received from it, and bore it along with its own rapid advance.

---

* The opinion that Finiguerra was the unconscious inventor of line engravings is now abandoned.

Then reappeared, following the new processes, the illustrations, in a measure abandoned by the Mayence workmen during the period of transformation. Our object is to speak at length of the Book ornamented and illustrated according to the means of relief engravings; to demonstrate the influence of painting, of sculpture, of art, on the production of the Book; and thus to help the reader at the same time to understand the almost sudden and irresistible development of typography, and to mention its foremost representatives.

CHAPTER II.

1462 TO 1500.

The Book and the printers of the second generation—The German workmen dispersed through Europe—Caxton and the introduction of printing into England—Nicholas Jenson and his supposed mission to Mayence—The first printing in Paris; William Fichet and John Heinlein—The first French printers; their installation at the Sorbonne and their publications—The movement in France—The illustration of the Book commenced in Italy—The Book in Italy; engraving in relief and metal plates—The Book in Germany: Cologne, Nuremberg, Basle—The Book in the Low Countries—French schools of ornament of the Book; Books of Hours; booksellers at the end of the fifteenth century—Literary taste in titles in France at the end of the fifteenth century—Printers' and booksellers' marks—The appearance of the portrait in the Book.

ONSIDERING the influence of printing on the book trade of the fifteenth century, as referred to in the preceding pages, the dealers in manuscripts were not disposed to give way at the first blow. An entire class of workmen would find themselves suddenly without employment if the new art succeeded; these were the copyists, miserable scribes, who for meagre remuneration frequented the shops of the merchants, where they transcribed manuscripts by the year. Before printing, the publication of books was done in this way, and the booksellers were rather middlemen between the copyist and the buyer than direct dealers with stock-in-trade. It is evident that they would not have provided themselves with

these costly books long in advance without being sure of
having a ready sale for them.

However small the remuneration of the writers was, still
they clung to it; and they were naturally the first to protest
against the new invention. At the same time, their opposition
and that of the booksellers was soon overcome, swamped, and
choked by the growing crowd of printers. Then, as always
happens in similar cases, in place of fighting against the current,
most of the former workers in manuscript followed it. The
caligraphers designed letters for engraving in wood, the booksellers sold the printed works, and the illuminators engraved in
relief their *histoyres*. For a long time the latter continued
to decorate books with the ornamental drawings with which
they had adorned the manuscripts, and so contributed to form
the fine school of illustrators who have carried their art to so
high a point since the end of the fifteenth century.

As previously related, the revolution of Mayence caused the
flight of a crowd of artisans who found their liberty suddenly
compromised by the conqueror. The want of money at this
time always entailed a diminution of patronage, and the
journeyman printers stuck at all times to their privileges. It
thus happened then that their guild, in place of remaining shut
up at Mayence many years longer, was, as it were, turned out,
and scattered to the four points of the compass by the
dispersion of its members, and thus spread many years before
the time that would otherwise have been the case. In point of
fact, in the common order of things, a workman here and there
quits the principal workshop to try the world. He makes his
way timidly, the unconscious apostle of a marvellous art. If he
succeeds, he gathers some pupils around him; if he fails, no trace
of him remains; in any case invention propagates itself more

gradually. With printing it was a thunderclap. No sooner had we realized its appearance than the exodus commenced. The greater part of the Mayence men bent their way to Italy : to Subiaco, to Rome, like Arnold Pannartz and Conrad Sweynheim, who printed that splendid edition of *Lactantii Opera*, 1468, in which the Greek quotations were printed for the first time, as well as the first edition of *Virgilii Opera*, 1469 (the excessive rarity of which is so great that a copy sold lately from Lord Hopetoun's library for £590), Ulrich Hahn, commonly called Ulricus Gallus, who was employed by Cardinal Torquemada to print his *Meditationes;* to Venice, such as Johannes de Spira, the printer of *Plinii Sec. Hist. Nat. Libri* (1469) ; Vendelin de Spira, the printer of *Petrarca's Sonetti* (1470), a book of the highest degree of rarity ; Christopher Valdarfer, Bernard Pictor (of Augsburg), Erhardt Ratdolt, Peter Loslein ; to Ferrara, like Andrew Belfort ; to Foligno, John Neumeister ; Henry Alding tried Sicily ; Andrew Vyel, of Worms, printed at Palermo. Lambert Palmart was at Valencia, in Spain, in 1477 ; Nicholas Spindeler at Barcelona ; Peter Hagenbach at Toledo. Nearer home to Mayence—that is, at Cologne—we find Ulrich Zell, a pupil of Gutenberg, who dated his first work 1466. It was Arnold Ther Hoernen who numbered a book with Arabic figures ; it was Koelhof, the printer of the *Cologne Chronicle*, who first used signatures to indicate to the binder the order of the sheets ; it was at Eltvil that Henry Bechtermunze, as we have already said, printed his *Vocabularium* in German, with the types of the *Catholicon;* at Basle, Berthold Rüppel, of Hanau, was the first established in that city, which, after Mayence, was destined to do the most for printing ; at Nuremberg we find Koberger, who took nearly the first rank among his contemporaries, set as many as twenty-four presses to work,

and was named by Badius the prince of printers. The very
year that followed the death of Gutenberg, a body of monks, the
Brothers of the Common Life of Marienthal, in the Rheingau,
themselves published a copy of the *Indulgences* granted by
Adolph of Nassau, Archbishop of Mayence. Before 1480,
presses were everywhere in Germany : at Prague, Augsburg,
Ulm, Lubeck, Essling, etc.

Fig. 15.—Imprint of Arnold Ther Hoernen, printer, of Mayence.

It is, however, to be remarked that the Mayence men
did not branch out in Holland. Is it that they found there
the descendants of Laurent Coster firmly established in their
workshops? Must we admit then the co-existence, the simultaneous advance, of the invention in Germany and in the Low
Countries? It is a problem for us as for many others. Let us
state, however, that Flemish printers were established at Utrecht
in 1473, at Delft, Bruges, Gouda, Zwoll, Antwerp, and Brussels.

At Louvain there was a Conrad of Westphalia, who published an undated work, the type of which denotes a very early age, but this seems an isolated instance of a German printer being

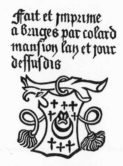

Fig. 16.—Mark of Colard Mansion.

established in the Netherlands, and perhaps he was only a simple dealer. La Serna-Santander does not think it unlikely that Conrad was the father of John of Westphalia, whose principal works, *Cicero de claris oratoribus*, 1475, *Virgilii Opera*, 1476,

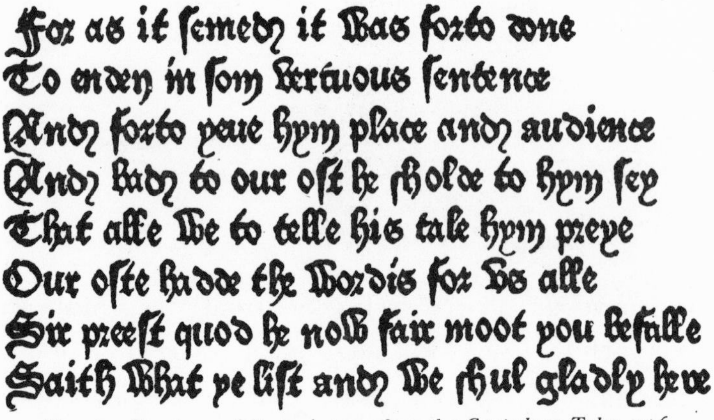

For as it semed it was forto done
To enden in som vertuous sentence
And forto yeue hym place and audience
And bad to our ost he sholde to hym sey
That alle we to telle his tale hym preye
Our oste hadde the wordis for vs alle
Sir preest quod he now fair moot you befalle
Saith what ye list and we shul gladly here

Fig. 17.—Specimen of Caxton's type, from the *Canterbury Tales*, 1476.

Juvenalis et persii satyræ and *Johannis de Milis repertorium in jure canonico* (sic), both of 1475, were all printed at Louvain.

Colard Mansion, who came from France and learned the art of printing either in Mayence or Cologne, was printing at Bruges about 1476. His first work was *Le Jardin de Devotion*, and his type is an imitation of the peculiar French type called *Grosse batarde*. He was also employed by William Caxton, who had been for some years trading as a merchant in the Low Countries, to print the *Recuyell of the Histories of Troy*, by Raoul Le Fevre, which Caxton had translated into English

Fig. 18.—Woodcut from Caxton's *Game and Playe of the Chesse*.

at the command of Queen Margaret. This was issued in 1474, and was the first book printed in the English language. In 1475 or 1476 Caxton returned to England with a fount of types, which he had employed Mansion to cut and cast for him, and established himself as a printer in the precincts of Westminster Abbey. In 1477 he produced the first book printed in England,

The Dictes and Sayings of the Philosophers (a copy sold lately from the Duke of Buccleuch's library for £670), followed by a large number of important works, amongst which we may mention : *Chaucer's Canterbury Tales* (no date) ; *Moral Proverbs*, 1478 ; *Cordyale*, 1479 ; *Chronicles*, 1st ed., 1480 (a copy sold for £470 at the Duke of Buccleuch's sale) ; *Myrrour of the World*, 1480 ; *Tully, Of Old Age* (a copy from Lord Crawford's library sold lately for £320) ; *Godefrey of Boulogne*, 1481 ; Higden's

Fig. 19.—The Knight, a woodcut from Caxton's *Game and Playe of the Chesse.*

Polycronycon, 1482 ; *Pilgrimage,—Festival,—Confessio,—Golden Legend*, 1483 ; *Knight of the Tour,—Æsop,—Order of Chivalry*, 1484 ; *King Arthur,—Charles,—Paris and Vienne*, 1485 ; *Good Manners*, 1487 ; *Directorium*, 1489 ; *Fayts*, 1490. For further particulars about England's greatest printer, we must refer the reader to the excellent work by Mr. W. Blades, *The Life and Typography of W. Caxton*, 1863.

William Caxton produced over sixty works, the colophons

of many of them revealing much of the personal life and character of the first English printer. Some of them were ornamented with woodcuts ; we reproduce two from the *Game and Playe of the Chesse*, printed in folio about 1474. The first represents a king and another person playing at chess ; the smaller cut is a representation of the knight, who is thus described in Caxton's own words : "The knyght ought to be maad al armed upon an hors in suche wise that he have

Fig. 20.—Music, a woodcut from Caxton's *Mirrour of the World.*

an helme on his heed and a spere in his right hond, and coverid with his shelde, a swerde and a mace on his left syde, clad with an halberke and plates tofore his breste, legge harnoys on his legges, spores on his heelis, on hys handes hys gauntelettes, hys hors wel broken and taught, and apte to bataylle, and coveryd with hys armes." The other Caxton block which we reproduce is a representation of music from the *Myrrour of the World*, a thin folio volume of one hundred leaves printed

in 1480, with thirty-eight woodcuts. These specimens will
serve to show the rudimentary character of English wood
engraving in the fifteenth century. No authentic portrait of
Caxton is known, and the one that is generally accepted is
really a portrait of an Italian poet, Burchiello, taken from an

Fig. 21.—William Caxton, from Rev. J. Lewis's *Life*.

octavo edition of his work on Tuscan poetry, printed 1554;
this was copied by Faithorne for Sir Hans Sloane as the
portrait of Caxton, and was reproduced by Ames in his
Typographical Antiquities, 1749. Lewis prefixed the portrait
here given to his *Life of Mayster Willyam Caxton*, 1737, which

is a copy of Faithorne's drawing with some alterations. John Lettou and William Machlinia, both contemporaries of Caxton, issued various statutes and other legal works.

Wynkyn de Worde, a native of Lorraine, and one of

Fig. 22.—Fyshing with an Angle.

Caxton's earliest co-operators, was the first who used Roman type in England. Four hundred books were printed by him, among them Voragine's *Legenda aurea*, with woodcuts, 1498; *Huon de Bordeaux* (from which Shakespeare derived his

Midsummer Night's Dream), and, perhaps his best known, *Treatyses perteynynge to Hawkynge and Huntynge, Fysyhing with an Angle, by Dame Juliana Barnes*, or *Berners*, 1496, from which we reproduce here the man with the angle. A copy of this book sold lately for £120.

Richard Pynson, who died in 1529 or 1531, was Henry VIII.'s first printer. There are more than two hundred of his works still extant, mostly in Old English and pro-fusely illustrated, such as the *Descrypcyon of Englonde*, fol., and he also was among the first who used Roman type in

Fig. 23.—Mark of Wynkyn de Worde.

England. From Westminster the art spread in England to Oxford, where Theodoricus Rood, from Cologne, printed an *Exposicio Sancti Jeronimi* in 1478 ; and to St. Albans in 1480 by a printer who has never been identified, and who produced the famous *Chronicle of England*, fol., 1483, and *Boke of St. Albans*, fol., 1486.

Wynkyn de Worde used no less than nine different marks, all of them bearing Caxton's initials,—evidencing the regard of the pupil for his master ; the mark which we reproduce is one of rare occurrence. Richard Pynson began in 1493, and continued well into the sixteenth century, and was

one of the first of the " privileged " printers, authorized to
issue the legal and parliamentary publications. One of the
marks used by him is here reproduced. Julian Notary began to
print in 1498, and established an office in London in conjunction
with Jean Barbier 1499. There are twenty-three books traced
to Notary's office. The only style of illustration used by any of
these early printers was the woodcut, and of this there was very
little beyond the title-page and printer's mark. The artistic

Fig. 24.—Mark of Richard Pynson.

form of the Book originated on the Continent, but England
was not slow to adopt it and fashion it to her own ends.

The invasion, we see, had been most rapid. In less than
fifteen years every important city had followed the movement,
and was ready to establish printing offices. If we may credit
a certain doubtful document, Charles VII. had on the 3rd
of October, 1458, sent to Mayence one of the best medal
engravers of the Mint of Tours to study the process of which
marvels were spoken. "The 3rd of October, 1458, the King

having learned that Messire Guthenberg, living at Mayence, in the country of Germany, a skilful man in cutting and making letters with a punch, had brought to light the invention of printing by punches and types, desirous of inquiring into such a treasure, the King has commanded the directors of his mints to nominate persons well instructed in the said cutting and to send them secretly to the said place to inform themselves of the said mode and invention, to understand and learn the art of the same, in order to satisfy the said Lord King. Thereupon was pointed out to the said King and was undertaken by Nicholas Jenson, who took the said journey to bring intelligence of the said art and of the execution of it in the said kingdom, which first has made known the said art of impression to the said kingdom of France" (*Bibliothèque de l'Arsenal*, Hf 467, pp. 410, 411).

Nicholas Jenson on his return met with a cool reception from Louis XI., who did not care to propagate the works of his father. It may be supposed that this coolness was the cause of his expatriating himself and retiring to a place where he could find freer scope for the exercise of his industry. Ten years after the above mission we find him established at Venice, his art of engraver of letters joined to that of printer. His *Præparatio Evangelica* by Eusebius, translated by Trapezuntius, and his *Justinian*, were composed in 1470, with such marvellous and clear Roman types that from that day the best typographers have imitated his founts. In spite of its success, he did not confine himself to these letters, but he made also Gothic ones, in which by preference he printed theological books.

Notwithstanding the attempts of Jenson in the name of the King of France—that is, if these attempts ever took place in the manner indicated above—the invention was not known to have

commended itself to the powerful University of Paris. It was
very difficult to introduce innovations into that learned body,
unless one had some powerful influence in the university.
We have seen John Fust, compelled suddenly to retake the
road to Germany, in a fair way to find himself taxed with
sorcery,—at that time no slight matter. For unauthorised

barbarum ac ferum legibus ad cultioré uitæ.ufum
traductu in forma prouinciæ redegit.

FINIS

Hiftorias.ue es peregrinaq; gefta reuofuo
Iuftinus.lege me:fum trogus ipfe breuis.
Me gallus ueneta Ienfon Nicolaus in urbe
Formauit:Mauro principe Chriftophoro.

IVSTINI HISTORICI CLARISSIMI IN TROGI POMPEII HISTORIAS LIBER XLIIII. FELICITER EXPLICIT.

.M.CCCE.LXX.

Fig. 25.—Imprint of Nicholas Jenson to a Justinian, printed in 1470 at Venice. This
type has prevailed up to now.

persons the sale of unlicensed books had had most unhappy
consequences, and Parliament was not able to interfere.

Thus ten years had passed since the journey of Jenson,
and ten or twelve since the first manifestations of typography
at Mayence, and yet the diabolical discovery had not found
admittance to the Sorbonne. What was still more extraordinary,
a Cologne printer issued about 1472 a small folio in Gothic

type, thirty-one long lines to a page, which was a work written in French. The *Histoires de Troyes* of Raoul Le Fevre, chaplain to the dukes of Burgundy, first found a publisher in Germany, and soon after another in England, before a single press was definitely installed at Paris.

As we have said of Peter Schoeffer, German students came in numbers to the university, where they pursued their studies, and frequently remained later as professors. It has been found that in 1458 a former student of the University of Leipzig named John Heinlein, a native of Stein, in the diocese of Spire, entered as director of the college of Burgundy, from whence he passed to the Sorbonne in 1462, the year of the troubles in Mayence. After the mania for latinising names so common at that time, he called himself Lapidanus, from the name of his native place, which means Stone in German. Heinlein met in Paris a Savoyard, William Fichet, born in 1433 at Petit Bornand, who became an Associate of the Sorbonne about 1461, and finally Rector, as he himself was in 1468. These two men, bound together with great friendship, and possessed of that instinct inherent to men of elevated studies, guessed at once what enormous help printing would bring to bear on their work. Besides, it grieved them to see through the whole of France, especially in Touraine, German canvassers carrying about their goods in bales under cover of other commerce, a practice from which the most grave inconveniences might result. It occurred to them that to prevent fraud they would themselves create a printing establishment; but if they deliberated on it, it must have been done secretly, for the registers of the Sorbonne are silent on their enterprise.

If Fichet conceived the idea, it may be believed that Heinlein, owing to his German connections, put it into execution. M. Philippe thinks that he was formerly at Basle. In all probability it was from that city he tried to obtain his workmen. It was in 1466, after six years had elapsed since the printers were dispersed and fled from Mayence. At all events, it was from Basle that Ulrich Gering, Michael Freyburger, and Martin Krantz, printers recommended to the two Sorbonnists, started, and in due course arrived in Paris. Of these three men, who were the first to establish a printing office on the French side of the Rhine, Ulrich Gering was a student as well as a printer, and so was Freyburger, a native of Colmar. As for Krantz, he probably was a letter-founder, and the only real workman of the three companions.

It is often regretted that there are no authentic portraits of these men, nor of Gutenberg, Fust, and Schoeffer, to transmit their features to us. As regards Gutenberg, every one will recall the fur cap and the tight breeches of Thorwaldsen's statue at Mayence, but there is really no genuine portrait of Gutenberg, except the traditional features of the inventor reproduced in the previous chapter. As to Gering, M. Philippe, in his *Histoire de l'Origine de l'Imprimerie à Paris*, publishes a grotesque figure muffled in the ruff of the sixteenth century, after a picture preserved at Lucerne, but it is not remarkable as a work of art.

The printing office of the three Germans was set up within the walls of the Sorbonne—*in ædibus Sorbonnicis*—in 1469. There they set to work at once,—no difficult matter, seeing that at that time a printing establishment consisted simply of a room, none too light, a table, and press, and some forms. Krantz doubtless cast the types chosen by the Sorbonnists; for there were then two sorts of letters in use, the German Gothic and the Roman. They kept to the Roman, as being more round and clear ; and when once the matrices were obtained and their type was cast, they entered on their task with ardour.

The tendencies of Fichet and Heinlein had no leaning

Gaſparini pergamenſis,clariſſimi orato/
riſ/epiſtolaꝛ liber foeliciter incipit;

Audeo plurimum ac lætor in
ea te ſententia eſſe:ut nihil a
me fieri ſine cauſa putes·Ego
enī etſi multoꝛ uerebar ſuſpi
tioneſ/ꝙ a me ſemproniū antiquū fami/
liarē meū reiiciebā:tamē cū ad incredibi͡
lē animi tui ſapiētiā iudiciū meū refere/
bā: nihil erat.ꝗre id a te improbari pu/
tarem·Nam cum & meoſ noſſeſ moreſ:&
illius naturā n̄ ignorares:n dubitabā qd
de hoc facto meo iudicaturus eſſes· Non
igit haſ ad te ſcribo lraſ/quo nouam tibi
de rebuſ a me geſtiſ opinionem faciā:ſed
ut ſi quando aliter homieſ noſtroſ de me
ſētire intelliges: tu q probe cauſam meā
noſti/defenſione meā ſuſcipiaſ·Hæc ſi fe/
ceris: nihil eſt quo ulterius officium tu/
um requiram·Vale ;

Fig. 26.—*Letters* of Gasparin of Bergamo. First page of the first
book printed at Paris, in 1470.

towards transcendental theology, but rather towards the literature of the ancients and contemporary rhetorical works. Besides, it may be said, considering that men are far from perfect, Fichet counted on making the authorised presses serve his own purpose.

We find him publishing a treatise on *Rhetoric* in quarto in 1471, and always engaged in supervising the work confided to his artists. The partners commenced with a large volume of *Letters* of Gasparin of Bergamo, which was set up in quarto with the Roman type, the character of which had then been accepted. At the end of the work, the production of which took much time—possibly a year—the three printers placed a quatrain in

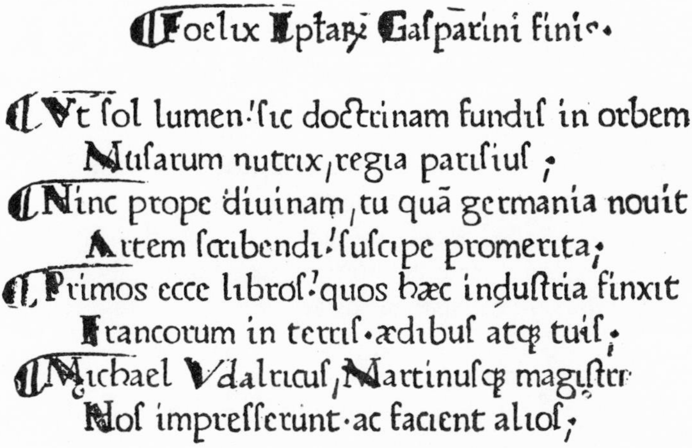

Foelix Iptar̄ Gaſparini fini·

Vt ſol lumen·ſic doctrinam fundiſ in orbem
Muſarum nutrix, regia patiſiuſ;
Ninc prope diuinam, tu quā germania nouit
Artem ſcribendi·ſuſcipe promerita;
Primos ecce libroſ·quos hæc induſtria finxit
Francorum in terriſ·ædibuſ atqʒ tuiſ;
Michael Vdalricuſ, Martinuſqʒ magiſter
Noſ impreſſerunt·ac facient alioſ;

Fig. 27.—Colophon in distichs in the *Letters* of Gasparin of Bergamo, first book printed at Paris at the office of the Sorbonne.

Latin distichs, which is at once a statement of identity and a promise for the future :—

> " Primos ecce libros quos hæc industria finxit
> Francorum in terris ædibus atque tuis ;
> Michael, Udalricus, Martinusque magister
> Hos impresserunt, ac facient alios."

If we try to apportion to each of the three printers his share in the production of the book, it may be supposed that the intellectual part of the composition and the correction fell to Michael Freyburger and to Ulrich Gering, while the heavier work of founding, placing in forms, and press work fell to

Krantz. This essay, satisfactory as it appeared, was far from perfect. The first Parisian printers had multiplied abbreviations and irregular contractions, and enormous difficulties and inevitable faults ensued. Further, either they had more than one punch, or the matrix got deformed, for the characters

Fig. 28.—*Rhetorique* of Fichet, printed at Paris in 1471. The marginals are drawn by hand.

frequently differ. In spite of these objections, we must commend them for having used, before all others, the *æ* and *œ*, which were uniformly written *e* in the manuscripts, thus giving rise to errors without number. Their punctuation was the comma, semicolon, and the full stop.

Fichet and Heinlein had become the modest librarians of the Sorbonne, and this new employment gave them greater facilities for superintendence. The printing office did not remain inactive. It issued successively the *Orthography* of Gasparin of Bergamo, the *Letters* of Phalaris, two books of Æneas Sylvius, the *Conspiracy of Catiline* of Sallust, the *Epitome of Titus Livius* of Florus, and finally the *Rhetorics* of William Fichet, which, if we may credit a letter addressed to Bessarion, was finished in 1471. Afterwards they produced the *Letters* of Bessarion, the *Elegantia Latinæ Linguæ* of Valla (the first folio volume issued from the Sorbonne presses), and many others; to wit, thirteen volumes in 1470-71 and seventeen in 1472.

At the end of 1742 the workshop was somewhat broken up, Fichet having left for Rome and Heinlein having gone to preach in Germany. The three printers had sufficiently shown by their works that they were in earnest; in addition, they had from the first presented gratuitously copies of their works to the nobles, who, being accustomed to pay highly for manuscripts, did not fail to note the difference. The Associates then resolved to quit the Sorbonne and to found an establishment for themselves, their patrons being no longer there to sustain them in case of failure; and if we judge by the sacrifice they made in giving up their presses and types they were not without anxiety on their new venture.

Their oldest dated books, the *Manuale Confessorum* 1473 (March) and the *Manipulus Curatorum* of Montrocher 1437 (May), were also the first that they printed in their new quarters, at the sign of the " Golden Sun " in the Rue St. Jacques. They remained there as partners up to the year 1477, when Gering alone signed at the " Golden Sun." Afterwards he took in associates, George Mainyal in 1480 and Berthold Rembold in 1494, who lived with him in the Rue de la Sorbonne, where he established himself on leaving the Rue St. Jacques. Ulrich Gering died on the 23rd of August, 1510, after a half-century of work.

The movement inaugurated by the Sorbonne was promptly followed. German workmen opened their printing offices nearly everywhere in France ; then the French themselves took the same course. At Lyons in 1472 a Frenchman was established, the same at Angers, Caen, Metz, Troyes, Besançon, and Salins. But in the central provinces we find Henry Mayer at Toulouse, John Neumeister at Albi ; in the east, Metlinger at Dijon ; and Michael Wensler, of Basle, at Macon, without counting others, between 1470 and 1480.

We have now arrived at an epoch of greater efforts. The Lyons printers used ornamental letters, from which engravings in the Book were developed. Since the block books, illustrations had been neglected, as the means were wanting to distribute the plates here and there in the form ; Schoeffer still employed initial letters in metal very like vignettes, like many others.

If we search for the precise epoch in which illustration appeared in the history of the Book, we shall perhaps have to go back to the time of Albert Pfister, printer of Bamberg, who issued in 1461 an edition of the *Fables of Ulrich Boner* with a hundred and one figures on wood, and the first book printed in the German language. This may be said to be the unconscious combination of xylography with typography, a kind of transformation of old elements to new things without any importance, for art counted for nothing in this adaptation.

Up to this time Germany had not, in its school of painters or illuminators, men capable of giving a personal impulse to ornamentation. In the German editions of the block books the influence of Van Eyck was remarkable, and the German printers who went to seek their fortunes in Italy fell into the midst of a circle admirably prepared to impart their ideas to them. It appears that the first book printed in Italy with woodcuts in the text and with an ascertained date is the work of a German established at Rome, namely Ulrich Hahn, in 1467. If we may believe an account in the *Annuaire du Bibliophile,*—which, being without citation of authority, we quote for what it is worth—but is no doubt a fable, as Joh. Winterberger 1482 is

Fig. 29.—Mark of Guerbin, printer at Geneva, 1482.

acknowledged as the first Vienna Printer,—Ulrich Hahn established a press at Vienna about 1462, but was driven thence by the publication of a pamphlet against the burgomaster of the city. Under these unfortunate circumstances, he was attracted to Rome by the famous Torquemada, who confided to him the impression of his work the *Meditationes*, which he wanted to adorn with illustrations. Hahn was himself an engraver, as were also most of his *confrères* at that time—that is, he cut in relief the design already drawn on wood so that it could be intercalated in the text like a large letter. Passavant relates that the designs of the *Meditationes* were taken from compositions

of Fra Angelico, who died in 1455. It is now impossible
to verify this fact, so much did the German artist preserve
the crude manner of his country in working these plates.
Be that as it may, the book, the printing of which was
finished on St. Sylvester's Day, 1467, is the first known with
engravings printed in Italy, and only three copies of it exist:

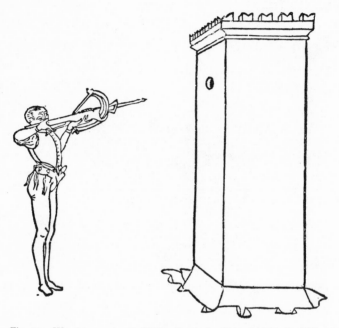

Fig. 30.—Wood engraving in Matteo Pasti, for Valturius' *De Re Militari*
(Verona : 1472).

one at Vienna, one at Nuremberg, and one in Lord Spencer's
library ; it is printed in Gothic type in folio.

Illustration found a true artist at Verona, in Matteo Pasti,
who furnished designs for a volume on military art by Valturius,
printed in Roman characters in folio, at the expense of John of
Verona, and dedicated to Sigismond Pandolfi. Pasti's eighty-
two wood engravings are simple outlines, cleverly executed,
of which we here reproduce one of the principal —an archer

shooting at a butt. Published in 1472, the volume of Valturius thus followed very soon after the *Meditationes*, but the engravings enable us already to see how the Italian process, consisting mostly of lines without shadows, differed from the Dutch and German. One thing to be remarked here is also the purity of the design, as compared with a certain irregularity of the engraving ; we feel in these figures Italian art at its height, despite the somewhat coarse translation of the wood-engraver.

At Venice the German discoveries had borne fruit. At the end of the fifteenth century, fifty years after the invention of typography, the printing offices and booksellers' shops were counted by hundreds. It was in this city that for the first time a title with frontispiece giving the contents, the place, the date, and the name of the printer, was given to the Book. We give here this ornamental title, placed before a *Calendario* of John de Monteregio, printed by Pictor, Loslein, and Ratdolt in 1476, folio.

The German Erhardt Ratdolt was probably the promoter of these innovations. He soon afterwards published the first geometrical book with figures, the *Elements of Euclid*, 1482, folio ; in the same year he produced the *Poeticon Astronomicum* of Hyginus, previously printed at Ferrara, in which he displayed illustrations on wood of excellent design, but heavily and comparatively unskilfully engraved. Yet the art of the Book could not remain inferior in this city, where so many artists were piling up marvels. Nicholas Jenson, the emigrant from France, of whom we have spoken above, had, in imitation of Italian manuscripts, introduced that Roman letter, the primitive type of which has come down to our time pretty well untouched. At the death of Jenson in 1481, his materials passed into the

5

hands of Andrew d'Asola, called Andrea Torresani, who did not neglect the good traditions of his master, and who produced before anyone else a book bearing signatures, catchwords, and pagination (*Letters of St. Jerome*, 1488). Torresani was the father-in-law of Aldus Manutius, who was to be for ever illustrious in the art of printing at Venice, and to conduct his art to the highest pitch of perfection.

Fig. 31.—Title-page of the *Calendario*, first ornamental title known. Printed in 1476 at Venice.

But if decoration by means of relief blocks found a favourable reception in Italy, and, above all, a group of artists capable of carrying it to success, there were at the same time other experiments which originated in a different direction. The discovery of Maso Finiguerra gave to the art a new process of reproduction, and printing presses were now able to make the working of engraved plates possible and practicable. In order to make that which follows comprehensible, we must enter into a few technical details, the whole subject having been so admirably and fully treated by MM. Delaborde and Duplessis.

In the engraved wood block, as in the printing type, it is a projection in the wood or metal which, being inked and passed under a press, leaves on paper its lines in black. Naturally then the intercalation of an engraving of this kind in typographical composition is made without difficulty, as the impression of both is taken at one pull. On the other hand, a line engraving is obtained from incised lines on a plate of copper; that is, an instrument called a burin traces the lines, which are filled with greasy ink. These incised lines are only inked. The surface of the plate is then cleaned off to avoid smudging. The sheet of paper destined for the impression has then to be made very pliable and pulpy, so that at the striking of the press it runs, so to speak, to find the ink in the lines and to reproduce them. It is therefore impossible to make simultaneous impressions from both raised and incised plates.

This kind of reproduction, however, which, contrary to that from wood, allowed of half-tints or shading, attracted in good time the workers in the production of the Book. It appeared to them possible to reconcile the two printings by the successive passage of the same sheet of paper through the press, to receive at first the impression from the type, and afterwards from the ink in the incisions of the copper plate. The first manifestation of this new method of illustration was made at Florence, the home of line engraving, by Nicholas di Lorenzo in 1477, for the work of Antonio Bettini, of Siena, called *El Monte Santo di Dio*. Here the artists were not the first in the field. If we accept the common opinion, Baccio Baldini borrowed from Sandro Botticelli the subjects of his plates.

In any case, Italian engraving seeks its source in Pollajuolo, Botticelli, and Baldini. It is not the simple work of a niellist, but it had not yet reached its perfect expression either in the work

Fig. 32.—Engraving on metal by Baccio Baldini for *El Monte Santo di Dio*, in 1477.

or in the impression; the illustrations of the *Monte Santo* are proof of this, as are also those of the *Dante*, by Baldini, in 1481, for the same Nicholas di Lorenzo. From this we reproduce the Misers.

At this epoch engravings by the burin were taken with a pale ink, the composition of which is not anything like the fine black ink of Schoeffer or of the old Italian printers. And besides in most cases the proofs were obtained by rubbing (*au frotton*) like the ancient block books, an eminently defective process. The press was not yet well adapted to the delicate work of line engraving, and the workmen, who did not insert the plates until after the text was printed, preferred not to risk the loss of their sheets by the use of inappropriate presses. These, with the insignificant attempts made by the Germans in

Fig. 33.—Metal engraving by Baccio Baldini from the *Dante* of 1481.

1479,[*] are the beginnings of the process of line engraving in the ornamentation of the Book. In fact, the process failed to take the position which was expected of it, owing to the inconvenient mode of working. Relief engraving still made great advances ; with it the sheets used for the impression did not require working more than once to produce the illustrations with the text; in a word, the labour was not so great. A century elapsed before line engraving completely dethroned the vignette

[*] *Breviarium ecclesie Herbipolensis :* Et. Dold., 1479, folio, copperplate engravings.

on wood, and a century in which the latter attained its height, and showed what able artisans could make of a process apparently the least flexible.

Not to leave Italy, which had the honour of making the book with engraved illustrations known to the world, we pass over some years, during which Arnold Bucking brought out at Rome a *Cosmographia* of Ptolemy, 1478, with incised plates, which is the first printed atlas that was produced, while as regards ordinary publications there appeared in all parts classical and Italian works, such as Cicero, Virgil, Tacitus, Pliny, Eusebius, among the ancients, and Dante, Petrarch, Boccaccio, etc., as regards the modern authors. Among the editions of Dante, we may cite that of Peter of Cremona, dated 18th of November, 1491 (Fig. 35), with one wood-engraving to each canto, of which the earlier ones are after Botticelli, and perhaps even drawn by him directly on the wood. Passavant believes these figures to be cut in relief in the metal. On some of the plates there is a signature, a Gothic ħ, the signification of which leaves a free field for conjecture, and perhaps for error. There is also another edition containing twenty plates printed, 1481, ten years before the woodcut edition, which is extremely rare ; one in the Hamilton Palace Library sold in May 1884 for £380 ; the Royal Library of Berlin recently agreed to pay £1,200 for a proof set of these plates.

As we shall see later apropos of German vignettes of the same period, the characteristic feature of Italian engraving was sobriety, the complete absence of useless work, and the great simplicity of the human figure. This special manner will be found in the famous first edition of Francesco Colonna's *Hypnero-tomachia Poliphili*, printed in 1499 by Aldus, which has been frequently reproduced, and even copied sixty years after its first publication by a French printer, a rare occurrence in the book trade. On account of its exquisite woodcuts this work has always been a great favourite with book-collectors, especially with artists, notwithstanding its continual increase in price. Mr. Beckford's copy sold for £130.

The Italian illustrators, whether they operated simply on wood, or, as some writers have it, engraved their cuts in relief

Fig. 34.—Plate from the *Hypnerotomachia Poliphili*, printed by Aldus Manutius, in 1499.

on metal, always brought their figures conspicuously forward, by making the surroundings more accentuated and often dotted over, thus forming a dark background. This was also the ordinary process in their ornaments, among the most interesting of which are the borders of the plates to an edition of Dante by Bonino de Bonini, Brescia, 1487, of which a specimen is here reproduced.

If we return from Italy, which then took the lead, to

Germany, we find at Augsburg about the year 1470 a school of *Formschneiders*, whose obscure workshops were of no great advantage to the booksellers. These ill-advised artists went even further Apparently furious at seeing printing so widely spread as to render their bad woodcuts difficult to pass off as original designs, they united in a body to forbid Günther

Fig. 35.—The planet Mercury and the city of Rome, engraving from the *Divina Comedia* (Venice, 1491).

Zainer and Schüssler to put engravings into their books. They must nevertheless have come to an ultimate arrangement, for Zainer printed in 1477 a *Book on Chess* by Jacopo da Cessole, with vignettes. He was besides one of the few German printers who employed Roman characters in place of the Gothic of Peter Schoeffer. At Cologne in 1474 Arnold Ther Hoernen published a work entitled *Fasciculus Temporum,* with small illustrations engraved on wood. A *Bible* without date contained most interesting illustrations. As to the celebrated *Todtentantz*, or *Dance of Death*, published about 1485, it contains forty-one plates in relief of the most ordinary

Fig. 36.—Plate from Bonino de Bonini's *Dante*, at Brescia, in 1487.

kind and the least personal mark, the same as in the *Chronicle of Cologne* of 1499, of which the figures, though less German and less distorted, do not come up to the more German, but more artistic Nuremberg books.

At Nuremberg, Antony Koberger, called by Badius the
prince of booksellers, directed an immense establishment,
employing more than a hundred workmen, without counting

Fig. 37.—The creation of woman, plate from the *Schatzbehalter*, engraved
after Michael Wohlgemuth.

smaller houses at Basle and Lyons. At Basle Johannes
Froben, born 1460, at Hammelburg in Franconia, established
a printing press in 1491, and printed chiefly the works of

Erasmus and the Latin Fathers, particularly the fine edition of *St. Augustin.* To many of his titles and borders Hans Holbein lent his hand. Koberger was a capable and a fortunate man. He had at first put forth a Bible very indifferently illustrated with the cuts of the Cologne Bible, but he had something better in view than copying others. Michael Wohlgemuth, born at Nuremberg in 1434, was then in the full vigour of his talent. To his school the young Albert Dürer came to study ; and as his business was to draw on wood as well as to engrave on copper and paint on panel, Koberger was attracted to him, and engaged him to make a set of illustrations for a book. The projected work was the *Schatzbehalter*, a sort of ascetic compilation, deficient both in interest and in arrangement. Michael Wohlgemuth set to work ; and, thanks to the ability of his engravers, of whom William Pleydenwurff was probably one, Koberger was able to issue the book in the course of 1491 in three hundred and fifty-two folios of two columns. Without being perfection, the designs of Wohlgemuth, very German, very striking, present the vigour and merit of the future school of Nuremberg. The figure is no longer a simple line, in the manner of the block books, but a combination of interlaced cuttings, intended to imitate shades. Such are those representing *The Creation of Eve* and *The Daughter of Jephthah* reproduced here. If we were to look for harmony between the text and engravings of this curious work, we should find grace and gaiety laid aside ; on the other hand, we should perceive a freedom and boldness that would fascinate and permit us to appreciate at their value the Nuremberg artists and Koberger, the printer. In fact, the German artists are here more individual, each one taken by himself, than the Italian illustrators could be, condemned as they were to the hierarchical

commonplace and to a certain form of forced idealism into
which the art of Italy was dragged little by little. The German
painters, naturalists and believers, presented their heroes in the

Fig. 38.—The daughter of Jephthah, plate taken from the *Schatzbehalter*,
engraved after Michael Wohlgemuth.

image of that robust nature that was before their eyes. It was
in this rude and unpolished spirit that Michael Wohlgemuth
illustrated the *Schatzbehalter;* he also designed the illustrations

for the *Nuremberg Chronicle* of Dr. Hartman Schedel, printed by Koberger in 1493 (Fig. 39).

With Dürer, at the latter end of the fifteenth century, the Book was no more than a pretext for engravings. Thausing, his biographer, says that the great artist felt the necessity of designing an *Apocalypse* at Rome at the time when Luther was premeditating his religious revolution in face of the worldly splendours of the pontifical court. The *Apocalypse*, published in 1511 in Latin, with Gothic characters, was an album of

Fig. 39.—Title of the *Nuremberg Chronicle*, printed by A. Koberger, 1493. Fol.

fifteen large wood engravings. *The Four Horsemen* is the best of these plates, and the boldest; but in this gross fancy, in these poor halting old hacks, the fantastic and grand idea which the artist meant to convey can hardly be seen. It may be said the genius of Dürer was little adapted to vignettes, so large they were, and did not easily lend itself to the exigencies of a spun-out subject. The title of his *Apocalypse* is of its kind a curious example of German genius, but, in spite of its vigour, it does not please like an Italian headpiece or like a French or

Flemish frontispiece. The other works of Dürer published in the fifteenth century, *The Life of the Virgin* and *The Passion*,

Fig. 40.—Title of the *Apocalypse*, by Albert Dürer, printed in 1498.
First edition without text.

were also sets of prints to which the text was afterwards added

For the rest of his illustrations Dürer belongs to the sixteenth century, and we shall have occasion to recur to his works. At present it remains to mention a curious work printed at Basle by Bergman de Olpe in 1497, which appears to be the

Stultifera Nauis.

Narragonice pfectionis nunqz

fatis laudata Nauis: per Sebaſtianū Brant: vernaculo vul-
gariqʒ fermone & rhythmo p cūctoʒ mortalium fatuitatis
femitas effugere cupiētiū directione/ fpeculo /cōmodoqʒ &
falute : proqʒ inertis ignauęqʒ ftulticię ppetua infamia/ exe-
cratione/& confutatione /nup fabricata : Atqʒ iampridem
per Iacobum Locher/cognomēto Philomufum: Sueuū :in
latinū traducta eloquiū : & per Sebaſtianū Brant : denuo
feduloqʒ reuifa:fœlici exorditur principio.
.1497.
Nihil fine caufa.
Io.de Olpe

Fig. 41.—Title of Sebastian Brandt's *Ship of Fools*, printed in
1497 at Basle by Bergman de Olpe.

first comic conception of fifteenth century artists : the *Navis Stultifera*, or *Ship of Fools* of Sebastian Brandt. This work of the school of Basle lacks neither originality nor boldness. At the time when it was published its success was immense,

from the strange tricks of its clowns, with fools' caps, with
which every page was adorned. Alas! the best things fell
under the satire of these jesters, even the Book and the Book
lover, if we may judge by the sarcasms which the personage
here reproduced volleys against useless publications. " I have
the first place among fools. . . . I possess heaps of volumes
that I rarely open. If I read them, I forget them, and I am
no wiser." Brunet saw in these humorous caricatures more

Fig. 42.—The Bibliomaniac. Engraving from the *Ship of Fools*.

art than is really to be found in them. Their value is owing
more to their spirit and humour than to any other artistic
merit. Even the engraving is singularly fitted to the subject,
with its saving cutting, and its close, hair-like texture. The
designer was certainly not a Holbein, but he is no longer the
primitive artisan of the first German plates, and his " go" is
not displeasing.

We have before spoken, apropos of engraving by the burin

in Italy, of the small share of Germany in the production of illustration by that means, and we do not therefore see any real and serious attempt in the two little coats of arms in copperplate in the *Missale Herbipolense*, printed in 1479.

The Flemish had not taken any great flight in the midst of this almost European movement. The school of Burgundy, whose influence was felt in all the surrounding countries, had lost its authority in consequence of the progress achieved at Mayence. Without doubt the great Flemish artists were still there, but they were honoured painters, and their inclination did not prompt them to work for the booksellers beyond making them offers of service. The first of these, officially esta-blished in Flanders, were two Germans, as we have mentioned before, John of Westphalia and John Veldener, of Würtzburg, who established themselves in the University of Louvain in 1473, three years after the first Paris printers. John Veldener edited the *Fasciculus Temporum*, a book which had enormous success in the fifteenth century, and the first book in which borders and ornaments occur, which later on, because these borders consisted of vine branches, were called in France *Vignettes*.

At Haarlem, in spite of the *Block-Books* attributed to Laurent Coster, illustration was backward. About 1485, a Dutch translation of the *Malheurs de Troye* of Le Fevre was issued. This French book was published at Cologne before France possessed the smallest typographical workshop. At Bruges Colard Mansion illuminated the cuts of his *Metamorphoses* of Ovid in 1484. Simple engraving appeared to him too far remote from manuscripts, the vogue of which had not yet passed away. At Zwoll, Peter van Os, from Breda, used the xylo-graphic plates of the *Biblia Pauperum*, while the master *à la*

6

navette, John of Vollehoe, an artist in the best sense of the word, was ornamenting certain popular publications with his designs. At Utrecht Veldener came from Louvain to establish a workshop. He published for the second time a *Fasciculus* in 1480 ; he created, as we stated, a style of decoration with flowers and leaves, which shortly after developed into the trade of *Rahmenschneiders.* Antwerp had attracted Matthias van der Goes, Gerard de Leeu from Gouda, and he produced the romance of *Belle Vienne* and the first Dutch translation of *Æsop's Fables,* 1485. Schiedam had an inventive engraver who illustrated an edition of the *Chevalier Delibéré* of Oliver de la· Marche, in folio, with Gothic letters, after 1483, as we read in the colophon :—

> " Cet traittie fut parfait l'an mil
> Quatre cens quatre vings et trois
> Ainsi que sur la fin d'avril
> Que l'yver est en son exil,
> Et que l'esté fait ses explois.
> Au bien soit pris en tous endrois
> De ceulx à qui il est offert
> Par celui qui *Tant a souffert,*
> La Marche.''

The French language, bright and harmonious, thus found hospitality in other countries. For many examples of French books published abroad, we cannot cite one German work printed in France. Spreading from the north to the south, typography had from 1490 its two principal centres at Paris and Lyons. After the success of the three Germans at the Sorbonne, events took their own course. In 1474 Peter Cæsaris and John Stol, two students who had been instructed by Gering and Krantz, founded the second establishment in Paris, at the sign of the " Soufflet Vert ;" and they printed classical works. Ten years later appeared Antoine Vérard, Simon Vostre, and

Pigouchet, the first of whom gave to French bookselling an impulse that it has not since lost ; but before them Pasquier-Bonhomme published his *Grandes Chroniques* in 1476, three volumes folio, the oldest book printed at Paris in French with a date.

The French school of illustration was at its most flourishing point at the end of the fifteenth century, but solely in miniature and ornamentation by the brush. The charming figures of the manuscripts had at this time a Flemish and naturalistic tendency. The most celebrated of the great artists in manuscripts, Jean Foucquet, could not conceal the source of his talent nor the influence of the Van Eyck school, yet the touch remained distinctly personal. He had travelled, and was not confined to the art circles of a single city, as were so many of the earliest painters of Flanders. He had gone through Italy, and from thence he brought with him architectural subjects for his curious designs in the *Heures* of Etienne Chevalier, now at Frankfort, a precious fragment of which is preserved in the National Library of Paris. Side by side with this undoubted master, whose works are happily known, lived a more modest artist, Jean Perréal, called Jean de Paris, painter to Charles VIII., Louis XII., and Anne of Brittany.

In joining with these two masters, Foucquet and Perréal, one who serves as a transition between them, Jean Bourdichon, designer to the kings of France from Louis XI. to Francis I., we at once obtain a not despicable assemblage of vital forces. Without doubt these men could not enter in the same line either with the admirable school of Flanders, or the Germans of Nuremberg, or the masters of Italy ; but, moderate as we may deem their merit, they did their work well, painting miniatures, colouring coats of arms, rendering to the kings, their masters, all the little duties of devoted servants without pretension, and leading the way, according to their means, for the great artistic movement in France of the seventeenth century. That these men, leaving the brush for the pencil, devoted themselves to design illustrations on wood is undeniable. It is said that one of them followed Charles VIII. to the Italian wars, and probably sketched the battles of the campaign as they took place. Now in the

Fig. 43.—A medical man of the fifteenth century, from *La Mer des Histoires.* Printed by Le Rouge. Paris, 1488.

books published at this epoch in France we meet with vignettes which so very nearly approach miniatures, that we can easily recognise in them French taste and finish. Such are, for example, the illustrations of the *Mer des Histoires*, printed by Le Rouge in 1488, where the delicacy of design is matched in some parts with extraordinary dexterity in engraving. Nevertheless, others leave something to be desired; they maim the best subjects by their unskilful line and their awkwardness of handling (Fig. 43). Were not these engravers on wood printers themselves : the Commins, Guyot Marchants, Pierre Lecarrons, Jean Trepperels, and others? We are tempted to see in certain shapeless work the hasty and careless labour of an artist hurried by the press. As mentioned above, considering the part taken by the booksellers in the making of the plates, our supposition does not appear inadmissible in itself.

Fig. 44.—Mark of Philip Pigouchet, French printer and wood engraver of the fifteenth century.

Printing had been established about twenty years in Paris when Philip Pigouchet, printer and engraver on wood, began to exercise his trade for himself or on account of other publishers. Formerly bookseller in the University, he transported his presses to the Rue de la Harpe, and took for his mark the curious figure here reproduced (Fig. 44). At this moment a true shopkeeper, Simon Vostre conceived the idea of launching forth *Books of Hours*, until then disdained in France, and

of publishing them in fine editions with figures, borders, ornaments, large separate plates, and all the resources of typography.
The attempts made at Venice and Naples between 1473 and
1476 warranted the enterprise. Entering into partnership with
Pigouchet, the two were able on the 17th of April, 1488, to
publish the *Heures a l'Usaige de Rome,* octavo, with varied
ornaments and figures. The operation having succeeded beyond
their hopes, thanks to the combination of the subjects of the

Fig. 45.—Mark of Jean Dupré, printer at Lyons.

borders, subjects that could be turned about in all manner
of ways so as to obtain the greatest variety, Simon Vostre
applied to the work, and ordered new cuts to augment the
number of his decorations. Passavant's idea is commonly
received, that the engraving was done in relief on metal,
because the line in it is very fine, the background stippled,
and the borders without scratches. Wood could not have
resisted the force of the impression; the reliefs would have been
crushed, the borders rubbed and badly adjusted. In all the

successive editions hard work and wear are not remarked, and we are forced to admit the use of a harder material than the pear or box-wood of ordinary blocks.

Fig. 46.—Mark of Simon Vostre, printer at Paris, 1501.

Fig. 47.—Ornament of Simon Vostre.

Fig. 48.—Ornament of Simon Vostre.

Fig. 49.—Ornament of Simon Vostre.

According to his wants, Simon Vostre designed new series of ornaments. Among them were histories of the saints, biblical figures, even caricatures directed against Churchmen, after the manner of the old sculptors, who thought that sin was rendered more horrible in the garb of a monk.

" Honorés sont saiges et sots,
Augustins, carmes et bigots,"

says the legend. Then there were the *Dance of Death* and

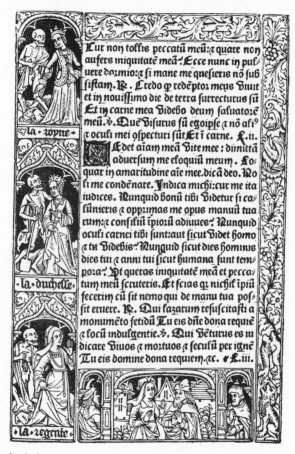

Fig. 50.—Border in four separate blocks in the *Heures à l'Usaige de Rome*, by Pigouchet, for Simon Vostre, in 1488. Small figures from the *Dance of Death*.

sibyls, allying sacred with profane, even the trades, all forming a medley of little figures in the margins, in the borders, nestled among acanthus leaves, distorted men, fantastic animals, and saints piously praying. The Middle Ages live again in these bright and charming books, so French in their origin, yet withal imbued with good sense and a tolerant spirit.

Fig. 51.—Plate copied from Schongauer's *Carrying of the Cross*, taken from the *Heures* of Simon Vostre.

The Book rose under Simon Vostre and Philip Pigouchet to the culminating point of ornamentation. Here design and engraving are at their proper value and sustain each other.

It is not only the stippled backgrounds of the borders that please the eye, but the whole effect is such as to compel the question, Who was this unknown designer, this painter of bold conceptions, whose work is so complete ? However, some of

Fig. 52.—The Death of the Virgin, plate taken from the *Heures* of Simon Vostre, printed in 1488. The border is separate.

the large full-page illustrations have not an originality of their own, nor the French touch of the borders. Thus the plate of the Passion here reproduced (Fig. 51) is inspired line for line by the German, Martin Schongauer. Are we to suppose then that already the trade with *clichés* from the original blocks was

established between France and Germany, or was it that a
copy was made of it by a French designer? It is difficult to
say. Still the coincidence is not common to all the missals
of the great Parisian bookseller. The *Death of the Virgin*
(Fig. 52) here reproduced is an evident proof of it. It forms
part of the 1488 book, and is certainly a truly French work.

It may be said that from the artistic association of Philip

Fig. 53.—Mark of Antoine Verard, printer at Paris, 1498.

Pigouchet and Simon Vostre emanated the art of book illustration in France; they worked together for eighteen years,
in steady collaboration, and, as far as we know, without a
cloud. When Vostre started in business in 1488 he lived
in the Rue Neuve Notre Dame, at the sign of "St. Jean
l'Evangeliste;" and in 1520 he was still there, having
published more than three hundred editions of the *Hours* for
the use of the several cities.

Contemporary with Simon Vostre, another publisher was giving a singular impulse to the Book by his extreme energy, true taste, and the aid of first-class artists. Antoine Verard, the most illustrious of the old French booksellers, was a caligrapher, printer, illuminator. and dealer (Fig. 53). Born in the second half of the fifteenth century,. he established himself in Paris on the Pont Notre Dame, both sides of which were then covered with shops, and about 1485 commenced his fine editions with a *Decameron* in French by Laurent de Premierfait. M. Renouvier remarks in his notice of Verard that his first books were not good ; the plates were often unskilful, and were probably borrowed or bought from others. This may be very well understood in a beginner whose modest resources did not permit bold enterprises ; moreover, the figures were in most cases groundworks for miniatures, outlines and sketches rather than vignettes.

Antony Verard was accustomed to take a certain number of fine copies on vellum or paper of each book published by him, in which qualified painters added miniatures and ornaments. It is curious now to find what the cost to one of the great lords of the court of Charles VIII. was of one of these special copies in all the details of its production. We find it in a document published by M. Senemaud in a provincial journal (*Bulletin de la Société Archéologique de la Charente*, 1859, part 2, p. 91), which enables us at the same time to penetrate into a printing office of a great French publisher of the fifteenth century. According to this document, Verard did not disdain to put his own hand to the work, even to carrying the book to the house of his patron if he happened to be a man of consequence. It is an account of Charles de Valois-Angoulême, father of Francis I. He was then living at Cognac ; and he ordered Verard to print separately for him on vellum the romance of *Tristan*, the *Book of Consolation* of Boetius, the *Ordinaire du Chrétien*, and

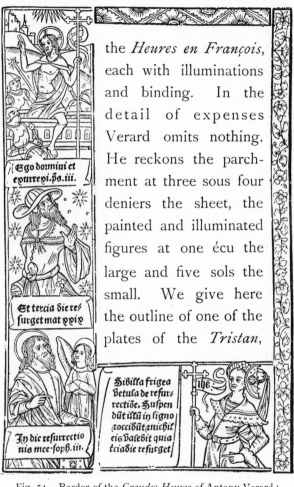

the *Heures en François*, each with illuminations and binding. In the detail of expenses Verard omits nothing. He reckons the parchment at three sous four deniers the sheet, the painted and illuminated figures at one écu the large and five sols the small. We give here the outline of one of the plates of the *Tristan*,

Fig. 54.—Border of the *Grandes Heures* of Antony Verard : Paris, 1498 (?).

ordered by the Duc d'Angoulême, reduced by two-thirds, and from its work (Fig. 55) it may be judged that the profession of the illuminator, even for the time, was by no means brilliant. The binding was in dark-coloured velvet, with two clasps

with the arms of the Duke, which cost sixty sous each.
The work finished, Vérard took the road for Cognac, carrying
the precious volumes. He was allowed twenty livres for his
travelling expenses; and this brings the total to two hundred
and seven livres ten sous, equivalent to £200 to £240 of
present money.

Fig. 55.—Plate from the *Tristan* published by Antoine Vérard, a copy of which
was illuminated for Charles of Angoulême.

Vérard had preceded Simon Vostre in the publication of
Books of Hours, but his first volume, dated 1487, was not
successful, owing to the want of borders and frontispieces. At
the most he had introduced coarse figures intended for illumi-
nation, which were rather wooden daubs than vignettes. In

1488, the same year that Simon Vostre commenced his
publications, Vérard put forth, by "command of the King our

Fig. 56.—Page of the *Grandes Heures* of Antoine Vérard : Paris,
fifteenth century.

lord," the book called the *Grandes Heures*, which is in quarto,
Gothic letter, without paging, twenty lines to the full page.

This *Grandes Heures* contained fourteen engravings, large borders in four compartments, smaller subjects and initials rubricated by hand. He thus published more than two hundred editions between 1487 and 1513, and among them the *Mystère de la Passion*, with eighty figures; the *Grandes Chroniques*, in three folio volumes, printed by Jean Maurand; the *Bataille Judaïque* of Flavius Josephus; the *Legende Dorée* of Voragine, all books for which he called to his aid rubricators, illuminators and miniaturists. From the outset he had two shops where he published his productions: one on the Pont Notre Dame, the other at the Palace of Justice, "au premier pilier devant la chapelle où l'on chante la messe de messeigneurs les présidents." After 1499, when the Pont Notre Dame was burned Vérard transported his books to the Carrefour St. Severin. At his death in 1513 he resided in the Rue Neuve Notre Dame, "devant Nostre-Dame de Paris."

Besides Vérard, Vostre, and Pigouchet, many others will be found who imitated them in the publication of *Books of Hours*. The first was Jean du Pré, who published a Paris missal in 1481, and who was at once printer and bookseller. Like Pigouchet, Du Pré printed *Books of Hours* for provincial publishers, without dreaming of the competition he was creating for himself. It is not the least curious feature in connection with the study of the History of the Book, to notice the encroachments of the publishers upon one another, as well as the friendly exchanges, the loans even of plates and type. Thielman Kerver, a German, also began to put forth *Books of Hours* in 1497 in Paris, ornamenting them with borders and figures on wood, and modelling his work completely upon that of Simon Vostre. But after having imitated him, he became associated with him in the publication and sale of the *Paris Missal.* The competition of these men was evidently an honest one, also the sale of pious works was sufficient to maintain all engaged in it. Established on the Pont St. Michel, at the sign of the " Unicorn," he sold his stock to Gilles Remacle about the beginning of the sixteenth century.

Thielman Kerver in his own works shows himself as the rival of Simon Vostre. The Hardouins, who followed the same

Fig. 57.—Typographical mark of Thielman Kerver.

profession, do not appear to have attained the success of their predecessors ; and, if we except the *Heures à l'Usage de Rome*, published in 1503 by Gilles Hardouin on the Pont au Change, at the sign of the " Rose," they servilely imitated their predecessors. There was also among the disciples of Vostre, Guillaume Eustache, bookseller to the king, "tenant la boutique dedans la grant salle du palais du çosté de messeigneurs les presidens, ou sur les grans degrés du costé de la conciergerie à l'ymage St. Jean l'Evangeliste." Eustache made use of the work of Pigouchet and Kerver, not to mention the printers of the end of the fifteenth century.

We have named the principal and the fortunate ones ; but

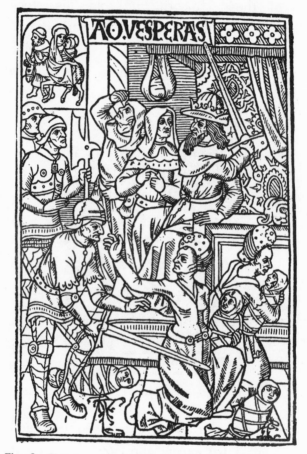

Fig. 58.—Plate from a *Book of Hours* of Simon Vostre, representing the Massacre of the Innocents.

what has become of the crowd of other publishers whose ambition was equally aroused before the success of Vostre and Vérard ? There were Denis Meslier, with his quarto *Heures de Bourges*, and Vincent Commin, bookseller of the Rue Neuve Notre Dame, who thus appealed to his customers :—

" Qui veult en avoir ? On en treuve
A tres grand marché et bon pris
A la Rose, dans la rue Neuve
De Nostre-Dame de Paris."

There were also Robin Chaillot, Laurent Philippe, and a
hundred others whose names have died with them or are
robbed of the fruit of their works.

But if pious books of this kind found vogue and a large

Fig. 59.—*Dance of Death*, said to be by Vérard.   The Pope and
the Emperor.

sale at this epoch, the dealers did not keep to ascetic publications only.   By a singular mixture of the sacred and the profane,
the book-men displayed also on their stalls the *Decameron* of
Boccaccio as well as the *Hours of the Immaculate Virgin*, and
the purchasers took an interest in the one as well as in
the other.   Besides, the end of the fifteenth century had its
literary preferences, its alluring titles, its attractive frontispieces.
At the commencement of the present century double titles—
*Atala ; or, The Child of Mystery : Waverley ; or, 'Tis Sixty
Years Since*—were common, although now out of fashion.

Afterwards came books of travels—*Voyages au Pays des Milliards, Voyages aux Pays des Révolutionnaires*, etc. Also in the fifteenth century, and even from the fourteenth, a series of titles was in public favour. There was first the *Débats*, or " Dialogues:" *Débat de la Dame et de l'Escuyer*, Paris, 1490, folio ; *Dialogue of Dives and Pauper*, London, Richard Pynson, 1493 ; and many other eccentric titles. There appeared also thousands of *complaintes*, a kind of lay in verse or prose ; *blasons*, light pieces describing this or that thing ; *doctrinals*, that had nothing to do with doctrine. And among the most approved subjects, between the piety of some and the gaiety of others, the *Dances of Death* established themselves firmly, showing, according to the different spheres of society then prevalent, Death taking the great ones of the earth, torturing alike pope, emperor, constable, or minstrel, grimacing at youth, majesty, and love. Long before printing appeared, the *Dances of Death* found their delineators ; they were some consolation for the wretched against their powerful masters, the revenge of the rabble against the king. They may be seen painted, sculptured, illuminated, when engraving was not there to multiply their use ; they may be seen largely displayed on walls, sombre and awe-inspiring, at Dresden, Leipzig, Erfurt, Berne, Lucerne, Rouen, Amiens, and Chaise-Dieu. It was the great human equality, which first tempted the French, then the inimitable Holbein. Death cries to the lords and fortunate of this world :—

> " Et après quant vous serez morts
> Tout ainsy que poures truans,
> Vous serez hydeus et puans,
> Des nostres et de noz livrées ! . . .
> Il ne souffist assez de dire
> De voz meschans corps la misere,
> Qui ne sont pas d'autre matère,
> Certainement, que nous ne sommes."

We can imagine the impression these bitter ironies made on the oppressed and disdained lower classes. The first *Dance of Death* was produced by Guyot Marchant in 1485, in ten leaves and seventeen engravings, in folio, with Gothic characters. Marchant describes himself as " demeurant en Champ Gaillart à Paris le vingt-huitiesme jour de septembre mil quatre cent quatre vingtz et cinq " (Fig. 60) The book must have gone off rapidly, for it was republished in the following year, with additions and new engravings. French illustration was

Fig. 60.—*Dance of Death* of Guyot Marchant in 1486. The Pope and the Emperor.

already moving forward, as may be judged by the reproductions here given from the folio edition of 1486. It is the pope and emperor, glory and power, that are led and plagued by Death, hideous Death, with open body and frightful grin.

We could wish that the tendencies and processes of what may be called the second generation of printers were well understood. In a few years they surmounted the difficulties of their art, and made the Book a model of elegance and simplicity. The smallest details were cared for, and things apparently the most minute were studied and rendered significant.

Speaking of titles, an enormous progress was here made in the
publications of the end of the century. In Italy subjects
of decoration were used as a framework for the front page,
wherein were included useful indications. The most ancient
specimen of this kind has already been referred to. A model
of this species is the *St. Jerome,* published at Ferrara by
Lorenzo Rossi, of Valenza, in 1497, folio; the title, much
adorned, is in Gothic letters; the engraved initial is very
adroitly left in outline, so as not to burden or break the text.

In Germany bad taste and prodigality already began to be

Fig. 61.—Mark of Guy Marchant, printer at Paris, 1485.

apparent; the letters become interlaced, the Gothic type is
covered with useless fantastic appendages and gets bewildering,
and the titles become intricate; later they became illegible even
to the Germans themselves. In France the front page gave
the most circumstantial indications of the contents of the work,
with the name and abode of the printer and bookseller. These
titles were often ornamented with moveable frameworks, printed
in Gothic, sometimes in two colours, which necessitated two
printings, one for the black and one for the red ink. The mark
of the printer or publisher generally appeared, and it was nearly
always a charming piece of work. These French marks were

all treated more or less heraldically ; that is to say, the initials occupy a shield, sustained by supporters and cut with extreme care. The first was that of Fust and Schoeffer at Mayence, of admirable simplicity and grace. In France this early specimen of the trade mark took with Simon Vostre and Vérard the shape of delicate illustrations, finely designed and carefully engraved ; but the custom of allusive marks did not prevail, as we shall have occasion to see, until the sixteenth century. The marks of Pigouchet, Vostre, and Vérard have already been given ; that of Thielman Kerver is conceived in the same principles of taste and art. The sign of his house being the " Unicorn," Kerver took as supporters to his shield two unicorns *affrontées.*

In these colophons are sometimes found philosophic aphorisms, satirical remarks, marvels of poetry. One bookseller pays homage to the powerful university, which dispenses glory and riches to the poor tradesmen by buying many books. Andrew Bocard engraved on his mark this flattery as a border :—

> " Honneur au Roy et à la court,
> Salut à l'Université
> Dont nostre bien procède et sourt
> Dieu gart de Paris la cité ! "

The Germans introduced into their colophons some vain-glorious notices. Arnold Ther Hoernen, already mentioned, who printed the *Theutonista* at Cologne in 1477, boasted in it of having corrected it all with his own hands. Jean Treschel (Fig. 63), established at Lyons in 1493, proclaims himself a German, as the Germans were the inventors of that art which he himself possessed to an eminent degree. He prided himself on being what we may call a skilled typographer ; " virum hujus artis solertissimum," he writes without false modesty. At times, in the colophons of his books, he attempted Latin verse, the Sapphic verse of Horace, of a playful turn, to say that his work was perfected in 1494.

" Arte et expensis vigilique cura
Treschel explevit opus hoc Joannes,
Mille quingentos ubi Christus annos
Sex minus egit.
Jamque Lugduni juvenes, senesque,
Martias nonas celebres agebant
Magna Reginæ quia prepotenti
Festa parabant."

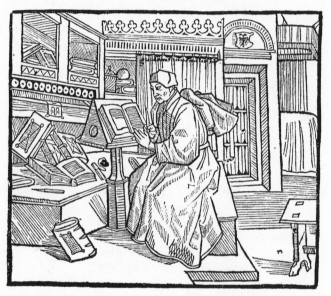

Fig. 62.—Frontispiece to *Terence*, published by Treschel at Lyons
in 1493.   The author writing his book.

The portrait is another element of illustration, the figure of the author is prefixed to his work. It had already been a custom in the manuscripts to paint on the first leaf of the work the likeness of him who wrote it, frequently in the act of presenting his book to some noble patron; and in this way is often preserved the only known portrait of either patron or author. Printing and engraving rendered these effigies more common, the portraits of one often served for another, and the booksellers used them without very much scruple. As we shall see later, this became in the sixteenth century a means of illustrating a book in the most simple manner, but only at the time when the portrait, drawn or painted, commenced to be more widely used. Previously the *clichés* of which we spoke went everywhere, from the Italians to the French, from Æsop to Accursius ; these uncertain features date back from the manuscript romances of chivalry, from whence they were

Fig. 63.—Mark of Treschel, printer at Lyons, 1489.

servilely copied in typography. The Italians from the first mixed the ancient and the modern. Thus in a *Breviarium des Décrets*, printed in 1478, there is an engraved portrait of Paul Florentin.

In France the author is often represented writing, and it was so up to the middle of the sixteenth century. In an edition of *Du Cas des Nobles Hommes*, by Jean Dupré, in 1483, Boccaccio is represented seated, having before him his French translator, Laurent de Premierfait. This plate is one of the oldest representations of authors in French books. In the

Roman de la Rose, first edition of Paris and Lyons, in folio, probably published by Guillaume Leroy about 1485, Guillaume de Lorris, the author, is shown in his bed :—

> " Une nuyt comme je songeoye,
> Et de fait dormir me convient,
> En dormant un songe m'advint. . . ."

There is also a portrait of Alain Chartier in his *Faits*, printed in 1489. In the *Terence* of Treschel, of Lyons, in 1493, we see a grammarian (Fig. 62) of the fifteenth century in a furnished room of the time, occupied in writing at a desk ; this is Guy Jouvenal, of Le Mans, the author of the commentary.

Thus was printing developed, carrying with it to the countries where it was established the rules of an unchangeable principle ; but, according to its surroundings, it was so transformed in a few years that its origin was no longer recognised. It was light in Italy, heavy in Germany, gay in France. Painting, of which it was accidentally the outcome, returned to it under the form of illustration a short time after its first and fruitful essays. The Gothic character which was general in Germany, continued to be used in France by the Vostres, the Vérards, and others up to the middle of the sixteenth century, although the earliest printers before this used Roman type ; it was also the prevailing type used in English books. In Italy it was Jenson, a Frenchman, who introduced the alphabet preserved to the present time ; and it was the Venetians and Florentines who were the first to learn the art of judicious ornamentation of the Book. The French came very near perfection, thanks to their printers and booksellers, at the end of the century ; and the Germans found illustrious artists to scatter their compositions in their large, heavy works.

CHAPTER III.

1500 TO 1600.

French epics and the Renaissance—Venice and Aldus Manutius—Italian illustrators—The Germans : *Theuerdanck*, Schäufelein—The Book in other countries
—French books at the beginning of the century, before the accession of
Francis I.—English printers and their work—Engraved plates in English
books—Geoffroy Tory and his works—Francis I. and the Book—Robert
Estienne—Lyons a centre of bookselling : Holbein's *Dances of Death*—School
of Basle—Alciati's emblems and the illustrated books of the middle of the
century—The school of Fontainebleau and its influence—Solomon Bernard—
Cornelis de la Haye and the *Promptuaire*—Jean Cousin—Copperplate
engraving and metal plates—Woériot—The portrait in the Book of the sixteenth century—How a book was illustrated on wood at the end of the century
—Influence of Plantin on the Book ; his school of engravers—General considerations—Progress in England—Coverdale's Bible.

UR simple division into chapters, it will be
understood, does not exactly correspond with
the most momentous epochs in the history of
the Book in France and abroad. Doubtless
it would be easy for France alone to find
some limits and to supply a framework within which contemporary publishers might be grouped. But in order to present,
as in a synoptical table, an essential and abridged sketch of
the Book in all European countries, it appeared to us
more convenient to take the confused and tangled notions
by centuries and to unfold them conjointly in Italy, Germany,

England and France, in taking up by the way the most salient features. Moreover, after the sixteenth century neither Italy nor Germany counts for much in comparison with France, which, less fortunate, perhaps, at the beginning than her neighbours, surpassed them in all the pride of her genius.

The commencement of the sixteenth century found the French army in Italy, under the command of Louis XII. Led from glory to glory, the French successively visited Pisa, Capua, and Naples, and that which has since been called the Renaissance impressed itself little by little on the conquerors. At Venice there lived Aldus Pius Manutius, then the greatest printer of the entire world. Aldus became proprietor of the celebrated printing office of Nicholas Jenson, through his father-in-law, Andrea Torresani, of Asola, who himself acquired it on the death of the French printer ; and he had in a few years conducted it to a position without a rival. We have seen him already printing, at the end of the fifteenth century, the admirable volume *Hypnerotomachia*, the renown of which became universal. Aldus was fifty-two years of age, having been born in 1447 ; and his learning was increased by daily intercourse with learned Italians, among others with the celebrated Pico de la Mirandola. His establishment at Venice ever since the year 1488 had for its object the creation of a chair in Greek, in which language he was well instructed from his youth. The idea having come to him of issuing editions of the principal Greek writers, which up to then remained in manuscript, he was induced to start a printing office with that purpose. He first published the *Hero and Leander* of Musæus in 1494, quarto, in a Greek character apparently designed by him, and engraved perhaps by Francisco da Bologna ; then the *Greek Grammar* of Constantine Lascaris, with the date of 1494 ; and the *Works of Aristotle* in five folio volumes. At the time of the Italian wars, Aldus was making a revolution in typography, by producing more compact sizes and finer characters, which would permit a volume of the smallest height to contain the matter of a folio printed with large type. Legend says that the new letters were copied exactly from the handwriting of Petrarch (of which author he published an edition in 1501, the first Italian work printed in Italic type), inclining like all cursive

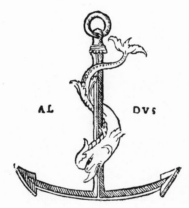

Fig. 64.—The anchor and dolphin, mark of Aldus Manutius, after the original in the *Terze Rime* of 1520, where it appears for the first time.

writing ; the name of *Italic* was given to this character, which was also called *Aldine*, from its inventor. It was engraved by Francisco da Bologna. Aldus also published in octavo size, with this kind of letter, an edition of *Virgil* in 1501. To procure a perfect copy of this first Aldine *Virgil* is almost hopeless, and the somewhat defective copies which lately turned up at the Sir John Thorold's and Wodhull's sale brought £145. Then he produced a *Horace*, a *Juvenal*, a *Martial*, etc. The following year, 1502, he gave an edition of the *Terze Rime* of Dante and for the first time took as his typographical mark an anchor encircled by a dolphin.*

His marriage with the daughter of Andrea Torresani, of Asola, brought together into his possession two printing houses. The burden became too heavy for Manutius to think henceforth of doing all the work himself. Besides, the wars did not allow him any repose, of which he bitterly complained in his prefaces. He therefore attracted young Greek scholars, who supervised, each one in his specialty, the works in progress, and founded a society, a kind of Aldine academy, in which the greatest names of the epoch were united. Aldus conveys the perfect idea of a great printer at those times, doing honour to celebrated men, in the midst of business preoccupations and of the annoyance caused by the war. It is said that Erasmus, passing through Venice, called on him, and as he was not duly announced to him, was rather badly received by the powerful printer. All at once, at the name of the distinguished visitor being mentioned, Aldus, for an instant taken aback, rose at once and showed him how highly he appreciated men of letters.

The war resulted in the alteration of this state of affairs. In 1505 Aldus quitted Venice to travel over the world, and on his return he found himself poorer than when he went away. Andrea Torresani, his father-in-law, came to his aid; but the great printer had received his death-blow; and in spite of the activity which he brought to the new establishment, he went from bad to worse until 1515, when he expired, leaving to his son Paul his affairs in a state of inextricable confusion.

* Tory in his *Champfleury* explains thus the mark of Aldus and his device, which was in Greek the "Make haste slowly" of Boileau: "The anchor signifies tardiness, and the dolphin haste, which is to say that in his business he was moderate."

He had early abandoned book illustration to devote himself to the scientific and useful in his publications ; moreover, the size of book chosen by him was badly suited for the introduction of plates ; but other publishers employed artists in the ornamentation of the Book. Lucantonio Giunta, the most celebrated

Fig. 65.—Aldus Manutius.

among them, was at once printer and engraver, a striking example of the affinity of the two trades from their origin. In 1508 Lucantonio Giunta, or Zonta, as he then spelt his name, published a *Roman Breviary* in large quarto, with twelve engravings in Lombardo-Venetian manner, signed " L. A.," in very good style. The same artist-publisher cut a portrait of

Virgil for an edition of that poet about 1515. Furthermore, Giunta did not alone illustrate the book from the resources of his own office. Other designers lent him their assistance. We find evidence of this in the *Bible* printed by him in 1519 in small octavo.

The most meritorious of the artists of Venice at this time was John Andrea, known as Guadagnino. He designed the vignettes for *Florus's Epitome in T. Livi Hist. lib.*, and for *Aretinus de Primo Bello Punico*, printed at Venice for Melchior

Fig. 66.—Mark of Lucantonio Giunta, of Venice.

Sessa and Peter of Ravenna (1520, folio); in 1516 he copied the plates of Dürer's *Apocalypse* for the edition of Alexander Paganini, of Venice. One of the Venetian works which signalised the beginning of the sixteenth century was the *Trionfo di Fortuna* of Sigismond Fanti, of Ferrara, printed by Agostino da Portese in 1527.

Venice was the home of Titian, and at the time which occupies us now, the great artist was at the height of his glory. In 1518 two brothers, Nicholas and Dominic dal Gesù, published a translation of the celebrated *Golden Legend* of

Voragine, the success of which was enormous in France. The plates which were added to the work were manifestly inspired by the school of the Venetian master. Unfortunately the engravers were not always equal to the genius of the drawings.

To resume, the city of Venice was, at the beginning of the sixteenth century, one of the most prolific in publishers and artists of talent. Since the first establishments of the Germans, typography had successively employed in Venice Nicholas Jenson, a Frenchman, the inventor of the Roman character; Erhard Ratdolt, the first to employ illustrations there; and Aldus Manutius, scholar and printer, whose progress in printing elevated that art to the highest rank among human discoveries; there were also remarkable engravers and draughtsmen, among others John Andrea and Giunta, without mentioning the anonymous masters of the school of Titian. The part of Venice in the movement was thus great, but it may be explained by the riches of its citizens, the extent of its commerce, and the genius of its own artists.

If we now return from Venice to the north, to Milan, we find the school of Leonardo da Vinci making itself apparent in the Book. In order of date we will mention the *Mysterii Gesta Beatæ Veronicæ Virginis*, published by Gotardo de Ponte, 1518, small quarto, with figures in the style of Luini, and *Vitruvius* in Italian by Cesariano. On the testimony of the author, the wood engravings in a book of Fra Luca Pacioli, *De Divina Proportione*, are even attributed to Leonardo da Vinci. But M. Delaborde, in spite of the declaration in the preface of Pacioli, does not believe in the direct collaboration of the master, although M. Passavant does.

In Germany, Nuremberg continued, with Albert Dürer and the artists of his school, to supply illustrations for books at the

8

beginning of the century.   The master reprinted his valuable
engravings of the *Life of the Virgin* in 1511, and also those
of the *Apocalypse.*   But after him the art already began
to decline ; a hundred years later nothing remained of the
honour and glory gained by Germany in the commencement.
Among the most interesting of the Nuremberg publications is a
chivalric poem by Melchior Pfinzing, composed for the marriage
of Maximilian and Mary of Burgundy.   As M. Delaborde
in his *Débuts de l'Imprimerie* well remarks, this was not a
book intended to be sold by a bookseller ; it was a work of art

Fig. 67.—Title of the *Theuerdanck.*   The flourishes of the
letters are printed.

destined originally by an emperor for his friends, and he took
care that it should be an unapproachable work.   Bold strokes,
majestic letters, intertwined ornaments, are here multiplied.   Three
persons worked upon it for five years ; these were, if we credit
Peutinger, Hans Leonard Schäufelein, the painter, Jost Necker,
the engraver, and Hans Schönsperger, the printer of Augsburg,
who must have changed his native city for Nuremberg.   When
they were able to take a proof, experts would hardly take it for a
book composed in movable characters ; they were sure, on the
contrary, that it was a true xylograph, cut in wood ; and, in fact,
from the title here reproduced, the error was excusable.   This

work, which is now called the *Theuerdanck*, from the name of
the hero of the romance, is ornamented with a number of wood
engravings, numbered by Arabic figures. We reproduce one of
the last plates, in which Theuerdanck—Maximilian—is conducted to the presence of the Queen—Mary of Burgundy. The
designs of Schäufelein almost recall the work of Albert Dürer,
his master; but, as we said of him, these works, heavy and

Fig. 68.—Plate taken from the *Theuerdanck*, representing Maximilian and
Mary of Burgundy. Engraved on wood after Schäufelein.

broad, although very clever, do not always suit as cuts inserted
in the text. However, our criticism does not refer so much to
the *Theuerdanck*, where the letters, excessively ornamented and
overwhelming, furnish a framework more suitable for the
engravings than to other works of a more slender character,
where the German plate completely overshadows the text.

When we have mentioned the *Passionale Christi* of Lucas

Cranach, published by Johannes Grünenberg at Wittemberg in 1521—twenty-six inferior wood engravings—we shall have mentioned the most important of the interesting and rare volumes published in Germany at the commencement of the sixteenth century.

The Netherlands, Spain, and England were working, but without great success. In the Low Countries Plantin and his gigantic enterprises may be recalled. In Spain the taste had hardly developed itself; and although the drawing of illustrations may be careful enough, the wood-cutting is pitiable. We will mention the *Seneca* of Toledo in 1510, and the *Chronicle of Aragon* in 1523.

Typography and the illustration of the Book in England in the sixteenth century did not make the same progress as in France and Italy. Much good work was done, but it was mostly with foreign material. Type was obtained from French and Dutch founders, and most of the woodcuts had the same origin. In the early part of the century most of the publications were translations of popular foreign books, such as Voragine's *Golden Legend*, Caxton's translations of *Cicero*, *Boetius*, etc. The numerous restrictions and privileges restrained the establishment of an English school, which was to come later with the spread of wealth and education. Books were mostly printed in Gothic type, or "black letter," and the woodcuts were of the coarsest kind. An exception was the beautiful Prayer-book of John Day, 1578, known as Queen Elizabeth's Prayer-book, from the fine portrait of the Queen, which we reproduce; but in this the woodcuts were designed by Albert Dürer and Hans Holbein. Pynson was the first to use Roman type in England, in the *Oratio in pace nuperrimâ*, 1518, quarto; and the first English Bible in

Roman type was printed at Edinburgh in 1576. It is thought that until about 1600 printers were their own

Fig. 69.—Portrait of Queen Elizabeth trom the *Book of Christian Praiers*, printed by John Day, 1578.

type-founders, as no record exists of founding as a separate trade until that time

The greatest achievement of the sixteenth century in

England was the printing of the first English Bible, in Coverdale's translation, in 1535, folio, but even this was printed abroad, the latest investigation giving it to Van Meteren at Antwerp.   The woodcuts in it are by Hans Sebald Beham ; we reproduce one representing Cain killing Abel.   Tyndall had previously printed abroad an English New Testament.   Another importation was Brandt's *Shyp of Folys*, printed by Pynson, 1509, and John Cawood, 1570, the woodcuts in both being copied from the originals before referred to.

Fig. 70.—Woodcut from Coverdale's Bible, 1535.
Cain killing Abel.

The size usually adopted was in folio, and in this size the series of *Chronicles* appeared : Froissart, by Pynson, in two volumes, 1523-5.; Holinshed, in two volumes, 1577 — the first and genuine edition of this chronicle, with numerous woodcuts.   In the same size Chaucer was first given to the world entire by T. Godfray in 1532, and many times reprinted, and Sir Thomas More's *Works* in 1557.   Polemical and religious treatises were mostly printed in quarto, as were the poets: Spenser's *Faerie Queene*, in 1590 ; Langland's *Pierce Plowman*, in 1550; and Sidney's *Arcadia*, in 1590.

Plays were also printed in quarto, in which shape at the end of the century some of Shakespeare's single plays were issued.

Richard Grafton, the leading English printer, first printed the English Bible, in an edition of 2,500 copies, at Paris, in connection with Edward Whitchurche (1538-9), which was confiscated by Francis I. ; then Cranmer's Bible, 1539-41 ; Edw. Halle's Chronicle and first Common Prayer Book, 1549 ; and he also printed Lady Jane Grey's proclamation of the first English Common Prayer Book, known as Edward VI.'s (a copy was sold lately from Lord Crawford's library for £155). Edward's book is curious as having on the last page a royal order as to the price at which it was to be sold : " No maner of persone shall sell the present Booke vnbounde aboue the price of two shillynges and two pence. And bound in Forell for ii*s*. x*d*., and not aboue. And the same bound in Shepes Lether for iii*s*. iii*d*., and not aboue. And the same bounde in paste or in boordes, in Calues Lether, not aboue the price of iiii*s*. the pece " Cranmer's *Catechism* was printed by Nicholas Hill in 1548, with twenty-nine woodcuts by Hans Holbein, one of which we reproduce, representing Christ casting out devils.

The Stationers' Company was founded in 1556, in the reign of Queen Mary, and was chiefly composed of printers. By Act of Parliament every book printed in England was to be entered at Stationers' Hall.

Hugh Singleton established a printing office in the City of London 1553, and was appointed printer to the City of London 1584.

Humphrey Powell carried on the first printing office at Dublin, 1551-66.

From the great perfection to which the liturgies, or books

of hours, had been brought by Vostre, Vérard, and others in France, it is not perhaps extraordinary that the service books for English use should have been mostly printed abroad. Those for Salisbury and York were produced at Paris, Rouen, and Antwerp. A Salisbury Primer in English was printed by John Kyngston and Henry Sutton in 1557, and Wynkyn de Worde printed a York Manual in 1509.

Fig. 71.—Woodcut by Hans Holbein from Cranmer's
Catechism, 1548.

Translations from the classics were popular, and in the second half of the century arose that passion for voyage and travel which has so largely contributed to the wealth and extension of England. This was begun by Eden's translation of Peter Martyr's *Decades of the New World; or, West India*, London, 1555, quarto, followed by Hakluyt's *Principall Naviga-tions, Voyages, and Discoveries*, 1589, folio. Many accounts of single voyages and discoveries were issued, and the taste thus created culminated in the establishment of the East India Company in the last year of the century.

The first specimen of copperplate engraving for books in England is a frontispiece to Galen's *De Temperamentis*, printed at Cambridge 1521; but the number of books containing copperplates engraved before 1600 is extremely limited, the most notable being portraits of Queen Elizabeth, Lord Leicester, and Lord Burleigh in Archbishop Parker's Bible of 1568; Saxton's Atlas, 1579, the first atlas in England; Harrington's translation of Ariosto, 1591, with forty-seven engraved plates.

The first printer at Cambridge was John Siberch, 1521. Peter of Treves established himself at Southwark in 1514. Among his productions is a Higden's *Polychronicon*, 1527, folio. John Oswen printed at Ipswich 1538, and among the English towns in which printers established themselves in the century were York, Canterbury, Tavistock, Norwich, and Worcester.

The establishment of the Reformed Church, and the diffusion of education among the people which followed, created an original English school of literature in the sixteenth century, and this gave employment and great impetus to typography in England, so that by the time we reach the end of the century we find a great improvement in the art of the Book, to be carried to still greater perfection in the next.

In France, on the contrary, we find an enormous commerce in books at the commencement of the sixteenth century. All the publishers mentioned in the preceding chapter were still living, and labouring under the effects of the French conquests in Italy. The dithyrambic literature then inaugurated, and which reached its zenith under Louis XIV., exercised a bad influence equally upon the printers and decorators of the Book. Doubtless the composition of the text and engravings was done hastily, for the great people did not like to wait for this kind of books. *Le Vergier d'Honneur*, written by Octavian de St. Gelais and Andry de la Vigne, was thus published

about the end of the fifteenth century and ornamented with
hasty vignettes, probably at the expense of Antoine Vérard.
Upon the accession to the throne of Louis XII., Claude de
Seyssel, his master of council, composed *Les Louenges du Roy
Louis XII.* in Latin, and soon after translated it into French
for the same Vérard, who printed it in 1508.

The taste for the history of the Gauls induced the publishers to reproduce *La Mer des Histoires*, which had already
been published in the fifteenth century; Thielman Kerver put
forth the *Compendium* of Robert Gaguin in 1500 on account
of Durand Gerlier and Jean Petit. The French version of
this work was given in 1514 by Galliot du Pré, with vignettes, and afterwards under the name of *Mirouer Historial*,
by Renaud Chaudière in 1520, by Nyverd, and others; the
same with the *Rozier Historial*, with figures, in 1522 and 1528.
Among the most popular works was the *Illustrations de la
Gaule et Singularitez de Troye*, by Jean le Maire de Belges,
printed everywhere in Paris and ornamented. In 1512 it was
published by Geoffroy de Marnef, in 1515 by Jean and Gilbert
de Marnef, by Regnault, by Philippe le Noir (whose curious mark
we here reproduce, and who also printed a hundred admoni-
tions in four hundred lines of verse, for the guidance of a true
knight, viz., *Les Cent Hystoires de Troye*, 1522, and a *Hystoire
du Sainct Greaal*, 1523), and others, always in the Gothic
characters which still prevailed in France at the beginning of
the sixteenth century.

We give from the *Illustrations de la Gaule* of Jean le Maire
an interesting woodcut (Fig. 73) representing Queen Anne of
Brittany as Juno, in which we can without much difficulty trace
the hand of a Bourdichon or a Perréal. The truly French style
of this figure leaves no doubt as to its origin. At the same

time, it may possibly have been inspired by the Virgin of a German master, say one of 1466, judging from the accessories, and even from the pose. This engraving will be found in the edition of 1512 of Gilbert de Marnef, in Gothic letter, quarto. On the reverse are the arms and device of Jean le Maire de Belges.

The time that elapsed from the death of Louis XI. until the accession of Francis I.—that is to say, from 1483 to 1515—

Fig. 72.—Mark of Philippe le Noir, printer at Paris, 1536.

was, to employ an old expression, the golden age of French printing and illustration. Under Charles VIII. and Louis XII. the designers on wood were not yet affected by the neighbour-ing schools; neither the accentuated Italian influence nor the German processes had reached them; they reproduced what they saw, and they did it in their own fashion and manner, without foreign influence. Neither did the kings ignore them, for Louis XII. preserved to the printers of the

university all their rights and privileges in a magniloquent
ordinance, in which the art of typography was extolled in the

Fig. 73.—Vignette taken from the *Illustrations de la Gaule et Singularitez de Troye.*
Queen Anne of Brittany as Juno.

highest terms. It restores to them all the advantages they
had lost. For instance, it recites, " In consideration of the great

benefit that has come to our kingdom by means of the art and science of printing, the invention of which seems more Divine than human, which, thanks to God, has been invented and found in our time by the help and industry of booksellers, by which our holy Catholic faith has been greatly augmented and strengthened, justice better understood and administered, and Divine service more honourably and diligently made, said, and celebrated, . . . by means of which our kingdom precedes all others," etc., etc. (Blois, 9th April, 1513).

Certainly Louis made the best of himself and his kingdom

Fig. 74.—Mark of François Juste, printer at Lyons, 1526. Printer of *Rabelais*.

in this preamble, but it must be recognised that France already held a predominant rank in the new industry, and that except from the Italians she had no fear of serious rivalry. The school of ornamentists made constant progress, not to forget Guillaume Eustace, who published some very fine works, missals and books of hours, with woodcuts; and François Juste, the printer of *Rabelais* and a translation of Sebastian Brandt's *La Grād nef des folz du Monde*. Before the books of hours, the booksellers contented themselves with miserable blocks, placed side by side, forming a framework of good and bad together; but after Simon Vostre, Vérard, and the others they had

remarkably improved. The borders, at least in the books of
hours, had become the principal part of the book ; they were
composed of flowers, architectural, complicated, and simple subjects, all of perfect taste and extreme elegance ; and, as we have
observed with regard to the representation of Anne of Brittany
in the *Illustrations de la Gaule*, the figure subjects were no
longer mechanical, commonplace, and tiresome blocks, but,

Fig. 75.—Mark of Guillaume Eustace, 1517,
binder and bookseller at Paris.

on the contrary, more often works specially designed and
engraved by artists of merit.

Geoffroy Tory, born at Bourges in 1480, continued after
Vostre and Vérard the onward march of illustration of the
Book. He was a sort of encyclopædist, who knew and fore-
saw everything, but with a singularly subtler and finer genius
than his predecessors. There is now very little doubt that by

trade Tory was an engraver and printer. However, he published with Jean Petit one of his first volumes, *The Geography
of Pomponius Mela*, in 1507, and Gilles de Gourmont printed
it. Tory was thus an erudite and diffusive commentator.

Fig. 76.—Title of the *Entrée d'Eléonore d'Autriche à
Paris*, by Guillaume Bochetel. Printed by Geoffroy
Tory in May, 1531, quarto.

He published later a book with poor engravings, entitled,
Valerii Probi Grammatici Opusculum, 1510, waiting until his
good star should place him on the right road.

He had for his mark, say the bibliographers, the cross of

Lorraine (‡), small enough to be lost in the ornamentation of his plates. In fact this sign is to be found again in Tory's mark—the " Pot Cassé "—the broken jar—and also sometimes in the letter G, which was his ordinary signature. This opinion, which we will not try to contradict in a popular work like this, appears to us to err, as others used this mark, as may be judged from the essentially different touches of engravings bearing the cross of Lorraine, and particularly those of Woériot in the middle of the century.

Fig. 77.—Mark of Geoffroy Tory,
printer at Paris, 1529.

If M. A. Bernard* may be credited, Geoffroy Tory cultivated all the sciences with equal success. For our purpose, suffice it to assign to him the first place in the art of decoration of books of hours. Doubtless his travels in Italy had contributed to modify his taste and to draw him aside from the sober and simple manner that then characterised French engraving ; but he nevertheless preserved the indelible

* *Geoffroy Tory, Peintre et Graveur, Premier Imprimeur Royal, Réformateur de l'Orthographe et de la Typographie :* Paris, 1857, 8vo.

traces of his original style, in the same way as some people cannot divest themselves of their provincial accent. The *Heures de*

Fig. 78.—Full page of the *Heures* of Simon de Colines, by Tory.

la Vierge, which he designed, and which he had engraved about
1520, for account of Simon de Colines, is marvellously surrounded
by ornaments, until then unknown in France; at the same time,

9

and in spite of other tendencies, it is purely a French work, and the specimen given here is a convincing proof. We should not here omit to mention the remarkable collection of *Voyages*, in fact the first which deserves this designation, printed by

Fig. 79.—*Heures* of Geoffroy Tory. The Circumcision.

Simon de Colines, under the title of *Extrait ou Recueil des toles nouvellement trouvées en la grand mer Oceane on temps du roy Despaigne Fernād et Elisabeth sa femme* (1532). This rare work fetched at the Beckford Sale £126.

Geoffroy Tory wrote a curious book, half poetic and half

learned, in which he studied at the same time the form of the letter from the typographic and the emblematic point of view, and also the French orthography of the time. He tells us himself that he set about to commence this book on the twelfth night, 1523, when, after a frugal repast, he was, he says, "dreaming on my bed and revolving my memory, thinking of a thousand little fancies, serious and gay, among which I thought of some

Fig. 80.—Mark of Simon de Colines,
printer at Paris, 1527.

antique letters that I had made for Monseigneur the treasurer for war, Master Jehan Grolier, councillor and secretary of our lord the King, amateur of fine letters and of all learned personages." Tory called his book *Champfleury, auquel est contenu l'art et science de la deue proportion des lettres . . . selon le corps et le visage humain,* and he published it himself in small folio, putting upon it the sign of Gilles de Gourmont, in 1529.

In reality Tory had been fascinated by the theories of

Dürer on the proportions of the human body ; for he says, "Albert Dürer, the noble German painter, is greatly to be praised in that he has so well brought his skill in painting to

Fig. 81.—*Heures* of Simon de Colines, with the mark of the Cross of Lorraine.

bear on the designing of geometrical forms, the ramparts of war, and the proportions of the human body." He wished thus to indicate to his contemporaries the true measure of letters, " the number of points and turns of the compass that each

one requires." The most amusing part of this curious treatise
is his short academical preface, where, with sportive fancy,
the great publisher studies the orthography of his time, and
exclaims against the coiners of new words, the Latinisers of the
language, "the skimmers of Latin, jesters and gibberers, . . .
who mock not only their shadows, but themselves." The
entire passage was copied by Rabelais, nearly literally, and he

Fig. 82.—Emblematical letter Y, taken from
the *Champfleury* of Geoffroy Tory.

indicates that its author was possessed of good sense, which,
unhappily, all his contemporaries were not.

He added to his theories a number of designs of geometrical
letters, technically considered, but he was afterwards carried
away in the train of the Greeks and Romans, as was then
the fashion, perhaps a little further than he meant, losing himself in a crowd of idle dissertations. To these geometrical
engravings he added small and charming figures, which he said
were by Jean Perréal, as well as emblematical letters of the

nature of the Y which is here given, with explanatory text and commentary. His Y had two branches: one of virtue and the other of vice; that of virtue carries palms, crowns, a sceptre, and a book ; that of vice, birches, a dagger, a gallows, and fire.

With the importance that cannot be denied to his works, Geoffroy Tory founded a school; and it was from his work-shop that the plates came for the book of Paulus Jovius on the dukes of Milan, published by Robert Estienne in 1549, 4to. The portraits of the dukes in this work have been attributed to Tory himself, but he died in 1533, and there is not the least indication that he engraved these sixteen portraits with his own hand sixteen years before their publication. Besides, our doubt as to the cross of Lorraine being the exclusive signature of Tory, as has been believed, leads us to think it the collective mark of a workshop, for we meet it on works long after the death of the master. As a proof, the mark is found on the engravings of *L'Entrée du Roi à Paris* (Roffet in 4to) in 1549, which cannot be taken as a posthumous work of Tory, for these engravings had their origin at a certain particular date. But in spite of the absence of the monogram, the admirable block from the *Diodorus Siculus* of Antoine Macault might, from its design and engraving, be considered as by Tory himself. Holbein—who, about the same time, designed a some-what similar scene, where the King of France, seated on a throne, received poison from the hands of Death—never did anything better. Within the scanty proportions of the design, all the figures are portraits. Duprat, Montmorency and the three sons of the King may be recognised ; Macault, on the left, is reading his translation to a circle of nobles and men of letters. This admirable woodcut, too little known, is one of the truest and

most skilful of the monuments of French engraving ; it is equal
to the best inventions of Holbein, which have never exceeded
it, and it marks the culminating point of the illustration of the

Fig. 83.—Macault reading to Francis I. his translation of Diodorus Siculus.
Wood engraving attributed to Tory.

Book before the exaggerations of the school of Fontainebleau.
Geoffroy Tory was not the publisher. The *Diodorus Siculus*,
doubtless prepared two or three years before, was not published

until 1535, in quarto, with his ordinary mark of the *Pot Cassé*. The original magnificent manuscript on vellum, from the Hamilton collection, of this celebrated book, with the miniatures by Geoffroy Tory, was sold lately for the sum of £1,000.

We have now arrived through him to the middle of the reign of Francis I., who was called the *father of letters*, and who for various reasons favoured the arts. Doubtless grand paintings and the decoration of the royal palaces attracted him more than vignettes in books or the efforts of printers ; but, at the same time, books interested him. He studied much, and even had books sent after him in his travels. An account in the French National Archives shows that Claude Chappuis, his librarian, and bookseller, packed entire cases, which were sent after him to Dauphiné at the time of the wars of Piedmont, the carriage costing twenty livres tournois. Francis was subject, moreover, to sudden outbreaks of curious fits of wantonness and mischief. It was perceived a little later that the doctrines of Luther were propagated by the Book ; and the Sorbonne was up in arms. She even attempted to impose her own expurgated text of the Bible on the publishers, to the exclusion of all others. Theodore Beza, an enemy of the Sorbonnists, said with regard to this, with all the amenity which characterizes him :

> " Nos grandz docteurs au chérubin visage
> Ont défendu qu'homme n'ait plus à voir
> La Saincte Bible en vulgaire language
> Dont un chascun peut congnoissance avoir ;
> Car, disent ils, désir de tout savoir
> N'engendre rien qu'erreur, peur et souci . . .
> *Arguo sic*, s'il en est doncques ainsi
> Que pour l'abus il faille oster ce livre,
> Il est tout clair qu'on leur devroit aussi
> Oster la vin dont chascun d'eux s'enivre."

This piece is only cited to show to what lengths matters had gone, thanks to printing. It is very certain that all the pamphlets, placards, and other horrors published to raise religious warfare, did not at all further the progress of the *Book*. The king was not, however, indifferent to the technical question ; books merited encouragement, at least as much as chastisement, and besides, as time passed on, gradually trans- formed men and ideas. In spite of his apparent severities, was not the King himself a little affected by coming in contact with the new religion, like his sister Marguerite, or his sister- in-law, Renée of Ferrara ?

Fig. 84.—Robert Estienne, after the engraving
in the *Chronologie Collee*.

However that may be, he twice showed himself a resolute partisan of the celebrated Robert Estienne, son-in-law and associate of Simon de Colines, whose work in point of erudition and typography assumed from day to day more importance. Robert Estienne had the great honour of being chosen from all his contemporaries by King Francis as the royal printer. This prince had ordered him to have engraved by Claude Garamond, after the caligraphic design of Ange Vergèce, the first cutter of matrices of his time, a special Greek character in three sizes, which was used in 1544 to compose the *Ecclesias- tical History* of Eusebius. These were the famous royal types —*typi regii*—the use of which Estienne did not fail to mention on the title-pages of his works. These types gave room for reflection and something to write about, since Francis I. founded the Royal Printing House, but the truth is that Estienne kept these characters in his own office for use in the royal editions ; and they may now be seen in the Imprimerie Nationale at Paris, where they are kept.

Robert Estienne married the daughter of Josse Badius of *Asch—Badius Ascencianus*, one of the first Parisian typographers

Fig. 85.—Mark of Robert Estienne, printer at Paris, 1541.

of the time. We reproduce the mark of Badius (Fig. 87), representing the interior of a printing house, and shall return in a special chapter to the functions of these workshops. Meantime it appeared proper to present to the reader a printing office at the time of Robert Estienne and Geoffroy Tory.

Robert Estienne does not appear to have concerned himself much about the decoration of the Book. The purity of the text and the characters were essentials with him, erudition, and

not art. He published many works in Latin and Greek, among
them the *Thesaurus*, a great Latin dictionary published in
1532, also a Bible, with notes by Vatable, revised by Leon de
Juda. Hence his trouble! Leon de Juda being a partisan
of Zwingli, the Sorbonne accused the Bible of leaning towards
the Huguenots; Francis I. took the part of Estienne, but
when that prince died Estienne fled to Geneva, where he was
accused of having taken the royal types with him. The truth
was that he simply carried off the matrices.

Fig. 86.—Mark of François Estienne, printer at Paris, 1538.

At this time everything served for the decoration of the
Book: there were portraits, blazons, topographical plates,
costumes, and emblems. Small portraits engraved on wood
usually ornamented the works of the poets, like that of Nicholas
Bourbon, for example, a marvel of truth and skill. The blocks
of frontispieces in the folios were multiplied; large initial
letters, ingeniously engraved and stippled, like that at the
commencement of this chapter, were used. Jacques Kerver
reproduced in 1545 for himself, and with plates made for him,

the famous *Songe de Poliphile*, published by Aldus in 1499. The widow of the publisher Denis Janot, Jeanne de Marnef, published one of the most delightful books of the time, *L'Amour de Cupidon et de Psyche* of Apuleius, with delicious figures on wood after Italian engravings. How many more might we not name in the extraordinary profusion of charming books!

Without entering into detail, something must be said about

Fig. 87.—Printing office of Josse Badius at the commencement of the sixteenth century.

Lyons, then a most extensive and prosperous centre of book-selling. Lyons had the signal honour of being the first to publish in France the celebrated cuts of the *Dance of Death* of Holbein, the Basle painter. Doubtless Treschel, the printer, was not the first, although a copy of a German edition is not known, because in the Lyons edition the cuts are already worn and broken. However, the Cabinet d'Estampes of Paris has some of the figures of the *Dance* with a German text, probably printed from the type of Froben at Basle. Treschel's title was

*Les Simulachres et Historiées Faces de la Mort autant elegam-
ment pourtraictes que artificiellement imaginées,* and the volume
in quarto was printed by Frelon. The *Icones veteris Testa-
menti,* which preceded the publication of the *Dance of Death,*
had also been printed at Basle with those of Lyons, as M.
Georges Duplessis states in a notice on the different editions
of this work.

With Holbein, as with Geoffroy Tory, we arrive at the

Fig. 88.—Portrait of Nicholas Bourbon. Wood engraving
of the commencement of the sixteenth century.

zenith of illustration and marvellous skill of the engraver.
It was Hans Lutzelburger who cut the blocks after the designs
of the Basle master, but, if we were to institute comparisons,
contrary to what generally happens, the translator reaches
almost to the height of his model; the line is perfection itself,
it is precise and intelligent, simple, and, withal, explicit. If the
work of Lutzelburger be admitted, it must also be admitted
that Holbein designed his cuts on wood before 1526, the date
of the death of the Basle engraver, for it was immediately before

1526 that Holbein lived in Basle, and it was afterwards that he travelled. We can add nothing to the universal praise of the book of Treschel, of Lyons ; every detail has been written of Holbein, and repetitions are unnecessary. We would ask the reader to compare the Francis I. of Tory and the King in Holbein's *Dance of Death;* there is a certain family resemblance between the two cuts, which is a singular honour for Tory.

At the commencement of the century Basle must have had

Fig. 89.—King and Death.   Vignette from the
Dance of Death by Holbein.

a school of *Formschneiders* working for export.   Besides the numerous products used at Lyons, it had also a trade in *clichés*, illustrations, which, having been used, were sold again.   Among these exchanges of engravings were many plates of Brandt's *Ship of Fools*, sold in 1520 to Galliot du Pré, publisher, of Paris, who used them in the *Eloge de la Folie* of Erasmus. It must be admitted that these blocks had a singular life, and a great success, for Galliot du Pré builds his hopes upon them :

"Va et cours selon tes fortunes,
Follie ! simulant tes faces ;
Mais quelques choses que tu fasses,
Rapporte force de pécunes."

The reign of Francis I. saw a great advance in the national art of illustration. The arrival at the court of Italian artists of the decadence, such as Rosso and Primaticcio, produced a revolution in taste. The exaggerated slightness of the figures brought by these artists from beyond the Alps was considered as of supreme distinction ; one saw in their twisted draperies and mannered poses some undefined and precious beauty that tempted the ready intelligence of the court of France. The simple and ingenuous figures of the old French artists were ranked among the refuse of another age, and their compositions were regarded with contempt, and deemed antique.

The rage for emblems and for allegories and mythological figures generally was well suited to these eccentric and bizarre inventions. On the other hand, an entire class of artists or artisans, book illustrators first, then enamellers and jewellers, seized on these Italian models, with which the King encumbered his galleries, and which, at great expense, covered the walls of Fontainebleau. One can understand what skilful men could make of such a movement and of so thoughtless an infatuation. The publishers put themselves to work, and composed works of which the sale was assured from the ideas that they furnished to other designers. This explains the quantity of Alciati's *Emblems* and Ovid's *Metamorphoses*, published at Lyons and Paris, and copied and recopied by the art industries of the time Without it the enormous success of such mediocre productions as the *Emblems*, in which the meaning of the enigma or rebus cannot always be graspd, is ill understood. It was Alciati who made this literature the fashion. He was a sort of Epicurean jurisconsult and miser, at once a Gargantua and a Harpagon, who had as many lords and

L'aage de Fer.

Laage d'Erain fut encor trouué pire,
Non vicieus, quoy qil il fust prompt aus armes·
Mais cil de Fer procedant à l'empire,
Reduisit tout à merci de gendarmes.
Le pere aus fils liure cruels alarmes:
L'hoste n'est point de son hoste à seurté,
Le seul recours du foiblet git aux larmes:
Bref, tout est sang, fraude, dol, malheurté.

Fig. 90.—Page of the *Metamorphoses* of Ovid, by Petit Bernard. Edition of 1564.

masters on earth, as there were kings and princes who would bid against each other to engage him. He had quitted Italy, seduced by the offers of Francis I., but when Sforza paid him a larger sum, he returned, giving as reason for his vacillation that the sun had to travel round the earth and warm it by its rays; this was an emblematic answer, for his emblems had all the coarse, sceptical, facetious humour of which few were then the dupes. At most these philosophical aphorisms, when they represented to be serious, have their droll side in that their author often practised the reverse of his teaching. A miser himself, he abuses the avaricious; leaving his country for the love of gain, he blames those to whom "a better condition is offered by foreigners." Yet he is sometimes logical and consistent, as when he assures us that "poverty hinders genius to succeed," and when, finally, lover of good cheer, he died of indigestion in 1550.

His book of *Emblems* had a vogue that lasted until the seventeenth century, and repetitions were infinitely multiplied: at Paris by Wechel in 1534; at Lyons by Hans de Tornes, who came from Suabia, one of the greatest Lyons publishers; by Roville, also one of the first Lyons publishers, and by Bonhomme; at Venice by the Alduses; in fact, everywhere, translated into French, Spanish, and Italian.

Bernard Salomon, called *Le Petit Bernard*, born at Lyons, was one of the designers of the school of Fontainebleau—that is to say, of the Franco-Italian school of which we have spoken above—who furnished many of the engravings for books printed at Lyons. He illustrated the edition of Alciati's *Emblems* published by Bonhomme in 1560; and designed skilful little plates, which, with the text, were surrounded by a border from the workshop of Geoffroy Tory, for Ovid's *Metamorphoses*, published by Hans de Tornes in 1564. Bernard had all the defects and all the good qualities of those of his time, from Jean Cousin to the least of them; he was

10

a Primaticcio on a small scale, but agreeably so. His designs
for the *New Testament* were also very careful, but in them
more than elsewhere the manner and the affectation of the
school of Fontainebleau are apparent.

Fig. 91.—Portraits of Madeleine, Queen of Scotland, and of Marguerite, Duchess of Savoy
after the originals of Cornelis of Lyons.

The workshops of the second city of France, we see, had
at this time attained considerable importance; but before the
books of which we are about to speak, Roville published two
anonymous books, one *L'Entrée du Roi Henri II. à Lyon*, in

Fig. 92.—Portraits of Francis, Dauphin, and of Charles, Duke of Angoûleme, after the originals
of Cornelis of Lyons. Woodcuts taken from Roville's *Promptuaire des Médailles*.

1549, ornamented with very graceful woodcuts, the other the
Promptuaire des Médailles, comprising a series of charming portraits under the guise of reproductions from the antique. The
designs of the *Entrée* are often attributed to Jean Cousin, as

it is a rule with certain amateurs to give a known name to a work ; but it must be remembered that Lyons then had celebrated artists, the Petit-Bernard, alluded to above, and Cornelis de la Haye, of whom we shall have more to say ; and it is therefore not necessary to go to Paris or to Rome to find the author of these illustrations.

Cornelis de la Haye was a painter who executed nearly the

Fig. 93.—Captain of foot, from the *Entrée de Henri II. à Lyon*, 1549.

same work as François Clouet in Paris, portraits on panel, in a clear and harmonious tone, then much the fashion. During a journey of the King, he had, if Brantôme may be credited, portrayed the entire court, keeping the sketches for himself. Ten or fifteen years after, Catherine de Medicis, passing through Lyons, saw these portraits again and highly praised them, recognising her old costumes, wondering at the courtiers of the day, who had never seen her in such attire. This artist is now known, thanks to various works that have been found, among others two portraits of the sons of Francis I., preserved by Gaignières, who attributed them resolutely to Cornelis, doubtless on the faith of inscriptions that have disappeared. Both of them were engraved on wood at Lyons, and published in Roville's book the *Promptuaire des Médailles*, mentioned above, with small differences of detail altogether insignificant. It is not impossible then that Cornelis designed these portraits and that they were drawn by him on wood after the cabinet models spoken of by Brantôme. The delicate figures of the *Promptuaire* are the work of a master; the differences mentioned are those of the artist, not of the copyist, who would not be permitted to make any alterations. It is the first time, we believe, that these comparisons have been made; they will perhaps help the learned Lyonnais to pierce the mystery, but in any case our suppositions are more favourable to Cornelis de la Haye than to the fancies of Robert Dumesnil (*Peintre-graveur Français*, tome vi., p. 343). To judge by the four little medallions here reproduced (Figs. 91, 92) the art of engraving on wood was rarely more skilful than in these portraits. What is there astonishing if a man like Cornelis had designed the figures of the *Entrée de Henri II.?* In any case, why should we choose Jean Cousin rather than Le Petit-Bernard? At this time, we know, the kings had their ordinary painters in their suite; but we do not know that Jean Cousin ever followed the court to Lyons in 1549, as he did not hold an official position, like Clouet.

This artist, however, produced well-authenticated works; one of them is signed and initialed, and leaves no doubt it is the *Livre de Perspective de Jehan Cousin Senonois, Maistre*

Painctre, published in 1560 by Jean le Royer, printer to the King for mathematics. This profession of printer for mathematics had its difficulties of engraving, for Le Royer tells us in his preface that he had himself to finish the plates commenced by Albin Olivier. In another practical treatise, entitled *Livre de Portraiture*, published in 1593, Jean Cousin is styled

Fig. 94.—Title of Jean Cousin's *Livre de Portraiture*, published in 1593 by Le Clerc. (The spot on the title is in the original, preserved among the prints of the Bibliothèque Nationale.)

"peintre géometrien." It is beyond doubt that this master produced figures and ornaments for many works, but what books were they? The custom was then to repeat the engraved borders of titles, the compartments, that is to say, the *passepartout*, in the middle of which the text was printed. Cousin must have designed many of these title-pages on wood, for that of the *Livre de Portraiture* affords a curious element of

comparison; but he was not by any means the inventor. In 1555 was sold at Antwerp a book printed from engraved plates after John Vriedman, by Gerard Juif, which is simply a collection of compartments for title-pages for the use of publishers.

It is about this time that metal plates may be seen in conjunction with wood engraving in the illustration of the Book, and the best artists soon attached their names to important publications of this kind. We have explained in a former chapter in what this process is least convenient in the impression of a book. In fact, two successive printings, that of the plates and that of the text, were additional trouble and a frequent cause of errors; but wood-cutting was in some measure abandoned in the middle of the sixteenth century, especially for separate plates, and engraved plates took a considerable importance under different artistic influences. The first was the facility of etching a metal plate compared to the difficulty of cutting a wood block. It thus naturally happened that the artists of the burin wished to employ their art in illustration, and taste was soon drawn to the new process.

In France the first volume of this kind was printed at Lyons, in 1488, by Topie de Pymont in folio: this was the *Pérégrinations en Terre Sainte* of Bernard de Breydenbach, with figures on engraved plates copied from the Mayence edition of 1486. Since, then, this process was abandoned until about 1550, as much for the reasons given above as for others, we only meet with a stray plate in a book now and again, which remains as a bait, and has but little reference to the text. Under the reign of Henry II. the smallness of the volumes did not always admit of wood engravings, and the artists in copper found a footing among illustrators; they made attempts, such as that of the *Histoire de Jason* of Réné Boivin in 1563, which brought about under Charles IX. a charming volume of engraved plates by P. Woériot.

The *Emblems* of Georgette de Montenay were also in the nonsensical style of those by Alciati, but they had an advantage, as the author assures us :—

> " A!ciat fist des emblèmes exquis,
> Lesquels, voyant de plusieurs requis,
> Désir me prist de commencer les miens,
> Lesquels je croy estre premiers chrestiens."

This pretension does not make them more intelligible, but the engravings of Woériot, unskilful as they are, import an element of interest which makes the rest passable. It was also at Lyons, the rival and often the master of Paris in typography, that the author printed his work.

By the privilege dated 1566, five years before publication, we see that it empowered Peter Woériot, engraver to the Duke of Lorraine, to portray, engrave, and cut in copper the said figures called emblems for the time and terms of five years (October 18th, 1566). Peter Woériot sometimes signed his prints with the small Lorraine cross adopted by Geoffroy Tory's workshop, as may be seen in our engraving.

Copperplate engraving had by this time established itself, and the works that were so illustrated increased. The architect, Du Cerceau, published his admirable collection of *Les Plus Beaux Bastiments de France* in folio 1576-79, in which he had lavished numerous plans and views of the royal and princely castles. Thevet put forth his *Cosmographie Universelle* and his *Hommes Illustres*, the latter adorned with skilfully engraved portraits. In Paris the publishers Mamert Patisson, who married the widow of Robert Estienne, the type and mark of whom he took, Adrien le Roy, and Robert Ballard, his *confrères*, published the celebrated *Ballet Comique de la Royne Faict aux Nopces de Monsieur le Duc de Joyeuse*, composed by Balthasar de Beaujoyeux, page to Henry III.; and in this book, in which were thrown slight etchings, the King displayed all his immodesty and lasciviousness. The Book has often had the unconscious mission of transmitting to posterity the unworthiness of

Fig. 95.—Engraving by P. Woériot for Georgette de Montenay's *Emblèmes*.

its author or of its heroes. From this time the Book has left its golden age to enter into the vanities of courtiers and political abstractions.

Among the publications opposed to the Government of the time, the two associates Jacques Tortorel and Jean Perrissin, of Lyons, had published a celebrated collection of plates on the religious wars that stained the reign of Charles IX. with blood. At first engraved on metal, these plates were worn out, and were gradually replaced by others engraved on wood, on which several artists worked, among them Jacques le Challeux and also Jean de Gourmont, one of the most celebrated wood-cutters of the sixteenth century. This was a work composed of single leaves in folio size, which had an extraordinary sale among the religious people of the time.

At the same time, illustration on wood did not stand still. The portraits of authors produced by the pencil of Clouet and his school were commonly put at the head of their works. We cannot say whether Clouet himself designed the portraits of Tiraqueau and of Taillemont in 1553; of Du Billon, the author of the *Fort Inexpugnable*, in 1555; Papon and Ambroise Paré in 1561; Grevin, Ramus, and others; but the precision of these physiognomies recalls the peculiar manner of the French artists of the sixteenth century. The *Poems* of Ronsard in 1586 contains a series of very clever portraits, among them that of Muret, his commentator, one of the most perfect of its kind. Christopher de Savigny, author of the *Tableaux Accomplis de Tous les Arts Liberaux*, published by Jean and François de Gourmont in 1587, is represented at full length in the frontispiece of his work, offering the book to the Duc de Nevers, to whom it was dedicated. This plate in folio, probably engraved by Jean de Gourmont, is the best finished that can be seen. The work of Savigny, forgotten as it may be now, had a great reputation in its own time; and Bacon took from it the idea of his celebrated cyclopædia, *Advancement of Learning: London.*

Speaking of the Duc de Nevers, it will not be without interest to our readers to mention here a manuscript found in the Bibliothèque Nationale, which enables us to give an account of the work then necessary for the publication of an illustrated book. In 1577 the Duke arranged for the impression of an apologetic book, of which, however, no trace remains ; and his *intendant* writes a long letter to him on the subject of composition and bindings. It was necessary that the work should be produced quickly, bound and gilt, for presents. The *intendant* thinks calf would be the most expeditious covering. " It would be much the best to use black or red calf, . . . well gilt above, and not vellum, which is a thin parchment that quickly shrinks." The statements of this man of business show that five proofs of each sheet were taken for typographical correction, and that twelve full days were wanted for the binding. The most interesting part of this memoir is that which treats of the engraving on wood of the portrait. The plate was designed by an artist who had afterwards gone away. If it was not satisfactory, but the ornaments would pass, the *intendant* proposes to "fix a little piece of wood in the block for another portrait to be drawn upon." Here we see correction by elimination. " The pear-wood on which the original figure was engraved was to be taken out and substituted by another piece of wood of harder material. The portrait of the Duchesse de Nevers was better, yet the pear-wood had given way under the work. That of Madame is more passable. Nevertheless, there is still something to say to one eye. The wood cannot carry the subtlety of the line." Here, in a few clear and explicit lines by a man of the time, we see the arrangement of a publication of the sixteenth century, at a time when wood engraving was declining, to give way to engraving on metal, which was soon to reign supreme, through the most important publishing house of the century, the Plantins of Antwerp.

Christopher Plantin, like Jenson, came originally from

Tours. After having learned his art with Macé at Caen, he went to Paris, from which the wars soon drove him. He left for the Low Countries, and there Philip II. nominated him as chief printer—*architypographus.* Established at Antwerp in

Fig. 96.—Portrait of Christopher Plantin, printer of Antwerp. Engraved by Wierix.

1555, he surrounded himself, as had done the Estiennes and Alduses, with most of the learned and literary men of his time, among them Justus Lipsius, to whom Balzac attributed the Latin prefaces signed by Plantin. It is certain, however, that he was neither an Estienne nor an Aldus. His artistic

probity caused him to submit the proofs of his works to
strangers, with promise of recompense for faults indicated ; the
Estiennes also had employed the same system.　Plantin, not
to be behind any of his contemporaries in typographical
perfection, brought from France the celebrated type-founder
Guillaume Lebé, and charged him to supply him with a special
fount.*　Under the orders of Philip II., he printed the cele-

Fig. 97.—Plantin's mark.

brated *Polyglot Bible*, in eight folio volumes, absolutely perfect
in its execution ; unfortunately the Spanish Government, having

* In the Bibliothèque Nationale is a copy of an octavo *Album de Caractères*,
in which Lebé has written, " This gloss, made in Paris (1574) by me, is my
fourteenth letter, and the text is made on the pattern of the preceding one for
size, but of a better art ; and from this was printed the great Bible of Antwerp by
Plantin, to whom I sold a fount " (folio 6).　On folio 20 he wrote, " I do not
know whence came this small Hebrew that I received from Plantin to make a
smaller one for him.　He sent me this half-sheet, and I have not seen at Venice
another part."

advanced him funds in the course of publication, prosecuted him with the utmost rigour to obtain repayment. This very nearly shut up his printing house, but he took courage and overcame his difficulties, and set his affairs in order, until he became, in 1589, the year of his death, the principal publisher of Flanders. His mark was a hand holding a compass, with the motto *Labore et constantia.*

Plantin, who died at the age of seventy-four, left a prosperous business to be divided between his three daughters. There was first the house at Antwerp, which employed seventeen presses even at the time when he was in trouble, and there were further branches at Paris and Leyden, of less consequence. His second daughter married Jean Moret, called *Moretus,* and to him descended the Antwerp establishment; he and his descendants continued the printing house until recently; in the present day the house of the great printer and publisher is a typographical museum. The Plantin printing office—*Officina Plantiniana*—is understood to apply to the founder as well as to his descendants. The fashion of engraving in metal spread itself before the death of the head of the house, and his successors continued it. The principal engravers with the burin of the Low Countries were employed by them: the Wierix, the Galle, the Pass, the Mallery, the Van Sichem; it was a real school of illustration, that created by degrees a precious and sustained style, not without influence on the artists of that epoch. It was from this particular manner that came Thomas de Leu and Leonard Gaultier in France; and it is from Antwerp that came those small religious engraved figures that have lasted to our time in their incomprehensible mysticism.

The title-pages of the Plantin printing office inaugurated

the *passe-partout* engraved by the burin, overloaded and complicated, of which the seventeenth century took advantage. To tell the truth, these elaborate displays, blackened by ink, do not well accord with the titles; and there is a long distance between this decadence and the books ornamented with wood blocks by the Italians and French of the commencement of the century. Exception must be made in favour of Rubens, who made the designs for many of these titles. The heavy and squat architecture of the time was least of all appropriate to these decorations, which wanted grace. It passed from Plantin into France through the engravers; it went to Rome with Martin de Vos and Jean Sadeler; it made its way everywhere; and from that day to this it has never ceased. At the time of which we write it had taken its flight in France, and spread itself in Europe with extraordinary success. Engraving in relief, holding its own until then, gave way little by little before this invasion. When Henry IV. mounted the throne wood engraving had well-nigh finished its upward movement; it still remained in the *canards*, or popular pieces sold at low prices, but it is easy to see what these hasty cuts are worth.

We have now seen, in broad outlines, the history of the Book and its decoration in the sixteenth century in France: at first there were the French epics in Italy, the *Books of Hours*, the Romances of Chivalry; then about 1550, with the reign of Henry II., the religious pamphlets commenced, bookselling spread itself; the strife between illustrations on metal plates and those in relief assumed shape, it continued under Henry III., and terminated abruptly by the victory of the first at the extreme end of the century. With political passions, printing has become a weapon of warfare, which it will never cease to be. They knew in the sixteenth century what perfidious accusations or excessive praises were worth. The

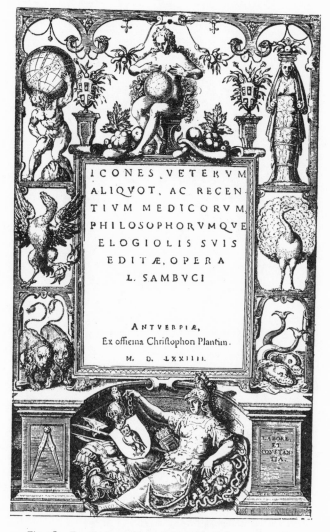

Fig. 98.—Frontispiece of a book from Plantin's printing office.
Metal engraving.

Book followed, besides, the fate of its author. If the writer was burned, so was his book, as was the case with Etienne Dolet, born 1509 at Orleans, who having learnt typography

at Gryphius's office, Lyons, and established a printing office
at Lyons, 1537, was burnt in Paris for his heterodox publications 1546. Witness also the *Christianismi Restitutio* of
the Catholic Servetus, printed at Vienne, in Dauphiné, and

Fig. 99.—Mark of Etienne Dolet, printer at Lyons, 1542.

consigned to the flames with its author at Geneva in 1553. A
single copy was saved from the fire, and is now preserved in
the Bibliothèque Nationale; it is the identical copy annotated
by Colladon, the accuser of the unhappy Servetus, and still
bears traces of fire on its leaves.

CHAPTER IV.

1600 TO 1700.

Tendencies of the regency of Marie de Medici—Thomas de Leu and Leonard Gaultier—J. Picart and Claude Mellan—Lyons and J. de Fornazeris—The Book at the beginning of the seventeenth century in Germany, Italy, England, and Holland—Crispin Pass in France—The Elzevirs and Enschedé and their work in Holland—Sebastian Cramoisy and the Imprimerie Royale—Illustration under Callot, Della Bella, and Abraham Bosse—The publishers and the Hotel de Rambouillet—The reign of Louis XIV., Antoine Vitré syndic at his accession—His works and mortifications; the Polyglot Bible of Le Jay—Art and illustrators of the grand century—Sébastien Leclerc, Lepautre, and Chauveau —Leclerc preparing the illustration and decoration of the Book for the eighteenth century.

Fig. 100.—Letter engraved by A. Bosse.

EVER did the art of printing pass through a more critical period than that at which we have now arrived, when the science of the old printers assumed a commercial character, in which taste lost itself under the influence of religious architecture. Changed into cathedral porticos, the Book is crowded with unsightly columns, mitred and crossed saints. Figures on copper plates replaced the foliage and the arabesques of the older booksellers. Through the Plantins and their imitators, the architectural passion was far spread. It inundated France, ran through Germany and Italy, and reigned

11

pre-eminent in Holland. Literary taste also underwent a
change ; manners were no longer those of the sixteenth century,
bold, free, and gay ; from the religious wars a certain hypocrisy
arose ; bombast replaced the natural ; the gods were preparing,
as a contemporary said, to receive Louis XIV. and his genius.

It is not that artists were wanting at the opening of the
seventeenth century who could, in giving free scope to their
talent, show themselves worthy successors of those who went
before them. Unhappily the booksellers had no longer a loose
bridle on their neck ; they rather had the rope round it, for they
were hung or burned at the least infraction of political or religious
propriety. Yet the reign of Henry IV. was relatively an easier
period for the workers at the Book, in which they were less
confined to the strict terms of excessive regulations ; but after
this prince severity increased, and during the year 1626 a new
law was promulgated punishing with death the printers or
distributers of prohibited books. Doubtless the books that were
thus secretly sold, and prohibited in defence of good manners,
were neither typographical nor artistic *chefs-d'œuvre*. The author
displays the indecencies by which he hoped to make profit
and fame, regardless of type or illustration. But during the
regency of Marie de Medici, it was not only the authors of a
bad standard that were in danger of being hung ; the printer
or seller of the pamphlet or book of a reputed heterodox author
was also hung, and it became difficult to steer safely among
these prohibitions. The consequence was, that enormous numbers
of works were made with frontispieces decorated with colon-
nades and mitred saints, and displaying high-sounding titles of
sound orthodoxy. The somewhat gross mysticism, from the
office of Plantin, formed the most solid stock of every
respectable dealer.

Under Henry IV. as well as under the minority of Louis
XIII., two French illustrators received from the school of

Fig. 101.--Title of the *Métanéalogie*, engraved by Leonard Gaultier.

Antwerp their inspiration for the ornament of the Book.
Thomas de Leu, probably from Flanders, was allied with the

old Parisian painter and engraver of celebrated portraits, Antoine Caron, in furnishing the engraved plates for the *Images de Plate Peinture des Deux Philostrates, Sophistes Grecs*, Paris, Claude Cramoisy, 1609, folio; and Leonard Gaultier, his contemporary worker in company with Jaspar Isaac and other artists in the Book. Leonard Gaultier contributed most to spread in France the Plantinian style, and his somewhat cold but characteristic talent suited this art more than that of any one else then could. He was also an engraver of portraits, now rare and valuable, in the style of Wierix or of Thomas de Leu; but, at the demand of publishers and booksellers, he composed other plates, at first historical figures representing the royal family and the nobles for the publisher Leclerc, in a simple and natural manner; he also designed pious figures, recording a miracle or representing the ceremonies of a jubilee and other devotional things. But he made his great success in the composition of frontispieces to theological and pious works, printed by nearly all the booksellers. Leonard Gaultier had a knack of his own for pilasters and Grecian columns, under which he boldly placed entire councils of cardinals and bishops, as in the heading of the *Bibliotheca Veterum Patrum*, into which he crowded nearly forty figures. He blended also with a certain grace the sacred and the profane, placing among ideal saints the wanton fine ladies of the time, with their large collarettes and jewels falling down on their naked breasts. The work of André Valladier, chaplain to the King, entitled *Métanéalogie Sacrée*, published by Peter Chevalier in 1609, was adorned with a title of this particular kind, in which Gaultier had no rival, and which preserves the precision of Flemish masters in the detail of ornaments of the toilet.

He was one of the first who worked for Sebastien Cramoisy,

printer and publisher, who had established his shop in the Rue St. Jacques at the sign of the *Stork*. We shall have occasion to speak of him later in connection with the Royal Printing House, of which he was the first director; he is mentioned now because in 1611 Leonard Gaultier engraved for him the frontispiece of *L'Aigle Français*, a collection of sermons by Thomas Girault. The publisher made a kind of *passe-partout* of it, for he used the same plate in 1618 for the *Sermons* of Raymond de Hézèque.

Besides the publications of Sebastien Cramoisy and Cheval-lier, Leonard Gaultier illustrated also those of Nicholas Buon and many other publishers of the time in Paris and Lyons. With such a profusion of works emanating from a single artist without reckoning those which were produced in great quantity by men of less note, wood engraving was dead. At most they ventured to put a wood block of a printer's mark on a title; more ordinarily this mark was not alone sufficient, and showed the disdain in which taste then held wood-cutting. Such is fashion, heedless of the most elementary rules of art. To put type within an engraved title, or to ornament a printed text with engravings, is a heresy of principle that was established in the eighteenth century, by dint of its cleverness and talent. But at the beginning of the seventeenth, in spite of Leonard Gaultier or Thomas de Leu, these overloaded titles, over-powering the very front of the Book, offend the eye by their excessive blackness, and incontestably make us regret the admirable frontispiece on wood of the preceding century.

This is, properly speaking, all the ornament at the accession and during the reign of Louis XIII. Leonard Gaultier composed also some small vignettes for an edition of Homer, but they are mediocre and but little to the point. The frontispiece was the resource of the unoccupied engraver, and many others followed the same path. Jean Picart made a frontispiece with architecture and figures for the *Histoire de la Maison de Châtillon-sur-Marne* for Sebastien Cramoisy. A cold and hard artist he was, the rival of Gaultier, and one of the most employed of the vignette engravers of Paris. There was also Jaspar Isaac, a mediocre craftsman, but a designer of clever titles, among which is that of the continuation of the *Annales* of Baronius for the publisher Denis de la Noue. Then Claude Mellan, whose great and clever talent did not disdain second-rate works, in which he gave free play to his burin. It must be said, however, that his bold touch did not accommodate itself well to reduced spaces, and that he was not working in the field which suited his inventive powers. We mention his portrait of Louis XIV. at the head of the *Code Louis XIV.;* the title of the *Perfection du Chrestien*, in which is included a portrait of Cardinal Richelieu, A. Vitré, 1647, folio; that of the *Instruction du Dauphin* for Cramoisy, 1640; that of the *Works* of St. Bernard for the Royal Printing House; and, lastly, perhaps the best of all, the *Poesies* of Pope Urban VIII., of which we here give a copy.

Lyons did not remain long behind in the movement, but how changed from its great reputation of the sixteenth century! J. de Fornazeris engraved the frontispieces to *Justus Lipsius*, published by Horace Cardon in 1613. Peter Favre and Audran imitated them. C. Audran designed for Claude Landry the *Theologia Naturalis* of Theophilus Reynaud, and the bookseller Picquet ordered from him the title for the *Annales Minorum* in 1628. Everywhere taste was modelled on the works of the capital, to name only the principal centres, Rouen, Rheims, Sens, down to Venes, a small town of the Department of Tarn, where Guillaume de Nautonnier published in 1603 his curious book *Mécométrie*, whose frontis-

Fig. 102.—Title engraved by Claude Mellan for Urban VIII.'s *Poesies*, printed at the Royal Printing House, in 1642.

piece was bordered by views of cities, with an equestrian portrait of King Henry.

And if we pass to Germany, we find at Mayence mediocre engravings for titles according to the pattern then prevalent everywhere. The title of the *Droit Civil* of Aymar

Vailius, that of the works of St. Bonaventura in 1609 for the bookseller Antoine Hiérat, and that of the *Viridarium Virtutûm*, rather cleverly treated by the burin in 1610. What a period had passed since Gutenberg, Fust, and Schoeffer! There was still one Ivo Schoeffer at Mayence, but only the name lived ; no trace remained of the old printers of the other century. It was the same at Bamberg, Cologne, Nuremberg, and Basle, in all the cities that were an honour to typography in former times. Cologne was neither better nor worse favoured than others. The booksellers Boetzer, Kinck, and De Binghy had passable engravings for their titles; and the *Commentaries* of Salmeron may be mentioned, with portraits after the original Germans of the fifteenth century. At Nuremberg we may cite a curious specimen treating of natural history by Basil Besler, in which the artist gives the interior of a zoological cabinet of the time; but what has become of the blocks and the typography in the city of Koberger? Basle held its own later in relief engraving. In the meantime there was a mediocre set of the *Dance of Death* on copper, published by Miegen, 1621.

At Jena and Frankfort-on-the-Main were prosperous printing houses, but engravings and ornamentation were neglected. Frankfort, however, employed the frontispiece in the *Traité du Commerce* of Sigismond Scaccia, published by Zuner in 1648 ; it was divided into compartments, in which the Bourse, the Exchange, and the quay of the city were represented.

It is hardly necessary to mention the Italian cities which followed the movement. Venice from the middle of the sixteenth century had used engraved frontispieces, among which was that of Domenic Zenoi for the *Portraits des Hommes Illustres* of Nicholas Valegio. In the same city James Piccini worked for

Sgava in 1648, but he was equally at the service of Roman publishers, for whom he designed a number of titles. By the side of him Frederic Greuter adorned the publications of Alexander Zanetti, not without talent, but without individuality. Bologna, Brescia, Florence, and Naples, had no original sentiment ; they followed indifferently the manner of the day.

In Holland, artists were somewhat numerous. The family of the Passes designed vignettes for books, and engraved frontispieces, admirably studied and composed. The clear and truly individual style of their works places their illustrations in the first rank among those of their time. They had, at the same time, the genius that created and the intelligent burin that faithfully represented an idea. They imagined with skill the scenes that they depicted without borrowing much from their predecessors. From 1599, the date of the publication of the *Hortus Deliciarum*, one of their best works, up to about 1623, they were in Holland, at Arnheim and at Amsterdam. In 1623 we find one of them, the most celebrated, Crispin the younger, designing figures for the *Manège Royal* of Pluvinel, published by Angelier in Paris, and for another edition, with folding plates, in 1624 for Guillaume Lenoir, at the sign of the *White Rose Crowned*. This magnificent work, in which the King, Louis XIII., is represented receiving lessons from the riding master Pluvinel, appeared in a third and more complete reimpression in 1625 with another publisher, Michel Nivelle. Here we see the Dutch appreciated in France, in Paris, at that time the city the most ready to understand and pay for the works of eminent artists. In 1624 Gombauld published an *Endymion*— Boileau later associated Gombauld with other poets to dub him a maker of pitiable sonnets —Nicholas Buon, the bookseller named above, undertook the publication, and employed Pass, Leonard Gaultier, and J. Picart to furnish plates in octavo size.   Heavy and black as were these vignettes, they none the less make a good appearance in the edition of the forgotten poet; and it is due to truth to recognise how much Pass was above his collaborators.   The following year, 1625, he engraved the *Dionysiaques* of Nonus, for Robert Fouet, and the *Roman des Romans* of Du Verdier, comprising more than ten engravings, in a very free and bold manner. The *Berger Extravagant* and the *Académie de l'Espée* came in 1628, among numerous others.

In point of fact, Crispin Pass did not devote himself entirely to Parisian publishers; he always kept up his interests in Flanders so as to return there from time to time; but he did not find in his own country the ready and assured sales of Paris.   Still the city of Leyden had then one of the most renowned workshops of typography; the Elzevirs had commenced to make a good place for themselves among the printers of Europe by the extreme correctness of their editions, the distinctness of their work, and their marvellous art in the taste and arrangement of the Book.   In reality, the sizes and characters of their books were too small, but if the smallness of the page did not allow room for vignette or ornament, they bore a certain practical elegance that was not without charm.   The origin of the printing house was due to Louis Elzevir, who published in 1592 an edition of *Eutropius* at Leyden.   He left sons, who went into partnership, and founded, as we know, a house which was unrivalled.

Bonaventure Elzevir, grandson of Louis, was the most illustrious of this family, so remarkably devoted to its art.   He took Abraham as partner, and together they published those little Latin classics in duodecimo of which the value is now so great.   Among others, *Pliny* issued from their presses in the year

1635, in three volumes, *Virgil* in 1636, and *Cicero* in 1642. To-day amateurs, above all those afflicted with bibliomania, hunt for unbound Elzevirs when they have full margins. From about 1633 to 1639 these volumes were composed of paper of rather small size, making a page of a hundred and thirty to a hundred and thirty-three millimetres; from 1639 onwards the

Fig. 103.—Title of Pluvinel's *Manège Royal*, engraved by Crispin Pass in 1624.

paper was larger, and the page in 12mo measured from about a hundred and thirty-five to a hundred and thirty-seven. One must be a book-lover to understand the interest attaching to these figures, and employ his entire activity in the discovery of these undiscoverable books, which are zealously kept under lock and key as soon as they are found.

One of the most esteemed of their works is the *De Imitatione*

of Thomas à Kempis, printed by Jean and Daniel Elzevir about
1653, and known as the edition without date. But as the
association of Jean and Daniel is known to have lasted only
from 1652 to 1654, the date 1653 appears to be most plausible.
We reproduce the entire title of this typographical *bijou*, which
merited a cleverer engraver.

Fig. 104.—Title of the *Imitation* of the Elzevirs.

The rarest of all the numerous Elzevirs, possibly by reason
of the popularity of its subject, is the *Pastissier François*, Louis
and Daniel Elzevir, Amsterdam, 1655, of which M. Morgand
had an uncut copy, measuring a hundred and forty-three millimetres, in 1878. The Benzon copy sold in 1875 for £140, and

another copy which lately turned up at M. Techener's Sale brought £96.

It is to be remarked that the Elzevirs frequently avoided dating or even signing their books, for reasons easily understood. Publishing numerous works, they were afraid of compromising themselves in the eyes of the powerful, and they let them go forth without any trade mark. These artists in typography were, besides, the most prudent and subtle of men. Working at a time when bookselling had become an acknowledged commerce, and a trade requiring all the skill and resources of others, they wisely availed themselves of these resources, gathering for

Fig 105.—Mark of Bonaventure and Abraham Elzevir,
printers at Leyden, 1620.

themselves honour and profit without having done anything more than seizing their opportunity. Using, as they did, the characters of Claude Garamond, of Jacques Sanlecques, and the paper of Angoulême, M. Didot thence claims them as French publishers.

After the Elzevirs another celebrated printer's family made its mark in Holland, who afterwards acquired the Elzevir fount, viz., the Enschedé family, who carried on a flourishing printing office and type foundry. Isaak, born in 1681, printed, in con-junction with his son John, a folio *Bible*. John began already as a boy of nine years, under the supervision of his father

to cut types in wood, and published in 1777 several classical
works and a pattern book of types, *Proef van Lettern*, which
even now is considered a very important contribution to the
history of printing.

In France the Elzevirs had no rivals; but a fashion was
introduced towards the end of the sixteenth century for the
association of several publishers in the production of important
and costly books. There were, among others, the company of
the *Grand Navire* in 1610, of the *Source* in 1622, and of the
Soleil in 1629. In 1631 several publishers united and founded
a second company of the *Grand Navire*. These were the two
Cramoisys, Sebastien and Gabriel, Denis Béchet, Jean Branchu,
Denis Moreau, Claude Sonnius, and Denis Thierry. The
associates took a ship as their mark, but without putting their
names on the masts, as the original company of the *Grand
Navire* had done. They published, at mutual expense and
divided profits, great works, of which each one of them had
the right of sale, but of course reserving to themselves the
right to publish such others as they pleased. Sebastien
Cramoisy passes as the chief, the moral director of another
company, formed to publish the Fathers of the Church, with
the royal types, a company affiliated to the *Grand Navire* and
signed in 1638 by Denis Moreau, Gille Morel, Etienne Richer,
Claude Sonnius, and Gabriel Cramoisy. But as regards their
personal works, if they had neither the perfection nor the
aspect of those of Froben, Aldus, the Estiennes, or even of
Plantin, they at least surpassed the French books of the time.
Formerly syndic of the Corporation in 1602, twenty-nine years
before the constitution of the *Grand Navire*, Cramoisy was
also sheriff of Paris, and carried on his trade in a shop in
the Rue St. Jacques which had been that of Father Nivelle,

the, *doyen* of booksellers, who died in 1603 at the age of eighty years.

The position of Cramoisy made it natural that Cardinal Richelieu should fix his eyes on him for the direction of the Royal Printing House. This establishment, founded by the King in 1640, was installed within the Louvre, in a long series of consecutive rooms which formed a workshop without rival in the world. Sublet des Noyers was named superintendent, Trichet du Fresne corrector; and under this triple direction the presses set to work. The first book was the *Imitation de Jésus-Christ*, dated 1640, folio, a fine book enough, but not to be compared to the Elzevir editions. The types used in this book are attributed to Claude Garamond, founder of the sixteenth century, to whom are due the Greek types of Francis I. With the Royal Printing House, as often happens with State enterprises, the cost was great, and the return nothing. Only a few years after its foundation it had swallowed up nearly 400,000 livres, a very heavy sum for a badly balanced treasury; it had produced sixty or seventy volumes of moderate value; and after Cramoisy the management was so little in earnest that it turned the workshops into a stable, called "the little stable of the King," at the commencement of the eighteenth century.

To return to the artists of the Book under Louis XIII. and Cardinal Richelieu, we must go back a little, before the foundation of the Royal Printing House, and we shall take up the French school of illustration at a time when Jacques Callot was giving it a vigorous lift and trying to do away with its affected and hard style. It must be acknowledged that Callot was not a vignettist, a special designer; his art aimed higher, and in most cases succeeded better; yet he did not disdain frontispieces, and made some for the *Coustumier de Lorraine*, the *Harpalice* of Bracciolini, and for a crowd of others of which the enumeration would be tedious. Certain of his works passed into Italy, where they helped to raise the debased level of the Book. He then adorned several works with etchings, among them the *Lumière du Cloistre*, published by François Langlois 1646. This was again one of the symbolic and sententious works with which the public taste is never satiated, and a kind

Fig. 106.—Plate taken from the *Lumière du Cloistre*.   Copper-plate by Callot.

of guide for the priest. At the bottom of the little etching here given, representing birds falling from a tree, we read,—

> " Ses petits hors du nid le courbeau jette en bas,
> Lorsque par leur blancheur ils lui sont dissemblables.
> Le bon prélat de mesme au cloistre n'admet pas
> Ceux qui n'ont rien d'esgal à ses mœurs venerables."

Callot also made another set of emblems on the life of the Virgin Mary, and even published in 1620 a series of prints in quarto for the tragedy of *Soliman* of Bonarelli, for Cecconnelli. France imposed herself on fallen Italy, where she dispersed her works, and if an engraver arose there, he did not disdain to be consecrated in France. Witness Della Bella, who went from Italy to France, where he was taken under the protection of Cardinal Richelieu. This was about the time of the establishment of the Royal Printing House, and it was expected that employment would be found for him sooner or later.

Callot was the model chosen by the young Italian artist, and this choice might have been less happy. Della Bella took from his master the philosophic vein, the drollery of design, which he exercised from the outset in humorous frontispieces, among others that of Scarron's works, where nine fish-women, taking the place of the Muses, dance around the poet. But he passed from gay and pleasant to severe, and made large designs of architectural titles. In 1649 he designed the plates for the large and ill-arranged volume of Valdor on Louis XIII., published by Antoine Estienne at the Royal Printing House. His success was not in that direction; Della Bella was a painter of groups, of ornaments, of subjects somewhat heavy and laboured, but which, after numerous transformations, opened a new road to the vignettists of the eighteenth century.

With Abraham Bosse the decoration of the Book took a wider range. Numerous and charmingly ornamented letters, heads of pages, and tailpieces appear. There are few artists that have done so much for graceful illustration and harmony between the vignette and the printed page. His prodigious fecundity made him attempt every style; and after the gaieties of the prints in which he laughed with his contemporaries, he adopted a graver mood and designed more serious sub-jects on copper. However, the book entitled *La Manière Universelle*, by Desargues, with numerous geometrical figures and a pleasing frontispiece, bearing the dedication to the

Seigneur de Noyers, superintendent of the Royal Printing
House, was a critical work, in which Bosse, under serious
pretence, did not spare an enemy. They were not, however,

Fig. 107.—Title of the *Manière Universelle*, by Desargues, in 1643, by Abraham Bosse.

angry with the artist, for the following year Bosse published
fourteen plates for the *Suetonius* printed at the Louvre.

He successively designed plates for the *Histoire de St.*

Louis, numerous vignettes for books of piety, figures for the *Pucelle* of Chapelain and for the *Larcins de la Fortune*. He was always himself, refined and ingenious, even in the most barren or the most complicated subjects.

Fig. 108.—Print by Abraham Bosse, representing the booksellers of the Palace under Louis XIII.

He has left us in a celebrated print a representation of a bookseller's shop of his time. It is for us an interesting work, inasmuch as it shows us in a simple and naïve manner the picturesque side of these stores, where the dealer and his wife offered and displayed new works to their customers. The shop is compact, and very much like the open-air stalls of to-day; posting-bills placed above the shelves indicate the " new books;" and if the inscriptions given by Bosse be credited, the Palace dealer offered his books with singular eclecticism: Boccaccio, Aretin, the *Astrée* of D'Urfé, the *Bible*, or Machiavelli. In the hands of the woman is seen the romance *Marianne:*

> " Icy les cavaliers les plus adventureux
> En lisant les romans s'animent à combattre;
> Et de leur passion les amants langoureux
> Flattent les mouvements par des vers de théâtre,"

says the text of Bosse. What was commonly done then is still done; they went shopping and rummaging the stalls, and those of the Palace were particularly attractive.

If we credit Sauval, the increase in the number of booksellers, in the middle of the century, was due to the wits of the Hotel de Rambouillet. The passion for novelty, for recent works, had produced that quantity of publishers, he says, that we have seen on the Pont Neuf, and that we still see to-day at the Palace and the University, the number of whom is so multiplied in all these places that in the Palace they amount to more than other dealers; and as to the neighbourhood of the University, they are obliged, in order to lodge the rest, to extend the ancient bounds from St. Yves to the river (Sauval, *Antiquités de Paris*, viii., 354).

In fact, each year saw an increase in the number of publishers in corporation, with syndic and adjuncts. During the reign of Louis XIII., the single year 1610 saw fifty new houses started, and among them Antoine Vitré, who was to become the most illustrious of his contemporaries. But, as there were no more than six printers, it may be inferred that all the rest were booksellers, in the true sense of the word, to begin with those who encumbered afterwards the great *salle* of which Sauval speaks. Antoine Vitré was syndic in May, 1643, on the accession of Louis XIV. He had four adjuncts. With him the Book marked the solemn style that the commencement of the century had imparted to it. Appointed royal printer for the Oriental languages in 1621, he undertook a Syriac work, the first that ever was attempted in Paris. The project of a Polyglot Bible suggested to him the idea of acquiring for the King the Oriental manuscripts and matrices of Savary de Brèves. The King left to him the care of negotiating the business, but did not reimburse him without numerous difficulties, in the midst of which the printer almost lost the means of conveniently continuing his trade. The advocate Le Jay charging himself with the enormous expenses necessitated by the Polyglot Bible, it was set up in the hope that Cardinal Richelieu would pay the cost. He was willing to do so, but required that his name should figure on the book; and as Le Jay, an independent man, formally opposed it, Vitré met with ill-will from the Minister, which increased from day to day. In 1645 the impression was finished, but Le Jay was ruined, and though we admire the paper, the type, and the extraordinary size of the nine volumes of the Polyglot Bible, we find in it so many faults, errors, and misprints that it has become almost valueless, being hardly worth its binding. There were terrible mortifications in the business, and Vitré had to bear the brunt of them more than any one. Nevertheless he did not let his presses stand still, but published successively Arabic, Turkish, and Persian works. His action against the Savary heirs, as representing the King, in the acquisition mentioned above, continued also after the printing of the *Bible*, and hindered its progress. He struggled on; and the Assembly of Clergy, of which he was the printer, sought to help him out of his difficulties. The matter being once terminated, the Cardinal being dead, and Vitré having been named by Colbert director of the Royal Printing House in place of Cramoisy, he also died, and was accused later of having destroyed the types and matrices of the *Polyglot Bible*, so that they should not be used after him. This fable, long accredited, has since been ascertained to be false, for the punches and matrices passed to the Royal Library, thence to the Royal Printing House, which was reorganised in 1691.

Antoine Vitré, in spite of his misfortunes, was a great personage. He was painted by Champagne and engraved by Morin, as was Richelieu himself. The portrait, which we here reproduce (p. 184), is from the book of M. Delaborde, *La Gravure*. Such was the man whom we meet at the beginning of the reign of Louis XIV. as syndic of booksellers; and it was by no means a sinecure, a canonry giving honour and profit; quite the other way. With the Draconian rules on the subject, the syndic assumed a heavy burden towards the King, as well as towards its *confrères*. Religious quarrels envenomed every question, and the revocation of the Edict of Nantes had for its immediate result new and more severe royal ordinances.

The reign of Louis XIV. saw the zenith of engraving with the burin, but not that of printing or illustration. Doubtless it would be puerile to pretend that typography had not made any material progress; it had done so in engraving and in setting up the type; work was done more quickly, because the presses had become more perfect. But the wise harmony of the old printers, their sure taste, even up to their old irregular *clichés*, were no longer there to form a graceful and charming

Fig. 109.—Frontispiece of the *Dictionnaire de l'Academie*, 1st edition, 1694.

whole, which to modern precision is as different as a picture

by Van Eyck from a chromo-lithograph. Under Louis XIV.,
titles became regular, following, as we have said in the
beginning, and modelling themselves on, the affected and
peruked people who read them. All art entered on this path
of sublimity and grandeur. The painter Le Brun is the

Fig. 110.—Antoine Vitré, printer to the King, by Ph. de Champagne.

highest exponent of this false Olympus, where an heroic pose
became necessary for the most simple movements. Made
popular by engraving by Pesne, Audran, Poilly, Edelinck, and
a hundred others, this tendency overran everything : art and
industry, painting and tapestry, illustration and typography

itself. All was grand, in reverse of other times, when all was small and mean. The embellishments of the Book were full of gods in perukes and goddesses in armour, Louis XIV. as Apollo, as the sun illuminating the world, as we see in the frontispiece to the first edition of the *Dictionnaire de l'Academie.* "Nec pluribus impar" was not the device of one man; it was the haughty and glorious cry of a whole people, from great to small, from the sublime painter to the modest printer.

In most cases these exaggerations are not beneficial to the art. Here they were. But, for the matter that specially occupies us, it does not appear that the Book was much advanced. It approached a marvellous epoch of a delicate and graceful art; but it did not find its true expression; it dragged painfully after the works of Plantin, throwing its etchings and line engravings heavily in the middle of texts, in gross and bad taste. Yet taste in literature had an onward tendency; Molière and La Fontaine produced on their contemporaries the effect that in our day the naturalists have produced on the romanticists; but this was not for long. Majesty recovered its rights with Bossuet, Boileau, and the others.

Sébastien Leclerc was one of the rare artists of the end of the seventeenth century who gave thought to the vignette in the midst of this outbreak of pompous commonplace. A successor of Callot in manner, sought after by the publishers, he began this style with a romance of La Calprenède, and continued with the *Promenade de St. Germain* of Louis le Laboureur, *bailly de Montmorency*, to whom Boileau said such curious things. This *bleuette* is one of the rarest books of Leclerc, and we reproduce one of the pages, with a charming tailpiece, which comes very near those of the eighteenth century. There was, moreover, the charm of this ingenious designer; he adorned the works of his contemporaries with graceful vignettes and decorations full of suppleness. It may be believed, besides, that he did not remain behind his *confrères* in figure composition or allegorical and Divine emblems. His art did not go far enough to throw off the errors of the existing school; he was content not to copy any one and to make his works truly his own.

JE laboure un champ plein d'épines
Qui ne rapporte fruit ny fleur,
Et me fens piquer jufqu'au cœur
Par mille pointes affafines.
Que mon deftin à de malheur !
Ce n'eft que labeur & douleur.

Fig. 111.—Tailpiece of Sébastien Leclerc for the *Promenade de St. Germain.*

Such were, for example, the vignettes of the *Histoire de Turenne*, where the heads of the chapters, the ornamented letters, and the tailpieces, harmoniously blend with each other, and make the book, although a little heavy as to impression, a most agreeable work. Leclerc then found himself ready to design vignettes for the works of Racine for the publisher Claude

Barbin, another name frequently encountered in Boileau. The title of Vol. ii. merits attention.

The same year of this last publication, 1676, Sébastien Leclerc illustrated the *Metamorphoses* of Ovid for Benserade, the engraving of which cost the King more than 10,000 livres. Thus adorned, the book had not a bad appearance, but a satirist of the time, Hardin very probably, made on it this quatrain :—

> " Mais quant à moi j'en trouve tout fort beau :
> Papier, dorure, images, caractère,
> Hormis les vers qu'il fallait laisser faire
> A La Fontaine."

It may be imagined what an engraver could produce working ever since 1650 and dying in 1715, that is, a life of work as long as could be hoped for. Leclerc was the absolute contemporary of the King. He died, like him, at the beginning of the eighteenth century, leaving work widely scattered among books, funeral orations, and placards. After the example of Callot and Bosse, he did not disdain satire. One of his prettiest vignettes served to illustrate some pamphlet of Richesource against the journalists of his time ; it represents a dandy of about 1679 offering his gazette :

> " Venez, savans ; venez me faire vos avances
> D'un louis tous les ans de contribution ;
> Vous aurez les lundis nouvelles conférences
> Dans des cayers volans de cette impression ;
> Je l'ai jusques icy pratiqué de la sorte,
> Et comme ce bâton soutenu qui me porte."

This proves that already the young pamphleteers understood the means how to frighten the authors of their time.

By the side of this unrivalled combatant we may be permitted to place Lepautre, twenty years older than Leclerc, whose studies had been principally directed on architecture. In the moments of leisure from his special work he devoted himself to frontispieces and vignettes; nevertheless, although he had before him the charming designs of Leclerc, he confined himself to a cold and hard manner, keeping, indeed, as much as

Fig. 112.—Small figure of Sébastien Leclerc for Richesource's pamphlet.

possible to titles, in which his particular talent could find scope. He designed also the *Chartreux Missal* of 1679, the *Gallia Christiana* after Marot, the *Dioptrique Oculaire* of P. Chérubin engraved by Edelinck, and a thousand other works of small repute.

Very different was Francois Chauveau, who, without having

the delicacy of Sébastien Leclerc or his art of arrangement, treated at least with grace small figures and illustrations. Certainly there is an enormous distance between these correct and commonplace engraved plates and the delightful wood

Fig. 113.—Frontispiece by C. Le Brun, for the first edition of Racine, 1676.

engravings of the time of Geoffroy Tory, for example. But, be their worth what it may, they were in excellent keeping; and even with Molière they did not cut such a bad figure. Chauveau was associated with many of the works of Leclerc, who induced him often to be less heavy, inasmuch as Leclerc corrected many of his compositions in engraving them. It was so with Molière, and still more so with Racine in the plate of the *Plaideurs*, in which Chauveau revealed himself a precursor of the eighteenth century. Unhappily he did not always follow this manner. Consecutively, and with various success, he illustrated *Alaric, Andromaque,* and the *Metamorphoses* of Ovid by Benserade, with Leclerc; the *Pucelle* of Chapelain, and the *Tragédies* of Racine, to which Le Brun did not disdain to put his hand.

In short, the connecting link between the beginning of the seventeenth and that of the eighteenth century in the development of illustration is Sébastien Leclerc. He had known the artists of the first period; he lived to see appear one of the precursors of the vignettists of the following century, Claude Gillot. Thanks to him, overloaded titles and unskilful vignettes underwent a gradual transformation. In the delicacy and slightness of his designs may be seen the dominant note of the eighteenth century, coquetry, and we get already a foretaste of Choffard. He was nearly the only one who did not fall into the exaggerations of the engravers of the time; he ran parallel with them without touching them, anxiously guarding his own well-accentuated personality. By the smallness and slenderness of his figures, Leclerc recalls somewhat the school of Fontainebleau; but he is above all the reflection of Callot, a Lorrainer like himself.

In Holland, a Frenchman, Bernard Picart, son of Etienne and pupil of Leclerc, was making a great name as an illustrator. He established himself as a print-seller at Amsterdam at the sign of *L'Etoile*, and successively designed vignettes for many works, among others the Boileau of 1718. His vignettes and tailpieces, without possessing either the spirit of Leclerc or the grace of the eighteenth century, express an ingenious and inventive art that had broken with the strained traditions of preceding epochs.

From these two artists the decoration of the Book rapidly advanced. The true form is found, and charming designers are not wanting to apply it.

The troubled state of England during the greater part of the seventeenth century no doubt accounts for the fact that the art of the Book made but very little progress. Theological controversies, the persecutions by the Puritans, and, above all, the great civil war and its antecedents and results, gave rise to a flood of publications of an ephemeral kind, which from their nature were hurriedly produced; and there was little room for pure literature and art. In the early part of the century, under the influence which Elizabeth left, and which James fostered, some important works were issued, with finely engraved illustrations; but wood engraving declined further and further, until it was artistically dead, to be revived in the next century. The works of the numerous poets and dramatists were printed in quarto, and collected editions of them in folio. Thus were issued the works of Shakespeare, first collected by Jaggard and Blount, 1623, folio, with an engraved portrait by Droeshout, the faithfulness of which was vouched in an opposite page of verse signed by Ben Jonson. *Don Quixote* first appeared in an English dress in 1612-20, published by E. Blount in quarto; and Jaggard, Blount's partner in the Shakespeare, published Boccaccio's *Decameron*, in two volumes folio, 1620. Among other notable works of the early part of the century were Drayton's *Polyolbion*, 1613; Chapman's *Homer*, 1611-15, folio, three volumes; Lord Bacon, whose essays and other

single publications appeared in the seventeenth, to be collected
as his *Works* in the next century; and William Prynne,
whose *Histrio Mastrix*, 1633, so offended Charles I. by its
references to the Queen and the court ladies, that the author
had to undergo a severe and degrading punishment. Many
of these works were illustrated with engravings of merit
on steel and copper by W. Hollar, P. Lombart, W. Marshall,
Hole, W. Pass, W. Faithorne, and R. Vaughan. So that here
were all the materials for the foundation of an English school,
to be cruelly broken up shortly afterwards by the distractions
of civil warfare.

In 1611 Robert Barker first printed the Authorised Version
of the Holy Bible, which has been more often reprinted than
any other book, and which exists to this day as the great
standard of the English language.

The taste for books of travel which arose in the last
century was largely increased by the voyages and discoveries
of the English in North America and the subsequent Puritan
exodus there. These early accounts of Virginia and New
England, many of which are tracts of a few leaves only, now
fetch fabulous prices. The great collection of voyages under
the name of *Purchas: his Pilgrimes*, was printed in five folio
volumes, 1625-26, while De Bry, Hulsius, and Linschoten
were enriching the world with their collections of travels,
printed in Germany and Holland. All of these works were
adorned with finely engraved plates, those to *Purchas* being
engraved by Elstrack, and, besides, it had a famous map of
the world, engraved by Hondius.

The controversial spirit engendered by the religious quarrels
of the century and by the great civil war gave incessant work to
the printers; and the many tracts and pamphlets thus produced

were frequently illustrated by crude and coarse woodcuts, of no value from an artistic point of view, but curious from the indications they afford of the costumes and manners of the time.

The first edition of Walton's *Angler* was printed by R. Marriott in 1653, 16mo, with plates in the text, engraved on steel by Lombart. Butler's *Hudibras* appeared in 1663-78, and Milton's *Paradise Lost* in 1667, quarto. · Fuller's *Worthies of England* was printed 1662, folio. We have roughly mentioned the principal English books of the century, and next approach the revival of literature and art in the eighteenth century.

13

CHAPTER V.

THE BOOK IN THE EIGHTEENTH CENTURY.

The Regency—Publishers at the beginning of the eighteenth century—Illustrators in France ; Gillot—The school of Watteau and Boucher—Cars—The younger Cochin; his principal works in vignettes—French art in England; Gravelot— Eisen—Choffard — The *Baisers* of Dorat; the *Contes* of Lafontaine — The publisher Cazin and the special literature of the eighteenth century — The younger Moreau and his illustrations—The Revolution—The school of David— Duplessis-Bertaux—The Book in Germany ; Chodowiecki—In England ; Boydell and French artists—Caslon and Baskerville—English books with illustrations— Wood engraving in the eighteenth century; the Papillons--Printing offices in the eighteenth century.

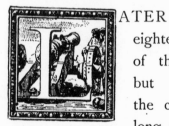

ATER on, about the beginning of the eighteenth century, the manners and tastes of the French produced an unconscious but tenacious reaction. It seemed as if the conceptions of romanticism had lasted long enough, and that the cycle of chevaliers and lords of the Middle Ages had passed away, and that a return to what is called the Natural was effected in literature and art. At the death of Louis XIV. the Olympes and its gods, the majestic poses and suns, had become wearisome. By a little half-open door, gaiety escaped from its prison and fled. For the Book that door was opened by the engraver Sébastien Leclerc.

Fig. 114.—Letter by Cochin for the *Mémoires d' Artillerie* of Suvirey de St. Remy.

The ancient school was replaced. Constrained during three quarters of a century, French manners began to be joyous under the regency of the Duc d'Orleans. The representatives of another age still lived, Rigaud still painted his portraits in wigs, but there were new comers, enlivened by the new fashions, less solemn and more bewitching. Le Brun was then far in the past, and as amusing to the ladies of the regency as are now to us the fashions of the Second Empire.

The Book, as its manner was, followed the movement, and gradually found the elements of its decoration in the tendencies of the day. Small sizes were multiplied, types showed elegance, and vignettes became more and more agreeable and spirited. Amateurs had their *ex-libris* or book-plates engraved. The smallest pamphlets were covered with ornamental letters, head and tailpieces, already very clever. Costume also, in its lighter form, gave to designers a means of agreeably composing a page of illustration and disseminating fancy in the figures. These revolutions were simply brought about from day to day, as taste became more pronounced and found its expression.

The commerce of the Book was still extending from the end of the preceding century; and if the number of printers was limited and arrested by certain somewhat hard laws, production in Paris was enormous. Among regulations that weighed most heavily on publishers figured the obligation put upon them by the ordinance of 1713 to deposit eight copies of illustrated books. In 1725 the King issued other regulations to affirm the rights of the university over the corporation, forcing the masters to assist in a body at the processions of the Sorbonne and to offer on the Day of the Purification a candle to the rector. In spite of this ordinance, more religious than useful to commerce, the fashion of vignettes increased. The principal shops were ransacked, as they are still, for novelties; the Rue St. Jacques and the Quai des Augustins, where they were grouped, were resorted to. The most important booksellers in 1727 were Coignard, the Barbous—who essayed afterwards, with Lengley Dufresnoy, to copy the Elzevirs,— Cavalier, Robustel, Fournier, Ballard, and D'Houry. Of the two last, D'Houry printed the calendars, and Ballard had the privilege for music. Another, Léonord, published the books of the Dauphin. At these and other publishers', recent works were examined, those who did not buy gave their advice and took ideas, and so this fashion slowly set in. It was thus that Houdart de la Motte published with G. Dupuis in 1719 a collection of fables, with illustrations by Claude Gillot, which was the talk at the booksellers'.

All was original in this book: the author, who had formed, five years before, the eccentric idea of translating the *Iliad* without knowing a word of Greek; the text, a kind of imitation of Lafontaine, without salt or savour; the size, quarto, admirably printed by Dupuis, in the Rue St. Jacques, with plates by Coypel, Massé, and, above all, the charming vignettes of Gillot, the most pleasing and clever of all his collaborators, a sort of Callot fallen into the eighteenth century, and who ought to take the first place in it by primogeniture. Gillot has been called, not without reason, "the last pagan of the Renaissance;" and this pagan had the honour to give us Watteau.

The Count de Caylus tells the story. Gillot had resigned the pencil for the etching needle on seeing the work of his pupil. He had no reason to complain; his pictures were of no value, and his prints gave other artists the idea of imitating them. The whole French school of the eighteenth century may have had its origin in this forgotten book, illustrated by the master of Watteau. In fact, in the manner of the little etching here given we may easily perceive the coquetry and affectation that were later the dominant tone of vignettes. For, it may well be said, the graceful, feminine, and arch manner of which we are going to speak was, above all, conventional and false. In opposition to the designers and engravers of the fifteenth and beginning of the sixteenth

Fig. 115.—Vignette by Gillot for the *Chien et le Chat*, fable by Houdart de la Motte, in 1719.

century, who reproduced naturally scenes of daily life even if somewhat idealized, it came to pass that, through the moral education of the artists, they put forth the ideal in the most ordinary things of life. Shepherds were no longer the gross and rustic peasants that we find in primitive Flemish paintings or in the *Hours* of Simon Vostre ; they were coxcombs, pomaded and adorned with ribbons, playing the bagpipes, and making love to court shepherdesses.

At first it was Watteau who influenced all the engravers

in the pretty and the smart ; Boucher did the rest ; and fatally the Book followed, and followed impetuously, surpassing, if possible, the painted works. If the severe poses, the grave touch, of the preceding century are no longer found, they often go too far in the contrary direction. It may be well said here that the arts are ordinarily the result of the manners of an epoch. The financial scheme of Law was not without influence on the entire eighteenth century, by the terrible manner in which it upset fortunes, awoke appetites, gave rein to aspirations hitherto held in check. Claude Gillot, the designer, was one of the first victims of the Scotch banker ; he lost his fortune on the Exchange ; but who may say what his artistic ambition dreamt of in the midst of all these disorders ? One thing is certain : that Watteau, his pupil, broke abruptly with the style of the seventeenth century.

Laurent Cars was the engraver who multiplied the compositions of Boucher, and set the fashion. He engraved also, after the painter of shepherds and nymphs, illustrations to Molière, the most agreeable that there are for style and spirit. In engraving certain works of Lemoyne, Cars did not completely desert the ancient school. He appears thus at the beginning of the eighteenth century as if divided between two manners, each equally possible to him.

The work of these engravers was almost exclusively done by etching, biting with acid a copper plate covered with varnish, on which the drawing was made by means of a point. This process, always previously used for sketches, served also for finishing vignettes, which up to then had been finished by the burin. The suppleness of the work was greater, and the artist remained more himself than he could be with the stiff cutting instrument of the seventeenth century.

The sizes of books had not yet all come to octavo or duodecimo. The *Œuvres de Molière* published by Prault in 1734 in six volumes quarto, under the direction of Marc Antoine Joly, give the idea of an enormous work, not at all of theatrical pieces. To tell the truth, these somewhat ex- aggerated dimensions gave artists more room for illustration ; later, when smaller forms predominated, text and engravings were so compressed that they were not always clear and readable to every eye. However, the quarto was not graceful, it was not in harmony with the delicate, the pastoral pieces, then in vogue, and as a current size it had to disappear in illustrated publications.

The class of artisans employed on the Book is hardly identical in the eighteenth century with that of printers and publishers. In the beginning, as we have seen, the engravers of wood blocks and the printers were often the same people, preparing their characters or their blocks, and afterwards putting them under the press. The great printing offices had very quickly changed that. Each particular work had its special workman. Typography had its type-founders, com- positors, forwarders, inkers, and pressmen. In the eighteenth century this was supplemented by designers, engravers, plate- printers ; and these different professions occupied themselves on the Book in manipulating the sheets in their turn. In the midst of this crowd, the designers and engravers, esteemed as was their collaboration, were not the most honoured. Their homes often reflected their life as reckless artists, quick to spend the money earned during the week ; and we shall have occasion to name some of the more miserable among them.

The booksellers, on the contrary, had become great person- ages. In the preceding chapter we have seen Cramoisy and

Vitré, to name only these two, acquire the greatest honours, the latter even having been painted by Philippe de Champagne, with many other lords of the court. In the eighteenth century there were Brunet, Ballard, Mariette, Chardon, François Didot, and a host of others, during the time of Watteau, Boucher, and Cars, of which we have just spoken; and these several publishers had houses of their own, and furnished shops and printing offices with the best appurtenances. Saved from falling into negligences by royal regulations on printing, they composed imperishable works, with admirable characters, on paper of the first quality; and, usual consequence of their high position, they paid the artists charged with their work badly. It would be long and tedious to enter into this matter in detail. They made progress by slow degrees, and in good time they united marvellously copperplate engraving to printed text, so marvellously that in comparing their works with the wood blocks of the sixteenth century, it may be asked which of the two styles is superior in elegance and good taste.

One of the ancestors of this group of vignettists was the younger Cochin, who had engraved the plate of the sparrows in the fables of Houdart, illustrated by Gillot. Cochin, in spite of his passion for allegory and his very marked taste for affectation, gave, it may be said, with the designer-engraver Saint-Aubin, an enormous impulse to the art of adorning books. From the beginning of his career he worked for the publishers, designing frontispieces, ornamented letters, and tail-pieces, or transferring to copper the drawings of others. Singular type of artist, educated, well brought up, epicurean and spendthrift, friend of great lords, and protected by Madame de Pompadour, whose young brother Abel Poisson he conducted over Italy, Cochin did everything, was ready at the least request, inventing curious menus, giving representations of fêtes, and yet finding the time to lavish on books and vignettes.

He worked chiefly for Jombert, a sort of learned bookseller, King's printer to the artillery, who dates from July 1736. Jombert held receptions to painters, gave little private soirées, which Cochin attended, and there he daily made numerous friends. It was in this house, of so special a character, and, it may be said, so little artistic at first sight, that Cochin

Fig. 116.—Vignette for *Daphnis et Chloe* by Cochin, for Coustelier's edition.

invented his best frontispieces, among them that of the *Calcul Differentiel*, that of the *Astronomie Physique*, and the plates of the *Méthode de Dessin*, after Boucher. He was one of the first to produce engraved titles, with which the publisher Prault ornamented his dainty volumes, and which were imitated, up to the end of the eighteenth century, by all the illustrators who followed. In the title to the works of Madame Deshoulières the letter itself is engraved. Since then the open letter has been employed in typography. These vignettes were used many times by publishers, sometimes simply effacing the inscription, sometimes reproducing the original design by a different artist. The cupid with the swan was used in 1744 to decorate a *Jerusalem Delivered* in Italian, by the same publisher, Prault ; it was then engraved by Aveline. Fessard engraved the second plate, which is here reproduced.

Nearly all the frontispieces of the Book with vignettes of the eighteenth century preserve this arrangement ; an ornamented and draped border, with garlands of roses, symbols, and cupids, in the middle of the title, in red and black, composed in open letter, often a scroll with the address of the publisher, but rarely a mark. It was the time of little winged cupids, goddesses, and gods. The goddesses were the favourites of the kings, Madame de Pompadour or the princesses, but rarely of the virtuous Marie Leczinska, too plain and too much ignored to tempt the artists ; the kings or the princes were the gods.

After Jombert, Prault, and Coustellier, Cochin worked for François Didot, syndic of the printers, for whom he prepared a set of illustrations for *Molière*. Unfortunately Didot died in 1757, and the project fell with him. Of the work of Cochin there only remains the set of *Tartufe* etchings in octavo.

In the vortex into which he was plunged, he successively illustrated the *Œuvres de Rousseau*, published at Brussels, quarto ; those of *Boileau*, published by David and Durand, octavo ; and Henault's *Histoire de France*, in the same size, with numerous vignettes. One of these should be noted in a book treating on printing ; it is that in which Cochin pretends to show to his contemporaries the interior of a workshop in 1470. Without doubt the sketch of this print was taken in one of the houses frequented by him—at Jombert's, Didot's, or

David and Durand s—for that room in which compositors are
working and printed sheets drying was not an invention
of Cochin, and served to reproduce a printing office of the
eighteenth century, such as it existed.

Around Cochin soon worked a number of designers and

Fig. 117.—Title-page engraved by Fessard after Cochin for the works of
Madame Deshoulières, 1747.

etchers, too prudent to lose the opportunity. The fashion set in
for books beribboned, festooned, and flowered. Hubert François
Gravelot had carried to London this style of new works, for
he knew, better than any one, how to decorate with letters,
figures, and tailpieces. He did not engrave much himself,
leaving this work to lesser artists, and contenting himself with

subtle invention and graceful subjects. With Eisen, Cochin, and Moreau, he is the French artist in the sense of the time,

Il Gravelot inven.   *N le Mire Sculp.*

Fig. 118.—Vignette taken from P. Corneille's *Théâtre*, by Gravelot.

free bold, and ingenious, but perhaps a little out of place in England. He published, nevertheless, his illustrations to the *Decameron* in 1757-61, five vols. royal 8vo, one of his most curious

sets of plates, and a hundred various vignettes. On his return
to France he designed the *Théâtre* of P. Corneille, from which
the *Galerie de Palais* is here reproduced, on account of the

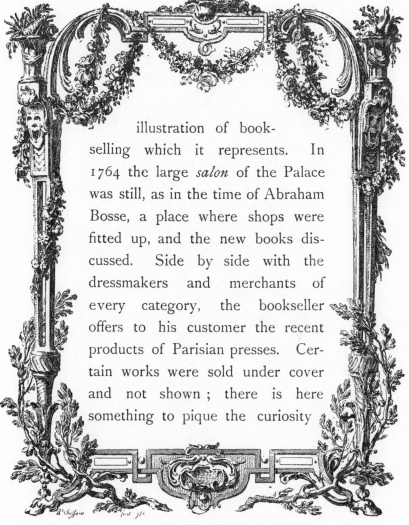

illustration of book-
selling which it represents. In
1764 the large *salon* of the Palace
was still, as in the time of Abraham
Bosse, a place where shops were
fitted up, and the new books discussed. Side by side with the
dressmakers and merchants of
every category, the bookseller
offers to his customer the recent
products of Parisian presses. Certain works were sold under cover
and not shown ; there is here
something to pique the curiosity

Fig. 119.—Border designed by Choffard in 1758.

of idle young seigneurs whose strolls in the galleries were
protracted.

Eisen has a simplicity, a good taste, and a special and

singularly perfect dash for artistic effect in combination with
typography. It is a pity that this designer had no consultative
voice in the choice of impression and getting up of the Book.

Fig. 120.—Frontispiece by Eisen for the *Voyage* by l'Abbé de la Porte, 1751.

The union of these two forces, the vignette and the composition,
is so close that we are tempted to believe that one was made
for the other, neither venturing to assert itself. In the pretty
and elaborate inventions of the artists reigned a lackadaisical

affectation that was delightfully becoming ; the rock-work, which it still had, suited admirably the borders of the first page. The *Lettres d'une Peruvienne* has a very pleasing title, differing little, on the whole, from that of *Madame Deshoulières*, by Cochin. It is the same with the *Lettres Turques*, published at Amsterdam in 1750, and generally with all the frontispieces signed by him. As to the other decorations of the Book, there were also a number of ingenious artists, combining cupids and flowers, heaping up blazons, delighting in playing with accumulated difficulties. Under this assuredly involuntary but real direction, publications attained proportions of luxury and coquetry until then unknown. The volume of *Les Baisers* by Dorat (La Haye et Paris, 1770) would not have lived but for Eisen and the delightful fancies with which he adorned it.

At the same time, we find Choffard, another designer and etcher of much repute, and the most sought after by the booksellers. Under his pencil the vignette became a *chef-d'œuvre*, the tailpiece was a delightful compound of judicious and sportive ornament, the taste for which grew more and more. From delicate foliage are suspended roses, shepherds' pipes, lyres, and zithers. With the zephyrs scrolls or ribbons float, carried by winged cupids. The initial letters are real pictures, of such fineness and precision that the difficulties of their reproduction prevent us from putting them before the reader.

When the *Fermiers généraux*, those great amateur financiers of the last century, conceived the idea of an edition of *Les Contes* of Lafontaine at their expense, their eyes naturally fell upon Eisen and Choffard, the artists best qualified to illustrate the inimitable fancies of the great poet. The first had for his task the composition of the separate plates, Choffard the general decoration. Ficquet was added for the portrait of the *bonhomme* Lafontaine—Ficquet, whose specialty in this *genre* was dazzling in its delicacy and spirit ; Diderot wrote a short introduction ; the composition was confided to a printer of the first order, and it was put on sale by Barbou (Paris, 1762).

Fig. 121.—Vignette by Eisen for the *Quiproquo* in the *Contes* of Lafontaine, in the edition of the *Fermiers Généraux*.

It is not a book to be recommended from a moral point of view, but never did typographical art, in combination with that of designers and engravers, obtain a more complete success : the size in octavo, the clear impression, united with the dimensions of the plates in a harmonious elegance, well calculated to please the very rich personages and the joyous amateurs to whom *Les Contes* address themselves. Although Eisen has dressed the greater part of the characters in the costume of his time, which is a little hurtful to one's feelings to-day, it might be imagined that it was Lafontaine who was mistaken, so completely do these delicate, equivocal tales appear to have been created for the seigneurs of the time of Louis XV.

All the special literature sought for then by rich people had not the value of the *Contes*. There was at Rheims a person, who has to-day become *à la mode*, as he was in the time of Louis XVI., who sold under cover of secrecy a quantity of licentious books of the better kind, adorned with figures by Eisen, Marillier, or Cochin; this was Cazin, an artist in his way, although his good name suffered under a scandalous trial. An order of the Council of State in 1764 enjoined him to cease his trade in the Place Royale at Rheims, where he sold his particular merchandise. It appears that the sentence was not without appeal, for we find Cazin at Paris about 1785. He was one of those who were ruined by the Revolution, after he had popularised the editions known as *Petits Formats*, printed by Valadel, of Paris.

We have come to the most beautiful illustrated books of the eighteenth century. To the illustrious artists of whom we have just spoken are to be added the younger Moreau, and St. Aubin, the former nephew by marriage of the publisher Prault, and therefrom a decorator of the Book, the other, thrown by Gravelot into full work, rapidly became the most subtle and clever of the etchers of the time. Moreau did not wait long after his marriage before setting to work. He began with ornaments destined for the *Histoire de France*

14

of President Hénault ; then he composed, in his own particular manner, titles and tailpieces for his uncle by marriage. In the Book he is the cultivator of garlands of roses, which he grouped with an ideal grace ; he twined them round the borders of his frontispieces, and applied them judiciously in his tailpieces. He excelled in inventing subjects referring to the text which were not merely commonplace ornaments suitable for anything. The tailpiece on p. 213, taken from

Fig. 122.—Card of the publisher Prault, uncle by marriage of Moreau le Jeune.

the works of Molière, brings forcibly to mind the *Médecin malgré Lui*, with its wood-cutter unmercifully beaten with sticks and muffled in a doctor's robe. It is the same with other illustrations, which cannot be displaced from the position assigned to them by the artist without loss of meaning.

The year 1773, which saw the publication by De Bret of the *Œuvres de Molière*, may perhaps be considered as that in which the French Book of the eighteenth century reached its culminating point. M. de Laborde, first valet de chambre of the King and governor of the Louvre, published with De Lormel, printer to the Academy of Music, his celebrated collection of *Chansons*, dedicated to the young Dauphiness Marie Antoinette, and partly illustrated by the younger Moreau. The work is exquisite, and of simple grace, by which the princess was particularly touched, and which anticipated his designs for *Le Devin du Village*. The sentimental note of the century was struck; in it the insipid love of shepherdesses tenderly sighed, and the designer has rendered delightfully this arch side of the pastoral song.

Fig. 123.—Tailpiece from the *Médecin malgré Lui*, by Moreau le Jeune.

Our task does not permit us to linger over the works of this prolific and charming artist, but we must mention his inimitable plates to J. J. Rousseau, the finest and most agreeable of his compositions and vignettes, also his masterpiece, the *Histoire du Costume*, containing the most typical designs of fashionable French life just before the Revolution.

As evidencing the activity of French artists of the Book in the eighteenth century, it may not be without interest to cite the number of works illustrated by the better-known artists as enumerated in the last edition of M. H. Cohen's

valuable *Guide de l'Amateur de Livres à Gravures du XVIII*
Siècle :—

Borel, 29 ;	Freudenberger, 7 ;	Moreau, 138 ;
Boucher, 47 ;	Gravelot, 86 ;	Patas, 65 ;
Cars, 13 ;	Le Barbier, 54 ;	Petit, 23
Choffard, 50 ;	Le Bas, 39 ;	Picart, 62 ;
Cochin, 143 ;	Lemire, 77 ;	Ponce, 65 ;
Duplessis-Bertaux, 22 ;	Lempereur, 68 ;	St. Aubin, 70 ;
Eisen, 135 ;	Longueil, 97 ;	Simonet, 83 ;
Fragonard, 10 ;	Marillier, 116 ;	

and we also should refer the reader to the valuable work by
E. and J. de Goncourt, *L'Art du* 18*ème Siècle,* containing
908 reproductions of the best works by Watteau, Chardin,
Boucher, Latour, Greuze, Les Saint-Aubin, Gravelot, Cochin,
Eisen, Moreau, Debucourt, Fragonard, Prud'hon. 2 vols., 4to,
Paris, 1882.

With the Revolution the decline of the Book in France
arrives, as that of all the arts. Moreau, a friend of David,
had become affected by the new ideas and the burlesque
renaissance in imitation of Greek and Roman art. He made
his sacrifice on the altar of the gods, and engraved simple souls
on wood to punish himself for having painted the elegancies
of fallen tyrants. At this game, vigour, as well as suppleness,
was lost ; and if he had had only the artistic propensity of the
Revolution, his daughter, married to Charles Vernet, could not
have written of him, " That which can be most admired is, at
the same time, the fecundity and flexibility of Moreau's talent,
that marvellous facility of conceiving a picturesque scene and
disposing it in an interesting and truthful manner in the least
extended space." This was true before,—but after ?

In spite of his passion for the ideas and men of the Revolution, Moreau found himself at the end of his resources

Renouard, the publisher, took him up as he had received St. Aubin, to whom he advanced sum after sum to prevent him dying of hunger Thus, like most of his contemporaries, Moreau pressed by want, "*prit, quitta, reprit la cuirasse et*

Fig. 124.—Vignette of.the *Pardon Obtenu*, designed by Moreau le Jeune,
for Laborde's *Chansons*, in 1773.

la haire." He had worked for everybody : for Louis XVI., for the Republic, for Napoleon I.

> " Moreau dota la République
> De la fleur de son dévoûment,
> Beau dévoûment !
> Il le jura sur une pique . . .
> Souffla le vent,
> Il emporta pique et serment ! "

The worst of it is, that after his designs for *Ovid*, *Molière*, and *Rousseau*, dating from the reign of Louis XVI., he should have done them again in 1804, 1806, and 1808. The difference was great, even probably for his publishers, Renouard and Dupréel. It does not appear either that the pontiff of the new school, David, knew of his distress, for Moreau succumbed in 1814 to a cancerous scirrhus on the right arm, forgotten, and in the greatest misery.

We have passed somewhat quickly to the end of the century because it is of no importance to name each of the publishers and artists, but only to sketch briefly their tastes or their manner. Nor have we dwelt long on the engravers so called, because of their number ; but their dexterity remains proverbial ; they handled the etching-needle with extreme suppleness, and often improved the drawings of illustrators during the process. Many of these, not to say all, made use themselves of the etching-needle, St. Aubin for example, who had the power of giving to the work of others his personal mark and character.

The Revolution passing over some among those, ruined them, and, as stated above, they followed the movement, and lost themselves in the school of David. It was Duplessis-Bertaux who, after having furnished to Cazin, the publisher, vignettes for his · *Recueil des Meilleurs Contes en Vers*, 1778, and many other books, after having worked for Didot, devoted himself to patriotic engraving and to the reproduction of scenes of the Revolution. When he published his *Tableaux Historiques*, in three volumes folio, adorned with nearly two hundred large plates, it was under the Consulate, that is to say, far from the time when the work was begun. Renouvier assures us, with his exclusive disdain for the eighteenth century,

that Duplessis-Bertaux was a mystifier, and that his scenes of
the Revolution were a hoax, " in the kind of spirit in vogue

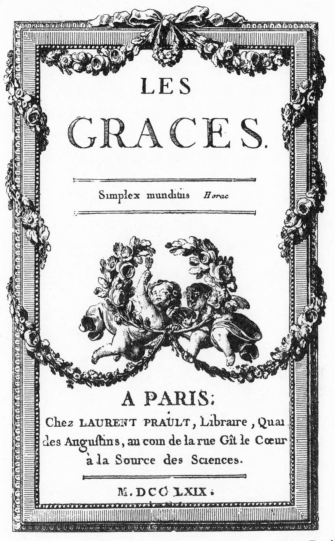

Fig. 125.—Title designed by Moreau le Jeune in 1769 for the publisher Prault.

under the Directory." The truth is that the artist, in place
of being a cheerful Callot, as might be thought from his
manner of engraving, so like that of the Lorraine artist, was

imbued with the emphatic and exaggerated impressions of the first Republic, its *sans-culottes* in the poses of the Sabines and its *tricoteuses* apeing Penelope.

The immense artistic advance made in France in the eighteenth century in the manufacture and illustration of the Book made itself felt throughout Europe. In Italy, Giambattista Bodoni, born at Saluzzo, in Piedmont, 1740, who was first employed at the Propaganda Office, Rome, 1758, devoted his attention chiefly to the study of oriental alphabets. He was placed, 1758, at the head of Duke Ferdinand's new printing office at Parma, and became one of the most celebrated printers of Italy. He printed *Epithalamia exoticis linguis reddita* in twenty-five languages, 1775 (in connection with the marriage of the Prince of Piedmont with Princess Clotilde of France), and a valuable edition of *Homer*, three vols., 1808, inscribed to Napoleon I., for which he received a pension of £120. In Spain we find Joachim Ibarra, born 1725 in Saragossa, "the Spanish Bodoni," with the title of Court printer. He raised the art of printing to a hitherto unknown height in Spain, and amongst his works we may mention the *éditions de luxe* of the *Bible*, a Spanish translation of *Sallust*, *The History of Spain by Mariana*, and above all his fine edition of *Don Quixote*, in 4 vols. 4to, with brilliant illustrations (1780), which is considered the *chef-d'œuvre* of Ibarra's press. After his death (in 1785) his widow continued the business, and issued the *Diccionario de la Langua Castellana*, fol., 1803.

In Germany, Chodowiecki, born at Dantzic of a family of apothecaries, developed his talent from ornamenting the boxes of his father, and from 1758 to 1794 he designed numerous plates for books and almanacs, a little heavy in engraving, but singularly clever in composition. In a diary of 1773, he depicted the incidents of his journey from Berlin to Danzig

Fig. 126.—Frontispiece of the *Glossarium* of Du Dange, Paris, Osmont, 1733.

on horseback; he illustrated besides Goethe's *Werther* and

Hermann und Dorothea, Lessing's *Minna von Barnhelm*,
Voss' *Luise*, and numerous other works. There were some
other clever designers and engravers, but the Book did not
make so much progress in Germany as in France and
England.

In England a vast improvement was manifested. Fine
types were cast by John Baskerville and William Caslon;
printing machines were perfected. Baskerville, born 1706, at
Wolverley, Worcestershire, is considered the father of modern
English typography. Commencing type-founding in 1750, for
Cambridge, he contracted with the University for printing a
folio edition of the Bible, also of the Common Prayer Book,
paying a royalty of £20 for every thousand copies. After 1756
he printed Latin, English, and Italian classics; the most
elegant specimen being his *Horace*, 1762.

The illustration of books by engraved plates was in the
first half of the century almost entirely done by foreigners, but
an English school was arising, which attained perfection in the
latter half of the eighteenth and first half of the nineteenth
century. Wood engraving also, which, with the exception of
blocks for head and tailpieces, had become almost a lost art,
was revived by Bewick, to become later one of the chief
adornments of the Book.

Before 1716 English printers obtained their best founts of
type from Holland, but the establishment of the Caslon
foundry rendered them independent. William Caslon, the first
great English type-founder, died 1766, but the foundry still
exists, pre-eminent in the beauty of its characters. We
must also mention the Foulis Press of Glasgow, celebrated for
its beautiful editions of classical works. The impetus given
to fine printing by these houses rapidly spread itself, and laid

the foundation of the perfection which English book-making reached.

As mentioned before, foreigners illustrated many English books in the early part of the century. Gravelot designed a set of plates to *Shakespeare* in 12mo, 1740, and another in quarto, 1744, besides numerous frontispieces and other plates in all kinds of books. Among other foreigners who engraved for English publishers were Grignion, Kip, Van der Gucht, Houbraken, and Bartolozzi. Bartolozzi, who was very prolific in the production of engraved plates, may perhaps be called the founder of that great English school of engraving which arose with the establishment of the Royal Academy in 1769, and the encouragement given by Alderman Boydell. A biographical and descriptive account of the life and works of Bartolozzi will be found in the splendid work by Mr. Andrew W. Tuer. Houbraken and Vertue engraved a set of fine portraits in folio for Rapin's *History of England*, 1736; William Hogarth designed plates for Butler's *Hudibras*, 1744; and among other curiosities of English engraving before 1750 were Sturt's edition of the Common Prayer, entirely engraved on copper plates, 1717, and an edition of *Horace* entirely engraved by Pine, 1733. That the taste for illustrated books soon grew to be great is evidenced by the publication of such expensive works as Boydell's edition of *Shakespeare*, in nine volumes folio, commenced in 1791, and adorned with a hundred plates from pictures specially commissioned by the spirited publisher; Claude's *Liber Veritatis*, with three hundred engravings by Richard Earlom, 1777, Sir Robert Strange's engravings of fifty historical prints about 1750, collections of views in Great Britain by Kip, Buck, and Boydell; Holbein's *Collection of Portraits*, 1792, a hundred and fifty plates to Shakespeare engraved by

S. and E. Harding 1793, all of which cost large sums to produce, and greatly contributed to the elevation of public taste. Among the artists of the latter half of the century who contributed to the decoration of the Book are Thomas Stothard and William Blake, whose very beautiful designs, extending into the next century, excelled those of all their contemporaries in their grace and spirit; Robert Smirke, best known by his plates for

Fig. 127.—Illustration by Stothard, from one of the *Keepsakes.*

Shakespeare, *Don Quixote*, and *Gil Blas;* Burney and Richard Westall, born at Hertford, 1765, well known for his illustrations to Boydell's *Milton*, and his *Shakespeare Gallery, Hume's History of England*, and the *Poems* of Crabbe, Moore, Scott, and Cowper. Thomas Stothard made more than five thousand designs. His best illustrations are to be found in the *Town and Country Magazine*, Bell's *British Poets, Novelists'*

Magazine, Boydell's *Shakespeare, Milton, Spencer, Don Quixote*, Walton's *Compleat Angler*, Rogers's *Italy, Robinson Crusoe*, 1790, and *Pilgrim's Progress*, 1794. William Blake attracted great attention by his eccentricity and artistic talents. Among the principal works which he illustrated are Young's *Night Thoughts*, 1779, with forty-three full page illustrations, and illustrations to Blair's *Grave*, 1808; illustrations to Milton's

Fig. 128.—Illustration by Blake, from Blair's *Grave*.

Comus, 1804; Mary Wolstonecraft's *Original Stories*, 1791. His designs are full of feeling and delicacy, and are looked upon with wonder. It may be said, generally, that the English books of the eighteenth century were of a more solid character than the French, although English art, especially in the direction of the Book, owes much to French initiation. It is curious to read now the opinion of a contemporary French engraver on English art. Choffard, in the preface to Basan's *Dictionnaire*, 1767, wrote : " They " (the English), "having been supported by some foreign talent, are trying to create talent among themselves ; but they are unable to kindle the flame of genius that vivifies all art in France."

Engraving by leaving the figure in relief, from which printing could be done with the letterpress, had, we may think, nearly disappeared in the midst of the continued invasion of the burin and etching. It only appeared from time to time in head and tailpieces, merely as typographical accessories, and lost in other directions. There were always wood

Fig. 129.—Tailpiece engraved on wood by Jean Baptiste Papillon (before 1766).

engravers, not very clever, capable only of working simple lines without charm. One of them resolved to resuscitate the art, and made various attempts about the end of the reign of Louis XIV. and beginning of that of Louis XV. He was named Jean Papillon, and was born at St. Quentin in 1661. His experiments did not go beyond a book of prayers, with thirty-six figures in relief after Sébastien Leclerc. His son, Jean Baptiste, succeeded him, and continued to engrave without ceasing subjects of ornament, letters, and often tailpieces, of a good style upon the whole, and taking an excellent place in an elaborate book. Unfortunately, grace had fled; the processes which the artists had taught each other were lost; and the Papillons reconstituted, we may say, a vanished art. Jean Baptiste also published in 1766 a theoretical treatise on wood engraving, abounding in historical errors, but in which something instructive may be found if taken with discretion. He says in his preface: " Now that excellent work is done on copper, wood engraving is neglected, and the art lost of designing and cutting the shadings of the pencil on the wood block; most of those who work in it have neither design nor taste, and only follow their own ideas; it is not astonishing that only very inferior pieces come from their hands, to say nothing stronger; the profound ignorance of nearly all who meddle with it contrives more and more to destroy the beauties of this art in which many people find neither pleasure nor grace. To obviate all this, if it be possible to me, I have undertaken to give my precepts and observations to those who wish to apply themselves to my engraving."

It was probably these essays of Papillon that provoked curious experiments on the part of other wood engravers. Duplat, at the beginning of this century, proposed to prepare a relief on stone, and as this would be broken under pressure, he invented a mould; that is to say, he took a leaden matrix from the stone cutting, and ran a resistant metal into this mould, thus obtaining a relief similar to the stone. Renouard, the publisher, made the trials; and the younger Moreau made the designs. Fancy Moreau making experiments in 1811! One of the plates of Lafontaine's *Fables*, published by Renouard in 1812, in two volumes, 12mo, is here reproduced.

It appears, however, that the publisher was thwarted by bad printing. The printers of Didot or Mame, much as they

devoted all their care to it, did not yet know perfect workmanship; they put the most intense blacks into fine sheets.
The great publishers trusted that better days would leave to
more clever men the task of perfecting the invention.

Wood engraving, as stated, owes its revival and almost
perfection in England to Thomas Bewick, who published his
first work in 1770, his *General History of Quadrupeds* 1790,
and his *Birds* 1797.   In these works he not only depicted his
subjects with the most scrupulous fidelity, but in the tailpieces
of the several chapters he drew the most quaint, humorous, and

Fig. 130.—Experiment in engraving in relief by Moreau le Jeune for
Renouard's edition of Lafontaine's *Fables*.

faithful representations of country life.   From the *Fables*, published in 1818, we reproduce an illustration, also a specimen from
the second volume of the *British Birds*.   He, with his brother,
John Bewick, and their pupils, among whom was Luke Clennell,
had an influence upon English art and the decoration of the
Book in England which exists to our day.   Not alone with us,
for he may be said to have repaid the debt which we owed to
France for her illustrated books of the eighteenth century by
stimulating the art of wood engraving, which was practised by
Tony Johannot and the other illustrators of the nineteenth
century.

To return to the eighteenth century, with which this chapter is specially occupied, we have said that the Royal Printing House, after various fortunes, still existed; and in 1788 it worked, for better or for worse, at the Louvre. According to

Fig. 131.—Portrait of Thomas Bewick.

the budget of that year, it cost the King 90,000 livres, of which the director had 1,400.

There were, on the other hand, a certain number of official printing offices, that of war, for example, which was devoted entirely to the work of the Ministry. It was situated at

Versailles, and was created in 1768.   It is told of Louis XV.
that, being one day in this workshop, he found a pair of
spectacles, left as if in inadvertence on a printed sheet.   As
his sight was weakening, he took the spectacles and looked
through them.   The sheet was a hyperbolical eulogium composed, as if at random,   by the director Bertier, in honour
of the King.   Louis XV., having read the dithyramb, replaced
the spectacles, and quietly said, " They are too strong ; they
make objects too large."

Fig. 132.—Wood block by Bewick, from his *Fables*, 1818.   The fox and the goat.

Who would believe that at the end of the century of
Voltaire and Rousseau a craftsman would be found desirous of
leading back the typographical art to its cradle, and of making
xylographs again, under the name of polytypes ?   A German
was the genius who conceived the plan.   He obtained an
order of council for the establishment of his presses in 1785,
but the same council suppressed them November 1st, 1787.
His process was to substitute for movable characters a plate
of fixed letters, and probably engraved.

Another eccentricity of typography at the end of the century was the introduction of "logography" by John Walter, by which system he issued *Gabriel the Outcast.* It consisted in casting whole the words in most common use, in place of separate letters. The system had soon to be abandoned, but he afterwards started the *Daily Universal Register,* which subsequently assumed the name of *The Times* (January 1st, 1785), and which his son John, born 1818, made what it is now.

In the eighteenth century there was a printing establishment in France for each of the constituted bodies; the King, the

Fig. 133.—Wood block from Bewick's *British Birds.* The common duck.

Queen, the princes, each had their own. The royal lottery occupied a special printing house.

The young inmates of the blind asylum worked under the direction of M. Clousier, royal printer. Louis XVI. authorised the celebrated Haüy, their master, to allow them to print; and in 1786 they composed an essay on the education of the blind. Pierre François Didot was in 1785 printer to the Prince, afterwards Louis XVIII. He published the *Aventures de Télémaque,* in two quarto volumes, from this special printing office.

The English colonies in North America early established printing there, their first book, the *Book of Psalms,* known

as the Bay Psalm Book, being dated 1640. By the middle of
the eighteenth century literature held a strong position in the
colonies, the greater part of it being, as might be expected,
English; but the revolution and subsequent establishment of
the United States created a national American literature, which

Fig. 134.—Benjamin Franklin, by C. N. Cochin.

has flourished to this day. Among the printers of North America
in the eighteenth century, the most famous was Benjamin
Franklin, born January 17th, 1706, but he is still more
celebrated as a philosopher and statesman. He established a
printing office at Philadelphia 1728, and as a curiosity we may
mention his *Poor Richard's Almanack*, which he conducted for

twenty-five years.   Interesting for printers is also his epitaph which he composed himself: " The body of Benjamin Franklin, Printer (like the cover of an old book, its contents worn out, and stript of its lettering and gilding), lies here, food for worms. Yet the work itself shall not be lost, for it will, as he believed, appear once more in a new and more beautiful edition, corrected and amended by its Author."

CHAPTER VI.

THE BOOK IN THE NINETEENTH CENTURY.

The Didots and their improvements—The folio Racine—The school of Didot—Fine
publications in England and Germany—Literature and art of the Restoration—
Romanticism—Wood engraving—Bewick's pupils, Clennell, etc.—The illustrators of romances—The generation of 1840—The Book in our days in Europe
and America.

OLITICAL imitators had not been found for
the French Revolution in all the neighbour-
ing countries of Europe, but its Greco-
Roman art established itself, and by degrees
was introduced into the studios of painters
and the printing offices. Prud'hon, Gérard, Girodet, and later
Desenne, without counting the younger Moreau and his
contemporaries of the older *régime*, rallied to the new study,
forming a school of illustrators and vignettists with which the
publishers could resolutely advance. England followed suit with
Flaxman, West, Fuseli, Barry, and a crowd of others. Among
the publishers the powerful family of the Didots took first
rank, and its members, at once type-founders, printers, booksellers, and *savants* of the first order, were the best fitted to
direct an artistic and literary movement. When Napoleon
crowned himself Emperor of the French, the elders of the
family had already brought about a number of perfections and
discoveries in their profession by which their workshops had

profited. François Ambroise, who died in the year of the Empire, had given an exact proportion to types, a free and elegant turn, but perhaps too regular and precise to be agreeable. He had already invented a press called the *presse à un coup*, in which the impression was taken by a single pull instead of being produced by a series of successive strikings. His brother, Pierre François, spoken of in the preceding chapter, was a type-founder and paper-maker at Essones, and counted among his official titles "printer to the Comte de Provence," as François Ambroise was to the Comte d'Artois.

Of these two branches equally faithful to typography, Pierre Didot, son of François Ambroise, became the head on the death of his father. Born in 1760, he had studied his art with passion, and had deserved the installation of his workshops in the Louvre, where he published the celebrated collection known as the Louvre editions, the *chef-d'œuvre* of which was the works of *Racine*. The splendid execution of this book, in three large folio volumes, was a true typographical revolution. Never in any country had scrupulous perfection of detail been joined to so masterly a knowledge of arrangement and form of characters. The great artists of the Davidian school were anxious of the honour of seeing their drawings reproduced as illustrations, and those named above designed the fifty-seven plates with which the edition was adorned. Pierre Didot displayed a great affectation in only printing two hundred and fifty copies of his irreproachable and marvellous work, of which a hundred were taken with proofs before letters. Published by subscription, the ordinary edition was issued at 1,200 francs, and with proofs 1,800 francs.

To these superb works Firmin Didot, his brother, added ingenious discoveries. Struck with certain difficulties of printing as well as of correction, he imagined the welding together of the types of a form, when once obtained perfectly correct, so as to avoid the trouble of new composition. This process, useless for books of small number, had a capital importance in case of reimpressions of popular and successful works. He named this method *Stereotype Printing*, and from 1799 he published a *Racine* in 18mo by this process.

This admirably directed house, we may indeed say this school of typography, formed with Renouard, Claye, Rignoux, and others, the greater number of the French publishers of the middle of the century. When the Czar Alexander went to Paris, he wished to do honour to the greatest French practitioners in the science of printing, in the persons of the brothers Pierre and Firmin Didot. But these were not the only ones. The sons of Pierre François Didot, Henri and Pierre François II.—the latter specially applied himself to paper-making, under the name of Didot Saint Léger— followed in the footsteps of their father and uncle. Pierre François made at Essones an excellent paper, which he brought to the perfection of making it in endless rolls, such as are made to-day for rotary machines. But perhaps the best known of the Didot family is M. Ambroise Firmin Didot, the eldest son of Firmin Didot, who died at an advanced age in 1876. He not only increased the reputation of his house by the publication of several great works, but also was himself a great collector of books. The extraordinary sale of his library from 1882 to 1884, which brought nearly three millions of francs, astonishing the literary world, is still in the recollection of all bibliophiles. He studied the old languages, travelled in Greece, Palestine, and Asia Minor, enjoyed a great reputation as a hellenist, and was in 1873 elected a member of the

Academie des Inscriptions et Belles-Lettres, all the time devoting his special attention to his favourite hobby, the history of printing, to which we owe his writings: *Gutenberg* (1863), *Essai sur l'histoire de la gravure sur bois* (1863), *Alde Manuce et l'Hellénisme à Venise* (1875), *Etude sur Jean Cousin* (1872), and other bibliographical works.

Fig. 135.—M. Ambroise Firmin Didot.

It was also at Essones where Bernardin de St. Pierre retired about the end of the last century, and there married the daughter of Pierre François Didot II. It is a curious coincidence that the same village contained at once the man whose works at the beginning of the century had so extraordinary a success and the great family of printers who had given definitive

impetus to typographical work.   It was in this tranquil circle
that the author of *Paul et Virginie,* at the age of sixty, sought
repose; that the publication of his book was resolved upon
with all the luxury due to its success, with admirable type and
with plates by Prud'hon and others.   He added to it the
Chaumière Indienne, written in 1790, on the eve of the Reign
of Terror, which is one of the most delightful novels of the
time.

The homely and sweet writings of Bernardin de St. Pierre,
the heroic inventions of Girodet, Gérard, and Chaudet in the
Greek or Roman style, the clever but severe typography of
the Didots—these are the characteristics of the Book at the
beginning of the century.   Under Louis XV. the nymphs
carried panniers; Polyeucte had a wig and sword.   It would
have been unbecoming not to give Juno or Venus the head-
dress adopted in paintings and vignettes.   At the time which
now occupies us fashion in clothing influenced designers also.
The hair of goddesses was *à la Titus;* the waist was under
the arms; golden circles were on the brow.   Simple mortals
walked naked on the roads, with plumed casques and splendid
shields.   There were heroes putting forth their disproportioned
arms, others raising their eyes to heaven in impossible attitudes.
Such were all the vignettes, from Girodet to the humblest,
and last, the most forgotten.

It happens, by an oddity of which the cause is vainly
sought, that this classic and revolutionary school of David
identifies itself so well with the Napoleonic epoch, and also with
the people of the Restoration, that it seems expressly made for
them.   At the same time, under Louis XVIII. and Charles X.
the Romans and Greeks had not the bold carriage of their
early days; they became more citizenized, and looked like the

national guards of the kingdom of which later an excessive use
was made.

A whole literature arose that was to react against the
Greek full of Gallicisms ; but the movement, by reversing the
ancient state of things, by wishing to replace antiquity by the
middle ages, old Romans by old French, completely changed
the physiognomy of the Book. The engraved vignette and the
copperplate of the seventeenth and eighteenth centuries were

Fig. 136.—Wood engraving by Clennell after West, for
the diploma of the Highland Society.

to lose their supremacy and to give way to etching and wood
engraving, which was also a revival of the Middle Ages.

After the unfortunate attempts of Papillon in France, wood
engraving was resorted to in England by Thomas Bewick,
who founded a school, as we said, of which, at the commencement of our century, Clennell and the brothers Thompson
were members. One of the Thompsons went to France
about the middle of the Restoration, doubtless with the

hope of profiting by his art, and he offered to the Print
Department of the National Library the diploma of the Highland Society, a large folio wood block, very adroit and very
curiously cut, after the drawing of the celebrated Benjamin
West, and copied from Clennell's original block of the same
subject.   M. Duchesne, then Keeper of the Prints, speaks of
this last process as of an apparition : " This print clearly shows
the long neglected and often reappearing art of wood engraving,
which, though it could never equal copper engraving, nevertheless merits the attention of amateurs when a capable hand is
exercised upon it." It was, we see, a curiosity then, this relief
cutting, the revival of which was to give an enormous
impulse to the Book from the facilities of printing and the
economies realized by the possibility of insertion in the text of
periodicals.   In fact, metal printing necessitated more trouble
for engravings than for the bookwork.   With wood blocks
surrounded by type the ordinary press sufficed.   The *Magasin
Pittoresque*, which was commenced in 1833, and the success of
which from the first was very great, was the fruit of these new
combinations.   Before it the *Messager Boiteux* of Strasburg
and other popular almanacs progressed very well with their
illustrations on wood.   A kind of association of engravers, at
the head of which were Best and Andrew, undertook the illustrations of the *Magasin Pittoresque*.   In a few years progress
was immense, other publications came into existence, and a
definitive return was made to the vignette in relief.   The
French illustrated paper preceded our *Illustrated London News*
by nine years.

     Lavish use was now made of wood engraving, which had
thus been suddenly revived in the very midst of the new
romantic effervescence, amid a war of books, which, in order

to please, had above all to captivate the eye, reacting at once against the spirit and the art of the Restoration. Never before had artists to such an extent taken active part in a purely literary warfare. All the fantastic tendencies of young France were embodied in the lame and halting lines of the time and similar wretched doggerel. Doubtless the leaders of the school did not go quite so far, and their reputation even suffered from such theories; but, as always happens in such cases, the disciples outstripped their masters.

The brothers Johannot were the first to enter the lists, in

Fig. 137.—Vignette by Devéria for the *Fiancé de la Tombe.*

the train of the poets and others of the romantic school, such as Victor Hugo, De Vigny, Paul Lacroix, George Sand, also Devéria, the most ruthless of illustrators. The last-named had designed vignettes on wood, of all others, for Baour-Lormian, that is to say, for the foe of the new ideas, for the Ossian and the Cockney bard, who assumed an excess of fury against everything in turn. The *Légendes, Ballades, et Fabliaux,* illustrated by Devéria in 1829, although a sort of compromise with the lovesick swains of mediæval times, did not escape the shafts of ridicule.

In the midst of this movement the Book became democratic ; it was printed on sugar-paper for reading-rooms and working girls. The generation of romancists diffused its paper-covered works, printing a thousand copies and selling five hundred with great difficulty. Poets publishing five hundred were happy with a sale of two hundred and fifty. Unheard-of titles were then needed to catch the eye, ridiculous and ghastly frontispieces to tickle the fancy of the riffraff. Paul Lacroix called himself the " Bibliophile Jacob," and invented surprising headpieces and foolish designs. And then, as in the fifteenth century, as in the old times, certain marks became popular with the reading public. In the place of the *Doctrinals, Complaints,* and *Disputes,* so common in the titles of those epochs, new fancies spring up and have their day. Eccentric devices recommend romantic trash, in which the assassin's dagger, blood, and the horrors of the tomb have replaced the insipid fancies of the fallen *régime.* Pétrus Borel, the werewolf, a sort of historic ghoul prowling about the graveyards enjoyed a monopoly, as it were, of the ghastly titles and contents of this charnel-house literature ; it was for his *Champavert (Contes Immoraux),* published in 1833, that Gigoux composed a kind of Bluebeard surrounded by female skeletons, that opened the eyes of publishers to his value as a vignettist.

Although he threw himself soul and body into the romantic movement, the young artist did not confine himself to the subjects called "abracadabrants," following the neologism of the time, any more than the booksellers only published romances. An attempt was made, by publishing them in parts, to popularise still further the old writers at all harmonising with the current taste. The publisher Paulin thus issued the *Gil Blas* of Le Sage, with illustrations in the text by the younger Gigoux, of which the best was expected. The history of this celebrated enterprise has been written by the artist himself in the curious *Causeries* published recently by him, fifty years after his work on *Gil Blas;* and this interesting view of an epoch already far distant gives us in a few words the ordinary getting up of these popular impressions in parts.

It appears that Paulin, publisher in the Rue de Seine, not being very well off, had associated himself with a man of business named Dubochet, who had before made an enormous

Fig. 138.—Vignette by Jean Gigoux for *Gil Blas.*

fortune with gas. The two represented fifteen thousand to twenty thousand francs, and they ordered a hundred drawings on wood from the young artist. He set to work with pre-caution, for Dubochet was hard to please; without knowing much about the business, he harassed the engravers for the least faults. Gigoux set himself to give his compositions in simple line, without complicated shadows, so as to allow the wood engravers to preserve a free outline. It resembled the process of the old artists of the fifteenth and sixteenth centuries

of Vostre and Holbein: true engraving in relief. The
success of the first sheets was extraordinary; new vignettes
were ordered from Gigoux; in place of a hundred they
wanted three hundred, then four hundred; at the end of the
work they amounted to six hundred at least. Money filled
the chests of the firm, but when the artist claimed a small
share of the profit, they laughed in his face. Dubochet
coolly said, " *There is no agreement.*"

Properly speaking, it was the first serious attempt at illustration by the recovered method of wood engraving in relief,
but it was not the only one. Curmer, the publisher of the
Rue Richelieu, prepared a Bible in 1835 and several other
volumes, among which were the *Paul et Virginie* and the
Chaumière Indienne by Bernardin de St. Pierre. He had also
collected around him a circle of artists which included Wattier,
Devéria, and Meissonier, the most perfect and correct of the
designers on wood, and whose dainty illustrations of *Les Contes
Remois*, by Le Comte de Chevigné, are very much coveted
by all bibliophiles. Meissonier made small designs, very sober
in style, and without much contrast of light and shade, which
were admirably cut by an engraver named Lavoignat, a master
in the best sense of the word. Curmer wrote in 1835 in the
preface to one of his books, " We hope that we have raised
a monument to wood engraving. It is easy to judge of the
resources presented by this art. We were compelled to have
recourse to England to accomplish our work. Peace to
publishers with such good intentions ! "

Curmer acknowledges the importance of English specialists
in this new process for vignettes, and the well-intentioned
publishers were not wanting ; they came from all parts. He
himself did not stop half way ; he continued his work on a large

scale ; and Charles Blanc was able to say of him later, as well as of Furne, " He desired to illustrate books for everybody, as the great booksellers of the last century had illustrated their rare editions for a small number of privileged persons." But he did not always confine himself to wood engraving ; he also employed etching and lithography. These, requiring separate printing, did not make intercalation with the text any easier than engraving with the burin ; but they served to illustrate

Fig. 139.—Vignette by Daumier for the *Cholera à Paris.*

periodicals, the *Charivari* and *L'Artiste*, as well as some books, where they replaced the engraved plates of the preceding century. At the same time, the latter process was not alto- gether neglected ; about 1840 it was revived, and steel was used in place of copper, as it resisted repeated impressions better. The publisher Furne, while he employed wood engraving, adorned with separate plates on steel his better publications. For him worked Raffet, one of the romanticists enamoured of

16

the Napoleonic era, which he had popularised, with Charlet and Bellangé, by the brush, wood engraving, and lithography. Raffet had transferred upon wood, as a labour of love, the three hundred and fifty-one vignettes of the *Histoire de Napoléon,* by De Norvins, which would to-day suffice for the glory and reputation of many artists. In fact, the analytical and inductive spirit of the artist led him to leave nothing to the chances of inspiration and ordinary tricks of illustration. He laboriously reconstituted,

Fig. 140.—Vignette by Gavarni for *Paris Marie.*

fragment by fragment, the physiognomy of the "old army;" and imbued with that perfect science of detail, he allowed his pencil full play in bold and luminous inventions, in which, with their peculiar bearing, the heroes of other days, the soldiers of the Rhine and Italy, of Austerlitz and Waterloo, live again before us.

A truly lively period was that of 1840. By the side of those great artists of whom we have spoken, and who will be more admired some day, there were the fantastic designers Traviès,

and Daumier, who adorned the illustrated journals with innumerable sketches, and also Grandville and Gavarni, one carica-
turing animals in a celebrated book, *Les Animaux Peints par
Eux-mêmes*, which is more than a *chef-d'œuvre;* the latter
pitilessly studying the vices and faults of his time, with the
precision of an anatomist, in *Les Anglais Peints par Eux-
mêmes* of Labedollière, in the *Diable à Paris*, without counting
many other works which his penetrating imagination produced.

Fig. 141.—Balzac writing his *Contes Drôlatiques.* Vignette by Gustave Doré.

Photography presently came, which was to reverse completely the conditions of illustration of the Book by the
numerous means of reproduction to which it gave birth. Wood
engraving then entered on a new phase, a complete transformation of its ordinary conditions, under the influence of Gustave
Doré. Little by little it had been attempted to produce in relief
the same effect which engraved plates only had hitherto done.
Black, half-tints, graduated tones, were tried where formerly
a simple line, bold and spirited, signified everything. The

house of Hachette, at the beginning of the century, was, together with Lahure, the promoter of relief produced and carried out in this manner. The numerous periodicals of these publishers spread the taste far and wide. England, for its part, entered on the same road, followed by America and Germany. At the present day wood engravings have reached perfection, finesse, and delicacy; but they are not, properly speaking, engravings on wood, but mostly mechanical reproductions.

We have seen that French publishers were largely indebted

Fig. 142.—Illustration by Cruikshank, from *Three Courses and a Dessert*, by Clarke.

to English wood engravers for their blocks. Luke Clennell, one of the most distinguished of Bewick's pupils, made some excellent engravings, among them the illustrations to an edition of Rogers's *Poems* (1812), from pen-and-ink drawings by Thomas Stothard. It was Stothard's opinion that wood engraving best reproduced pen-and-ink drawings. Other pupils of Bewick were J. Jackson, John Thompson, who engraved Harvey's beautiful illustrations to Milton and Henderson's *History of Wines*, S. Williams, Orrin Smith, Robert Branston, and C. Nesbit. Thomas Rowlandson, 1756—1827, was celebrated for his illustrations to Combe's *Dr. Syntax's Three Tours*, etc., but his greatest ability is displayed in his well-known *Caricatures*. The most prolific and perhaps the most popular book-illustrator of the century in England, was George Cruikshank, who engraved most of his own designs on wood, steel, or with the etching needle; *The Catalogue of the Works of G. Cruikshank* (1871), by Mr. G. W. Reid, formerly Keeper of the Prints in the British Museum, occupies three quarto volumes, with 313 illustrations. His best known works fetch large prices in spite of many unpleasing mannerisms and faulty draughtsmanship. The illustrator of *Oliver*

Fig. 143.—Wood engraving by Clennell after Stothard, for Rogers's *Poems* 1812.

Twist, the *Sketches by Boz*, the *Comic Almanack*, 1835-53 (a set of which sold lately for £30); of Pierce Egan's *Life in London* (for which £34 was given lately in a sale-room), and other famous books that achieved a hitherto unexampled popularity in the earliest years of the Queen's reign, delighted, like his artistic ancestor Hogarth, "to paint a moral and adorn a tale." The fearless directness and sturdy realism with which he depicted romantic incidents imparted a zest to his vigorous sketches which has manifestly not declined. The designs of "Phiz," as H. K. Browne called himself, largely contributed to the popularity of the works of Charles Dickens; and the mere mention of Richard Doyle and John Leech will recall the palmy days of *Punch*, although both of these artists did excellent work in book illustration. Richard Doyle's bird's-eye views of society and the allegorical illustrations of remarkable personages are well known; also John Leech's *Pictures of Life and Character*. Randolph Caldecott's illustrations to Washington Irving's *Old Christmas* should be mentioned also, as well as Sir John Gilbert's illustrations to *Shakespeare*, and Birket Foster's *English Landscapes*. From the days of the Bewicks to the present, wood engraving has formed the most widely used means of illustration in England and the United States. Its adaptability to the printing machine renders it admirably suited to the production of books in large numbers and at low expense. Without it we could not have our *Graphic* and *Illustrated News*, nor the floods of cheap but splendidly illustrated magazines which are appearing on both sides of the Atlantic. True, many of these blocks are due to the "processes" which photography has made available, but they are nevertheless the outcome of wood engraving.

The most prominent Book illustrators in Germany in the nineteenth century are Moritz Retzsch, Schnorr von Carolsfeld, Ludwig Richter, Adolf Menzel, Wilhelm von Kaulbach, Moritz von Schwind, Friederich Preller (renowned for his landscapes to the *Odyssey*), and Anton von Werner, the celebrated painter and illustrator of Victor von Scheffel's works.

Moritz Retzsch, born 1779 at Dresden, excelled in romantic subjects; his best known works are his outlines to Goethe's *Faust*, 1812, twenty-six etchings. Later on he undertook for Cotta the illustration of *Schiller's Works* in outline; he also began a *Shakespeare Gallery* and produced several single etchings, among which his *Chessplayer* (1836) is the most esteemed.

Julius Schnorr von Carolsfeld was born in Leipzig 1794 and after several years' sojourn in Italy he published in 1852 his celebrated Bible pictures, *Die Bibel in Bildern*, with two hundred and forty woodcuts, a work which has made his name known in every country. He also illustrated an edition of the *Nibelungenlied* for Cotta.

Ludwig Richter (1803-84), born at Dresden, received his first instruction from his father, who wanted to bring him up as

Fig. 144.—Illustration by Ludwig Richter, from Bechstein's *Märchenbuch*.

an engraver; but, assisted by the bookseller Arnold, he soon took his own course, and excelled in homely landscapes, enlivened by human figures, with which he illustrated the most popular German works. His best known works are his illustrations to the *Deutsche Volksbücher*, the popular stories of *Musæus* and *Bechstein*, the *Lords Prayer*, and a number of *Albums* for the house.

During the time when Richter's illustrations appeared, a

work of quite a different kind was created under the hand of a young artist, which marks an epoch in the history of German art. This work was Kugler's *History of Frederick the Great*, with four hundred illustrations by Adolf Menzel, born in Breslau 1815. He also executed, some forty years ago, the celebrated illustrations to the *Works of Frederick the Great*, by order of King Frederick William IV. Adolf Menzel is one of the first artists now living. It is not too much to say that the modern school of Book illustration was initiated by him. He was the first to depart from the conventional modes of illustrating history that were in vogue during his youth, and one perceives in his illustrations the artist who is in love with nature, life, movement, and historical accuracy.

Wilhelm von Kaulbach (1805-74) possessed a great power of imagination, and combined with his large and correct designs the art of clever colouring. As a book illustrator he is best known for his trenchant and satirical designs to Goethe's *Reinecke Fuchs*.

In our days, the great Paris publishers have returned to the reproduction of the books of the eighteenth century, orna- mented with vignettes on copper ; many of them purely and simply imitate by photographic processes the pretty editions of Eisen and Moreau, but they cannot be compared with the original editions. The processes of illustration are now without number : wood, metal, heliogravure, phototype, autotype, and others. And if these mechanical means have at present some importance, they by no means add to the intrinsic value of wood engravings as works of art, but merely to the rapidity and economy of their manufacture. The Book has nothing to do with all these inventions and innovations, and may well confine itself to the burin or the relief block.

But as regards the Book, properly so called, it never was the object of more excessive care, or of more unfortunate precipitation. It may be remarked that works least destined to live in the libraries, those thousands of lame pamphlets on questions of small provincial erudition or the cap-and-sword romances, are ordinarily the best and most carefully printed, in comparison to other more important works composed in worn-out type and printed on rotten and inferior paper. There are in reading-rooms a good number of pamphlets that will not easily be found fifty years hence, and will be worth their weight in bank-notes, even if dirty and tattered, on account of their intrinsic value.

TYPES, PRESSES AND PAPER.

 HISTORY of the Book would be incomplete without a brief account of the mechanical processes by which it is produced; and we propose in the present chapter to deal with this important part of the subject, describing first some of the earlier methods used, and types produced, by the first printers, and

afterwards giving a short account of the modern practice of typography.

The first printers were their own type-founders. The secret of the invention was the discovery of movable types. Of the preliminary experiments of the inventor we know nothing. If, as the Haarlem story alleges, he began by attempting to cut letters in wood, or perhaps by separating the letters from a fixed wooden block, he would only convince himself of the impossibility of printing a book by means of such types. His next step was probably to attempt, by some rude process, to cast his letters in sand or clay from moulds fashioned after the manner of those in use among the trinket-makers of the Middle Ages. Finally, after much fruitless labour, he would arrive at the excellent invention of the first German typographers, namely, the cutting of a punch of each letter in relief on hard copper or steel, sinking the punch into a matrix of hard lead or copper, adjusting the matrix to one end of the cavity of a bipartite iron mould, and so casting his leaden types therefrom in the same manner and by the same methods as those by which type continued to be cast for four centuries after. The shape of the body, or "shank," of the type was given by the mould; the "face," or letter at the end, was given by the impressed image of the punch in the matrix. When a fresh letter was required, a new matrix would be attached, and so on through the alphabet.

Fig. 145, from an old Book of Trades by Jost Amman, represents the interior of a German type-foundry about 1568. The founder, seated before the furnace, is in the act of pouring his molten metal into the mould, in the interior of which the matrix is fixed. In the basket beside him are a number of types already cast, while on the shelf may be seen

some more moulds, sieves, crucibles, and other implements made
use of in the industry.

The form of character adopted by the first printers invariably followed the models of the national scribes. In Germany,
for the Bible and Service Books, the Gothic or Black letter
was used; while for the more secular books, such as grammars,
law-books, and theological treatises, a mixed letter called Bastard

Fig. 145.—Type-founder in the middle of the sixteenth century.
Engraving by Jost Amman.

—half Black letter, half Roman—was employed. In Holland
the secular hand was the Black letter. In Italy the first
printers copied the elegant hand of the scribes of that country,
and produced the character afterwards known as Roman. This
character was perfected by Jenson, the most elegant of the
fifteenth century Italian printers; while in 1500, Aldus, imitating, it is said, the handwriting of Petrarch, produced the
Italic. In France, the first printers of the Sorbonne made use

of a Roman letter, which however shortly gave place to a Gothic. In Flanders and Burgundy, the first printers naturally adopted the flowing secretary hand of their scribes. In this character Colard Mansion printed at Bruges, and from his office William Caxton transferred the same character to his infant press at Westminster in 1477.

The Roman letter did not appear in England till 1518, when Pynson used it. During the early years of the sixteenth century, when printers gave up buying type from abroad and attempted to cast it themselves, printing became very poor. John Day, the English Plantin, was the first to revive it, about 1560. Many of his founts are handsome; and some of them remained in fashion for many years. But although there were many printers in England in the sixteenth century, the best printing was executed, and the best types were cast, abroad.

To mention only a few famous names, the Aldine family in Italy, Claude Garamond in France, Froben in Switzerland, and Plantin in Holland, all produced types which advanced printing into a fine art, and left for future generations models which are admired to our own day.

One or two interesting attempts were also made during the same century to reduce to definite rule the form of printing letter. Chief among these was the celebrated *Champfleury* of Geoffroy Tory, the Paris printer, who, while fantastically deriving the shape and proportion of each letter from the symmetry of the human body, gave the Roman letter an elegance and style which brought about a revolution in French typography, and led to the abandonment of the old Gothic for the new fashion. The brilliant school of French letter-cutters who succeeded Garamond,—the Estiennes, under whose auspices the Imprimerie Royale of Francis I. was started; Lebé, who cut types for Plantin's famous Polyglot; Sanlecques, Grandjean, Fournier, and the Didots, were all more or less indebted to the inspiration of Tory for their art.

In England the artistic perfection of the Roman type was neglected until Moxon in 1676 attempted to correct it by the model of the neat and serviceable letters designed by Christoffel Van Dijck, and used with success by the celebrated Dutch printers, the Elzevirs. Moxon's rules, however, failed to accomplish their object, and the Roman letter used in England till the commencement of the eighteenth century was of the most debased kind, and came for the most part from Holland. The English founders of the day lacked the skill to amend it, and it was not till Caslon turned his attention to letter-cutting in 1720 that English printing began to recover the ground it had lost. Caslon's types, modelled on the best form of the Elzevir types, rapidly became popular. Baskerville attempted to refine them, and produced some beautiful founts, which, with the aid of exquisite presswork and highly-glazed paper, bade fair to eclipse those of his predecessor. The English public, however, grew tired of the dazzling types of the Birmingham genius, and settled down once more to the more serviceable models of Caslon. Baskerville's types were bought by the French for the great edition of Voltaire printed at Kehl at the end of the eighteenth century.

About 1800, chiefly owing to the influence of the Italian typographer Bodoni, the old-style Roman was abandoned for a more modern style, which still remains the common printing letter of Europe, although in our own country the Caslon old-styles have been successfully revived and largely used in artistic work.

During the four centuries, as we have said, the method of type-casting has remained practically the same as that invented by Gutenberg before 1454. A gradual improvement has taken place in the materials used. Punches are now cut on hard steel and sunk into copper; the mould is hard iron carefully "justified" and finished, and the types themselves are cast in an alloy of lead, tin and antimony, calculated to combine sharpness and toughness, and endure the severe strain of modern machinery.

At the present time there are about twenty different sizes or bodies of type, ranging from an inch to $\frac{1}{24}$ of an inch. A fount of type consists of capitals, "lower case" or small letters, small capitals, points, figures, reference marks, signs, spaces, and italic. The quantities of each letter are regulated according to a "bill" calculated on the ordinary requirements of the language. In the English "bill," containing, say, 3,000 "m's," there would be 9,000 "a," 14,000 "e," 800 "k," 700 capital "A," 300 notes of interrogation, and so on, each sort in fixed proportion.

The types are distributed into cases, partitioned into small boxes, one for each sort. From these they are picked up one by one by the compositor and set in a tray-like iron frame called a composing-stick, in words and lines, according to the "copy" to be printed. As the stick is filled, the matter is carefully lifted out on to galleys, on which the pages are made up. These pages of type are then imposed, usually eight or sixteen at a time, and wedged fast in an iron frame or chase, represented by the black lines in the accompanying diagram. The imposition follows fixed rules, the pages being so placed that when the sheet is printed and folded they shall follow one another consecutively in their proper order.

The following would be the form of imposition of a four-leaf tract printed on both sides, making eight pages.

4 (inverted) except the name of Meyden-bach; but their office was limited exclusively to that of money-lend-ers.	**5** (inverted) During his residence at Strasbourg Gutenberg pub-lished by means of his new process two pam-phlets writ-	**6** (inverted) ten for the schools, of which he had in consequence of their fire-of their use, quickly to sell the print-ed copies.	**8** (inverted) first expen-ses. Their association increased later on by several mem-bers, whose names have not come down to us.
1 trade of a goldsmith, other histo-rians say of a banker ; and they formed together an association, to which the one contri-1	**8** the defects of the blocks for such par-ticular pur-pose, con-ceived the idea of com-posing them with sepa-rate letters,	**7** The general belief is that Fust, initi-ated by him into the se-crets of the art which he had just in-vented, and struck with	**2** buted his in-dustry, a probable source of future bene-fits, and the other a cer-tain sum, appointed to cover the

It will be seen that these sheets placed back to back and folded once across the breadth and once perpendicularly down the middle, will give the eight pages in consecutive order, and be a regular " quarto."

The first printers usually printed only one page at a time.

The imposed form is now ready for the press, on to which the chase is lifted. The pressman first takes a proof or rough impression of the type, which is carefully read and all corrections marked. These corrections are made in the type, and the form is then ready for printing.

The printing press dates back to the invention of printing. The first used was probably a modification of the old domestic press in common use among the people for a variety of purposes. It was gradually adapted and strengthened for the special purpose of taking impressions from type. The woodcut overleaf represents the press of the Parisian printer, Badius Ascensius, about 1535. The wooden screw press continued to be used for three centuries, until Lord Stanhope, about 1790, produced an improved model, much stronger and more accurate. From that time till the present improvements in this branch of the art have been very rapid. The Stanhope press gave place to the simpler and more perfect Columbian and Albion presses, while, early in the century, mechanical presses, or printing machines, were introduced into newspaper offices, and these have since developed into the monster perfecting machines of the present day,—machines which, fed by an endless reel of paper, will, at a single revolution, print both sides of a large newspaper at the rate of twelve thousand an hour and upwards, and not only print, but cut and fold ready for delivery. In the year 1814 the first steam printing machine was used in England. It was the invention of a man named Friederich Kœnig (born at Eisleben, 1774), who a few years before its introduction in England had offered it to Gœschen, the celebrated German publisher, and grandfather of the present Chancellor of the Exchequer of England :—" You are," Kœnig wrote to Goschen, " the only printer in Germany who works with ambition ; therefore I address myself to you. So far as I can judge, you are the only man in Germany who can make the most profitable and at the same time the most useful use of the invention which I bring before you."

To return to the press. The form being laid on the iron bed, the surface of the type is inked by means of a roller. The paper is then laid upon it, and the bed passed under the descending " platen " of the press. This platen is brought down with an even pressure by means of a lever or screw, pressing the paper

17

upon the inked surface of the type. The result is that the mark of the type is transferred to the paper, and we have a printed impression. The recent mechanical inventions in printing machinery all start from this simple process. Instead of the flat platen, the pressure is now usually produced by the passing of a cylinder over the face of the type, while the leverage,

Fig. 146.—Mark of Jodocus Badius of Asch. Engraving *à la croix de Lorraine.*

instead of being applied manually, is given by steam-power. In the press of Ascensius, as will be seen, the pressman makes use of balls instead of rollers to ink the type. These remained in use for presswork till comparatively recently.

With regard to paper, it is unnecessary to point out that its manufacture was understood long before the invention

of typography or even block printing. We have here a
block representing the paper-maker at work in the sixteenth
century.

The process of making paper from rags by hand was briefly
as follows.

The rags, having been thoroughly cleansed, were put into
vats, where they were worked up under a beating press until

Fig. 147.—Workman engaged on the vat with the wire frame.
Engraving by Jost Amman.

they became pulp. This pulp was thrown into hot water and
stirred until a uniform mixture was produced. Then a mould
of fine wire cloth, fixed upon a wooden frame, and having a
" deckle " to determine the size of the sheet, was taken ; in the
middle of this frame was disposed, also in brass wire, a factory
mark, intended to appear in white in the sheet of paper, and
called the " watermark." This mould was dipped into the
vat of pulp and drawn out again. After gently shaking it to

and fro in a horizontal position, the fibres of the pulp became
so connected as to form one uniform fabric; and the water
escaped through the wires.   The deckle was then removed
from the mould, and the sheet of paper turned off upon a felt,
in a pile with many others, a felt intervening between each
sheet, and the whole subjected to great pressure, in order to
absorb the superfluous water. After being dried and pressed
without the felts, the sheets were dipped into a tub of size and
again pressed to remove surplus size.   This primitive method
of paper-making is represented in fig. 147, and the same principle is still in use for the production of hand-made paper.
Machinery has effected many improvements and economies in
the production of laid paper.

China and Japan have their special paper manufacture.   In
Japan the material employed is the bark of the Japanese
mulberry tree (*Morus papyrifera sativa*).

According to their fineness, size and weight, papers have
received different names, proceeding from the watermark.

Fust at Mayence used paper marked with a bull's head.
Jenson at Venice used a balance, of which the form varied.
This latter came from a mill which furnished Vicenza, Perugia,
and Rome. Jenson used, besides a crown, a cardinal's hat.

The bull's head underwent transformations; it had stars and
roses, and was special to Germany, and it may sometimes be
found in Italy.

The laid wires and chain-wires served to determine the
size of a book.   Looking at a folio leaf against the light, the
laid wires will be seen to be horizontal, and the chain-wires
vertical.   In quarto they will be reversed, the paper having
been folded in four instead of in two.   The chain-wires become
horizontal.   They return to the vertical in octavo, and so on.

Such, then, is a brief account of the mechanical processes undergone by the printed book in course of production. It will be obvious that, for book ornament, the ordinary relief wood-block is at once the simplest and most suitable. The block will work with the type as part of the same page, and

Fig. 148.—Balance used by Jenson, at Venice.

receive its impression at the same time, in the same press, and by the same process. The old art, made famous in the block books of the old xylographers, has taken its place as handmaid to the newer art of typography; and its chief function now is to lend itself sympathetically and harmoniously to the adornment of the page of which the type is the most important feature.

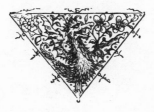

BOOKBINDING.

Early bindings; superiority of English work
— Panel-stamps invented in the Low
Countries — The binding of the first
printed books—French binding in the
time of Louis XII.—Influence of German
and Netherlandish binders on the art
in other countries — Italian bindings —
Aldus — Maioli — Grolier — Francis I. —
Henry II. and Diana of Poitiers —
Catherine de Medici — Henry III.—The
Eves—The "fanfares"—Louis XIII.—Le
Gascon—Florimond Badier—Louis XIV.

—Morocco leathers—Cramoisy—The bindings of the time of Louis XIV.— The regency—Pasdeloup—The Deromes—Dubuisson—Thouvenin—Lesné —The nineteenth century—English binders—Roger Payne—Francis Bedford —Blocking.

 EAVING the book itself, we must now direct the reader's attention to the means adopted to protect it from injury; in other words, to the art of binding. Originally the binder was simply a workman whose business it was to arrange in proper order the quires or gatherings of which a manuscript was composed, sew them on to thongs of skin or bands of parchment, and by means of these fix the volume to the boards of oak, or other wood, of which the sides were made, and finally to cover these and the back with deerskin, pigskin, or leather. As luxury increased, the wooden boards which protected the book were either covered with some precious silken stuff, or encrusted with plates of gold or silver, adorned with cloisonné enamels and precious stones or plaques of ivory, according to the taste of the owner. Generally these precious bindings were reserved for books of the Gospels (as on that formerly in the Cathedral of Noyon, now in the Museum of the Louvre, Fig. 150), Psalters, and Bibles, which alone were deemed worthy of such magnificent clothing. Other books were covered with leather, either left plain or simply adorned with ruled lines. The next step was to decorate the covers with interlaced and other patterns, produced by means of a style. Stamps were probably not introduced until the eleventh century, but by the middle of the twelfth the art of adorning the covers of books by stamping, generally called blind tooling, had, especially in England, attained a very high degree of perfection. For some

reason, probably owing to the introduction of plates of copper gilt, and of the champlevé (much less expensive than the cloisonné) process of enamelling, the art of ornamental leather binding declined in this country. An example of a book-cover thus decorated, representing Merlin, is given on p. 266. In France, Germany, and the Netherlands it developed more slowly, but continued to progress during the fourteenth and fifteenth centuries.

Fig. 149.—Bookbinder's shop in the sixteenth century.   Engraving by Jost Amman.

The invention of printing led to a great increase in the number of books produced, and as a consequence stimulated the art of bookbinding. When books were produced singly by copying, the binder could devote more time to the covering; but in the Netherlandish monasteries and towns where there were a large number of copyists, it was found that the orna-mentation of the covers by means of small tools absorbed too much time, and this led in the fourteenth century to the

A.VINET F

Fig. 150.—Cover of the *Evangeliarium* of Noyon, made of skin, copper and horn, with reliquaries.

invention of panel-stamps. These very commonly bore an inscription with the name of the binder, who was generally a bookseller as well. Each bookseller applied himself to the work, or at least covered in his own house books intended for

Fig. 151.—Cover of a book in enamelled goldsmith work of Limoges, fifteenth century, representing Merlin l'Enchanteur transformed into a scholar.

sale. The fashion was not then to expose for sale, as now, unbound books. Purchasers wanted an article easy to handle,

whîch they were not obliged to return for ulterior embellishment.

So to the public the first printed books were presented
bound in wooden boards covered with calfskin. At the four
corners of the larger sized volumes, brass bosses prevented
rubbing against the shelves of the bookcase, for at that time
books were ranged on their sides, and not as they are to-day.
We must return to the bibliomaniac of the *Ship of Fools*

Fig. 152.—Bibliomaniac of the *Ship of Fools.*

(Fig. 152), to get an idea of these depositories ; before him
may be seen ranged on a desk large folios, with bosses on
their sides, in the shelves, so defying the dust, instead of
being placed upright on their edges, which rendered them
liable to spots and stains.

Unhappily the wooden sides had in themselves a germ of
destruction, the worm, capable first of reducing the sides to
powder and then ravaging the body of the work. Certain

preparations destroy the insect, but the precaution often has
no effect, and this may to some extent account for the dis-
appearance of volumes formerly abundant, but now almost
impossible to find.

From the beginning the operations of the binder were what
they still are, except for improvements. They consist in the
gathering and collation of the sheets of a book, folding them,
beating them to bring them together and give them solidity,
and sewing them on to the strips of strong leather or the cords,
which form the four, five or six bands seen on the backs.
Primitively these bands were brought into horizontal slots cut
in the thickness of the wooden boards, fastened down with
little pegs, or sometimes with brass nails; the head-bands into
similar diagonal slots. Over both boards was placed a resistent
skin, on which, from metal or wooden stamps cut in intaglio,
were struck the most pleasing decorative subjects. Calfskin,
brown and fine, lent itself especially to ornamentation of this
kind. In Central and Northern Germany pigskin was more
generally employed.

The inside of the board was generally lined with parchment,
vellum or paper. We reproduce here the binding of a volume
in purely French style (Fig. 154), belonging to the late M. Dutuit,
of Rouen, executed at the commencement of the sixteenth
century for Louis XII. and his Queen, Anne de Bretagne; not
more than nine or ten specimens of such bindings remain.
They are of coarse aspect. The workman who tooled them
crowded his subjects one upon another. Coats of arms, porcu-
pines, ermines, are treated so as to be confusing, and form a
medley that is not pleasing. Very similar bindings were executed
for Francis I., but with the salamander and an F surmounted
by a royal crown in the place of the porcupine and ermine.

The workmen who introduced printing into the other countries of Europe were either Germans or Netherlanders,

Fig. 153.—Binding in gold, ornamented with precious stones, having been used for a cover of an *Evangeliarium* of the eleventh century (Louvre)

who for a long time were the chief dealers in books. These printers were either themselves bookbinders, or were accompanied in their migration by binders. In France the ornamentation of binding was influenced and modified to a very great extent by both Netherlanders and Germans. In Italy there was no national style of binding, what little there was of ornamental leather binding being a mere servile imitation of Arabian work. The influence of German, especially of Swabian, binders made itself felt there until well into the first quarter of the sixteenth century, when Oriental designs again prevailed. These were often richly gilt and coloured, so much so that the leather itself was almost completely covered, as on the binding of a Koran (p. 275). Into Spain the Germans introduced their system of ornamentation, which, however, was quickly modified by the adoption of Moorish details. In no country, however, was the style of ornamentation so completely denationalised as in England.

Towards the middle of the second half of the fifteenth century a charming innovation was introduced, by whom we know not, perhaps by an Italian, more probably by a German working in Italy. This is now known as gold-tooling. At first it was confined to gold dots sprinkled here and there in the openings of interlaced work; then to leaves or flowers in the angles formed by the borders; then the borders were adorned alternately with plain and gilt ornaments; but the gilt work was, during the remainder of the fifteenth and the earlier years of the sixteenth century, generally used with moderation and good taste. Venice quickly gained pre-eminence over the other towns of Italy; this is easily accounted for when we call to mind the number of foreign printers, artists and craftsmen gathered together in that city, where bindings in the Persian, Arabian, Greek and Swabian styles were produced at the same time.

The art of decorative bookbinding was greatly developed

by Aldus' Manutius. The covers of books issued from his press and bound in his offices before 1502 were all bordered with a rectangular frame adorned with designs in gold, in imitation of Persian or Arabian work produced by the repetition of a stamp.

Fig. 154.—Binding for Louis XII. Collection of M. Dutuit, of Rouen.

About 1512 Aldus made the acquaintance of a wealthy financier employed as French treasurer and receiver-general of the Duchy of Milan. This distinguished lover of books, named ·Jean Grolier, was, above all his contemporaries, even

King Francis, the greatest patron of the art of binding. It is not too much to say art, for if better had not been done before, it may safely be said that nothing better has been done since ; and the books of Grolier remain as the most perfect and most admirable types of this kind of decoration.

Born of a Veronese family established at Lyons, Jean Grolier had the good fortune to succeed his father, Etienne Grolier, as treasurer and receiver-general of the Duchy of Milan. The position of the treasurers during the campaigns of the French in Italy was important ; they handled the pence levied with great trouble in the cities of France "for making war." Many abused their trust, and were punished, and among others the Lallemants, whom documents show us to have been in connection with Grolier, and who suffered, with Semblançay, the most terrible trials of the time.

Italian art then treated the decoration of books with the greatest freedom. Of the interior we have spoken in our first chapters on wood engravings ; for the exterior, the cover of the volume, foliage, golden flowers worked with a hot iron, and polychromatic compartments obtained by coloured pastes were multiplied. Thus was produced on the outside that which it was no longer sought to obtain in the interior, the variation of tints so highly prized during the middle age, but generally forsaken since the invention of printing. In the midst of these literary men was a lover of books and fine connoisseur who, not content with choosing the best editions, such as those of Ferrara, Venice, and Basle, bound them superbly, with compartments of admirable taste, and had his name and device inscribed on the sides in the fashion of the time. He was named Thomas Maioli, and following the

custom of the book-lovers of the time, he offered the enjoy-
ment of his library to his friends. " THO. MAIOLI ET AMICORVM,"
he inscribed, as did later Mark Lauweryn of Watervliet,
Grolier, and others, but he somewhat modified the enthusiasm
of his friendship by a sceptical device, "INGRATIS SERVIRE

Fig. 155.—Arms of the University of Oxford, in which a bound book appears.

NEPHAS," which might very well be the cry of the owner of
books betrayed by his borrowers.

Maioli more often inscribed on his book-covers the phrase
"INIMICI MEI MEA MICHI, NON ME MICHI." He also sometimes used a cypher, which was composed of all the letters
of his name.

The relations of Grolier with this unknown and mysterious

18

book-lover, whose name is not always found outside his volumes, are not doubtful. Brunet possessed a volume that had belonged to Maioli and had passed through the hands of Grolier. What better proof could be wished of the communion of ideas and tastes between the two collectors?

But these book-lovers were not alone. Beside them were princes and great lords, lay and ecclesiastic. From the commencement of the sixteenth century bookbinding had received an enormous impulse from the tastes and the predilections of these wealthy collectors. And it cannot be ascribed to the simple skill of the workmen experimenting in that line. The century that saw Italian artists occupied in making designs for raised pies, painting beautiful ladies and the courtesans of Florence, could not be alarmed at finding them painting models for bindings, with compartments of varied tone and style. Maioli affected white on a background of dark leather. His book-covers are adorned with scrolls of foliage in white or clear paste with a very happy effect (see Fig. 157).

This was the time when Grolier travelled in Italy, sojourning sometimes at Naples, but generally at Milan, and often visiting Venice. He had already acquired the reputation of being a great lover of books, and was soon in communication with the Alduses, and through them with the principal learned men and binders of the time.

Following the fashion, Grolier put his name on the obverse side of his books—" IO. GROLIERII ET AMICORVM "— in gold letters, and on the reverse the pious ejaculation of the Royal Psalmist : " PORTIO MEA DOMINE SIT IN TERRA VIVENTIVM." Generally all the Grolier books which came from the Alduses have the name on the obverse and the motto

Fig. 156.—Cover of an old Koran.

on the reverse side; the title was placed above the name and often disposed in rows. Some large volumes had the cover ornamented with an architectural design, like the Iamblichus of the Libri collection, which had on the front the façade of a temple, with the title in rows on the door. This volume was printed by Aldus in 1516, and probably decorated by him for the great French amateur.

Jean Grolier is said to have himself designed some of the subjects of his ornaments, and their perfection indicates an active and enlightened supervision. He returned to France in 1530, took up his abode at Paris, in a house near the Porte de Bucy, before 1537, when he held the office of treasurer of the king's finances in the Isle of France and the district beyond the Seine and Yonne, until 1545, when he became treasurer-general of France, which office he held until his death. At Paris he came into relation with Geoffroy Tory, the artist best fitted to understand him, and who was himself painter, engraver, printer, and binder. It was there that, in the leisure of his financial functions, between two projects for revictualling the forts of Outre Seine and Yonne, Grolier invented combinations, sought interlacings, and laid out foliage. Tory himself tells us of these works undertaken in common. It was for Grolier, as he relates in his *Champ-fleury*, that he invented antique letters. It was for him, too, that he interwove so finely his designs in compartments for binding, and that he reproduced the delightful ornaments of his Books of Hours in golden scrolls.

As we have said, Grolier placed his titles on the sides of his books on account of the arrangement of the works on the shelves of the library where they were laid. For this reason also the back was neglected, and no ornament used upon it ; thick and heavy with its projecting bands, without any decoration between them, this part of the bound volume was a kind of waste in a splendidly cultivated garden. The profusion of books brought about a revolution. There was no longer room to place on their sides the innumerable books that were produced; they were then placed

Fig. 157.—The fourth part of a binding for Thomas Maioli (sixteenth century).

on their edges, as now, and the back also was decorated. For this the bands were made to disappear, and were replaced by decorative subjects in compartments like the sides. Then with Grolier the bands reappeared, and the title was placed between them, as it still is.

In the centre of each side was almost always a square,

lozenge or shield-shaped space reserved for the title on one side and for his motto on the other; at the foot of the obverse, between the lines of the border, was printed in small Roman capitals: 10. GROLIERII ET AMICORVM. Sometimes, however, this was placed immediately beneath the title; in four instances on the obverse side, and in three on the back. On two others a second motto is inscribed: TANQVAM VENTVS EST VITA MEA.

The books of Grolier have been divided into two series: those bound for himself, and those originally bound for others, but which he subsequently acquired by gift or purchase. The bindings of many of these were too remarkable to be destroyed, and he merely had his name and motto impressed on them, or if this could not well be done, he wrote them on the fly-leaf. The volumes bound expressly for him are all covered either with morocco or yellow or brown calf, and may be grouped in four classes: first, those ornamented in compartments, with scrolls, full-gilt or adorned with parallel gilt lines. After these come the bindings in the style of Geoffroy Tory, with gilt compartments; then, the polychromatic bindings, in which, by the aid of colour or mastic, the alternating tones are mixed. Grolier also had some mosaic bindings, composed of little pieces of leather connected by incrustation or paste, pure Italian bindings; but these were not numerous, especially if compared with those conceived in the manner of Geoffroy Tory.

One of these latter works is here reproduced from a beautiful volume in the collection of the late M. Dutuit. This copy has the back flat, and the interlacings of the decoration are most complicated and clever.

Grolier got his Levant moroccos through the dealers of

Venice, to make sure of the excellence of the material he
employed.

Born in 1479, the treasurer-general of France lived until

Fig. 158.—Binding for Grolier in the collection of M. Dutuit.

22nd October, 1565. In 1563 an original manuscript shows
him much occupied with finance at over eighty-four years of
age ; but his passion for bindings had cooled down, for few

book-covers bearing his name are found the execution of which can belong to a later date than the reign of Henry II. After

Fig. 159.—Binding for Francis I., with the arms of France and the salamander.

great trials, after having seen Semblançay suffer at Montfaucon, Jean Lallemand beheaded, and himself having narrowly escaped losing life and fortune at one blow, Grolier passed away quietly in his house, having collected most of the fine books of the time and many curious medals. Christophe de Thou, his friend and *confrère* in the love of books, had saved his reputation before the Parliament of Paris. After his death his library was transported to the Hotel de Vic, and from thence dispersed in 1675, a hundred years after.

Fig. 160.—Mark of Guyot Marchant, printer and bookbinder. He published the *Danse Macabre* of 1485.

Thus from Italy came a change in the style of French binding, which, however, still remained original. The kings did not fail to follow the movement, and even to anticipate it, thanks to the means at their disposal. We shall see Francis I. occupied with bindings, and we know the name of one craftsman who worked for that monarch ; but Geoffroy

Tory must have been his principal inspirer, and who knows but that he also himself carried out the best work executed for the prince, as he did for the great financier?

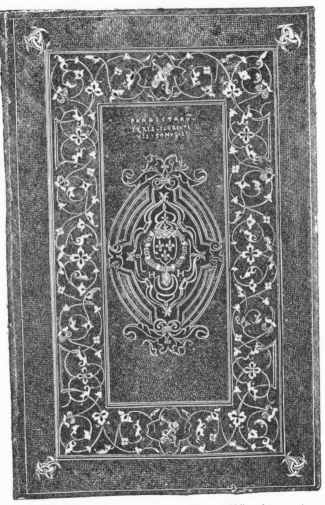

Fig. 161.—Binding for Henry II., with the "H" and crescents.

We have said that Louis XII. knew nothing of fine bindings. During his travels in Italy he had received presentation copies of magnificently covered books, and among others the poems.

of *Faustus Andrelinus*, bound in calf in his honour. He, who knew so little of the fine arts, purchased the entire library of Louis de la Gruuthuuse, and substituted his own emblems for

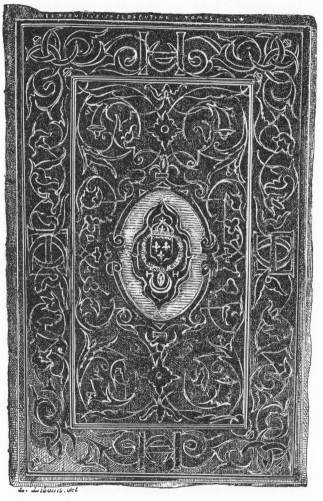

Fig. 162.—Binding for Henry II. (Mazarine Library).

those of that wealthy Fleming. Francis I., with innate sentiment for masterpieces and the powerful protection he had given them, did not allow the experiments of Grolier to pass unnoticed. The king did not wish to be behind the treasurer, and so the binders were set to work for him. He had adopted the salamander as his badge ; this emblem he used on his castles and furniture and the liveries of his people ; he lavished it also on the sides of his books, together with an " F " ensigned with a crown, and the arms of France with the collar of the order of St. Michael. The design of the binding here represented (Fig. 159), if not by Geoffroy Tory himself, was certainly suggested by his works. It must not be thought that this ornamentation was produced at a single blow by means of an engraved plate or a block. On the contrary, every detail was separately impressed by a hot tool applied by the workman's hand to the gold laid on in advance, making it, so to speak, enter into the skin or morocco. That was art binding ; blocks were only used for commercial bindings, quickly impressed and intended for ordinary purchasers.

During the reign of Francis I. the binders were the booksellers, as Vérard and Vostre had been. The king generally employed a publisher named Pierre Roffet, and it is his name that most frequently figures in the accounts that have been preserved. Roffet not only bound, but it appears also rebound books to patterns which the king desired. Philippe Lenoir and Guyot Marchant were also royal workmen. The latter, placed beneath his mark, here reproduced (Fig. 160), the figures of Saints Crispin and Crispinian, patrons of the leather-dressers, who prepared the leather for the binder.

The binders in Grolier's time had not much time to be idle. Thousands of volumes were then destroyed to make the boards for sides. Owing to this, many discoveries are made in our days by pulling to pieces sixteenth century work,—unknown playing cards and portions of early printed works. To mention only one instance, twenty leaves of the *Perspective* of Viator were discovered in the binding of a volume in the National Library at Paris. The board thus formed was covered indifferently with sheepskin, parchment, calf, morocco, or goatskin; the books were sewn on bands or cords, according to the

Fig. 163.—Italian binding for Catherine de Medici, with the initials "C. C."

owner's taste; the edges were gilt, sometimes gauffered, and designs often impressed upon them to match those of the sides. For large folios wooden boards were still used, more solid, and protected from rubbing by nails in relief. But the inside of the cover was as yet only covered with paper. Leather linings were extremely uncommon.

The reign of Henry II. increased yet more the importance of bindings; it was the time when Grolier collected, and clever artists came from all parts. Geoffroy Tory had given the best models for letters and interlacings. The Queen, Catherine, derived from her parents the taste for decoration in gold and colours, and patronised the artists called by her from the court of Florence; and the favourite, Diana of Poitiers, Duchess of Valentinois, rivalled her in luxury and expenditure. Henry II. in the decoration of his castles, as well as his books, introduced doubtful emblems. He interlaced two reversed "D's" with an "H," in the form shown in the border on page 283. Strictly speaking, we ought to see there two "C's" back to back; but as we find the "D" on all the bindings displaying the arms of Diana, there can be little doubt. Other emblems of Diana are to be found in the bows and crescents that are plentifully displayed. The library of Diana was large, owing to the king not hesitating to take valuable books for her from the royal collections. Two centuries after her death it was dispersed, and the greater part of the books belonging to the royal collections were restored on the deaths of those who then purchased them. Hence the largest number of the bindings of Henry II. and Diana of Poitiers will be found in the National Library of Paris.

Queen Catherine also had special patterns with a monogram identical with the double "D" mentioned above, but the branches of the "C" were a little longer than the branches of the "H;" she also used a "K" on the sides of her books. The specimen which we reproduce (Fig. 163), is a purely Italian work.

Frcm kings and queens the fashion passed to the great lords, it having come to the kings and queens from a private individual. The Constable Anne de Montmorency adorned his

Fig. 164.—Binding with the arms of Mansfeld, with lined scroll work, from the Didot collection.

bindings with a cross and spread eagle. Among the book-lovers of the sixteenth, seventeenth, and eighteenth centuries using distinctive marks, we may mention Philippe Desportes, the poet, who used two Φ enlaced, as did also Superintendent Fouquet in the seventeenth century. The brothers Dupuy adopted the double Δ, arranged as a star. Colbert had a curled snake (*coluber* for Colbert!), the Gondis two war-maces, Madame de Pompadour three towers, etc. Fouquet beside the Φ used a squirrel on some of his bindings.

In Germany, Count Mansfeldt adopted the ornamental style with arms (Fig. 164), of which a specimen is here given. Among the lords of the French courts who favoured polychromatic ornament and bold compositions were the young Valois, Louis de Sainte Maure, Marquis of Nesle, and Henri de Guise, called "Le Balafré."

Charles IX. had his emblems and devices, the double "C" crowned the legend "PIETATE ET JVSTITIA," but his brother, Henry III., loved the decoration of books more than he did. The passion of this king for miniatures which he cut out of books is known; his love of golden things showed itself also on bindings, for which he chose special designs. Henry III. was an amateur of dances of death; he visited cemeteries, attended funerals, and took a death's-head for his emblem. This emblem was, however, not his invention; long before him Marot had addressed an epigram to a lady in which he brought love and death into close conjunction. However that may be, the king chose skeletons and penitents' tears to ornament his books. He also tolerated diamonds, although he absolutely prohibited them in the adornment of ladies or fixed the number *pro rata* with the rank of the authorised person. There was in this prince a singular mixture of taste and artistic acuteness by the side of a mania or hallucination which was reflected on the most intimate objects of his apparel or of his furniture. Thus if we find, at the end of the sixteenth century, a death's-head

Fig. 165.- - Part of a binding having belonged to Jacques de Thou (sixteenth century).

on the sides or the back of a volume, the binding is of the
period of Henry III.

The binders of his time are known by the mention that is
made of them in the royal accounts; the Eves were the most
celebrated among them all. Nicholas Eve was charged with
the binding of the Statutes of the Order of the Holy Ghost,
with which the king gratified his friends. Mention of this work
is found in the Clairambault manuscripts, where we read, "To
Nicholas Eve, washer and binder of books and bookseller to

Fig¹ 166.—Mark of Nicholas Eve, binder of Henry III.
and Henry IV.

the king, forty-seven and a half escus for washing, gilding, and
squaring the edges of forty-two books of statutes and ordinances
of the Order, bound and covered with orange Levant morocco,
enriched on one side with the arms of the king, fully gilt, and
on the other with those of France and Poland, with cyphers at
the four corners, and flames on the rest of the ground, with
orange and blue ribands," etc.

Louisa of Lorraine, wife of Henry III., counted for little in
the life of her husband; nevertheless she had a certain number
of books decorated with their united escutcheons.

The bindings attributed to Eve were decorated all over the sides and back with interlacing patterns of geometrical character,

Fig 167.—Sixteenth century binding, called *à la fanfare*. In the Dutuit collection.

the spaces between the parallel lines and in the middle of the figures left at first quite blank, but afterwards filled in with palm branches and wreaths of foliage; to these delicate and elaborate yet brilliant toolings have been given the name of bindings *à la fanfare*. The origin of this designation is doubtful, and is a good example of the peculiar terminology adopted by modern amateurs.

The fine work of that time prepared the way for the coming in the seventeenth century—about 1620—of the artist known as Le Gascon, with whom in our days are connected the bindings executed during the reign of Louis XIII. Under Henry IV. the fleur-de-lys occupied most of the covers of the royal books, from vellum to Levant morocco; works in this class had nothing very remarkable. The first years of Louis XIII. revealed a new process, inspired by the Eves. Le Gascon embroidered delightfully on the fanfare ornaments; showing the fibres of the leaves, he made a new kind of ornament, consisting of minute gold dots elaborated into lines and curves of singular brilliancy and elegance. Of this style, called *pointillé*, we give a specimen from the collection of M. Dutuit (Fig. 168). The fashion had sprung up all at once; lace, banished from clothing by severe edicts, found a refuge on the covering of books.

The times were hard then for binders in France; they were constrained to live in the university and to employ only its workmen. A binder was never his own gilder; he employed the *gaufreurs* of shoe-leather, more expert and bolder, to gild his leather. Among these artisans at Paris was one named Pigorreau, whom the edict found living in the midst of publishers and working for them; he was compelled to choose either to remain a bootmaker or become a bookseller; he chose the latter, against the wish of the syndics of the trade, against everyone, and he so made enemies for himself.

He revenged himself by turning the masters into ridicule in a placard.

Le Gascon was probably the assumed name of an artist

Fig. 168.—Le Gascon binding.

in this style, perhaps of Clovis Eve, son of Nicholas. The *Guirlande de Julie*, tooled by him for Mademoiselle de Rambouillet, gave him great honour in the special circle of this

little literary court.   It was the fashion then for poor authors
to put a fine covering on their works and to offer them to
the great for their own profit.   Tallement des Reaux notably
signalises the poet Laserre, who displayed his luxury in
irreproachable bindings.   And then the farmers of the revenue,
successors of Grolier in financial trusts, formed libraries for
pure fashion's sake, never opening the volumes covered for
them in sumptuous attire.   If we may believe Sauval, author
of the *Antiquités de Paris*, they went further, and on the covers
of sham books inscribed imaginary titles and fantastic squibs
to mislead their visitors.   The bookcase being carefully closed,
it was difficult to discover the imposition.   Sauval writes, " In
place of books, they are content with covers of levant morocco,
on the backs of which, in gold letters, are inscribed the names
of the most celebrated authors.   A binder of the university
assured me that not long since he and his *confrères* had made
sham books for a single financier to the amount of 10,000
crowns ! "

The bindings of Le Gascon will be found more often
covering books belonging to great personages than to this class
of collectors, who did not appreciate their grace and charm.
The king's brother Gaston possessed them, as did Mazarin,
an example from whose library is here reproduced (Fig. 170).
On this binding Le Gascon worked gilt compartments and
elaborate arabesques ; in the middle of the sides are the arms
of the Cardinal and his pretentious device : " ARMA IVLII
ORNANT FRANCIAM ! "—" The arms of Julius adorn France ! "
In spite of the profusion of subjects, nothing could be produced better calculated to please the eye or indicate a man
of taste.

But if Le Gascon be a legendary personage, he had an

imitator or rival, very near to him, named Florimond Badier, whose works had at least the advantage of being signed. At the bottom of the inside cover of an inlaid morocco binding

Fig. 169.—Binding executed by Le Gascon for the MS. of Lafontaine's *Adonis*, having belonged to Fouquet (seventeenth century).

in the National Library at Paris is the inscription " Florimond Badier fec., inv." The analogy between this work and those known as Le Gascon's is palpable ; inside and outside, the cover is stippled with small tools (*au petit fer*) in the same manner. Florimond Badier was not appointed bookseller until 1645, and so could not have composed earlier bindings attributed to Le Gascon, but this resemblance of style proves the existence of a Parisian school, the adepts of which copied one another, as they do nowadays.

The work was soon simplified; pallets and wheel-shaped tools were invented to produce that which was improperly called *dentelle ;* this mechanical work was done by a wheel-shaped tool, previously heated, on sized gold leaves, on which it impressed its projections.

With Louis XIV. the passion for gilding increased. Charming festoons were designed, but they were soon abused, and inundated the libraries. On the sides were seen rising suns, arms, and golden garlands. Cramoisy directed the royal bindings, the king having devoted large sums to the purchase of Levant leathers. In 1666 the Director of Works ordered red moroccos ; in 1667 he received twenty-two dozen skins, amounting, with the expenses of transport, to 1,020 livres tournois. Successive supplies were obtained, and were used for the royal library, sixty-nine dozen in 1667, forty-six dozen in 1668, and three hundred and thirty-three dozen in 1670, costing the king more than 12,000 livres. On these admirably dressed skins, which, in spite of incessant use, still remain now as in their first days, the king caused to be applied tools of borders, and placed in the middle the arms of France, with the collar of the Order of the Holy Ghost.

Among the binders mentioned in the very useful work of M. J. J. Guiffrey on the expenditure of Louis XIV., we find Gilles Dubois, who died before 1670 ; Levasseur, binder to Huet, Bishop of Avranches ; La Tour, Mérins or Mérius, who died before 1676 ; and also Ruette, the reputed inventor of marbled paper for fly-leaves of books: to him the bindings of the Chancellor de Séguier, with their ornament of the golden fleece, and of Madame de Séguier, are attributed.   It

Fig. 170.—Le Gascon binding for Cardinal Mazarin.

was probably these men who decorated the books of the brothers Dupuy, Fouquet, and Colbert, marvellous works of solidity, if not always of elegance, which have resisted all assaults.   Unhappily, in many instances the mechanical *dentelle* overburdened the work, and gave it a commonplace regularity. In the Condé, Colbert, and perhaps even Madame de Longueville's collections, there are many specimens of this kind with two or three filleted borders.

We have come to an epoch when the difficulties resulting from confusion between the booksellers' and binders' trades began to be understood. The revocation of the Edict of Nantes entailed a crowd of measures and rules in all branches of national industry. It was a good occasion to prevent the artisans of binding from unduly parading themselves as booksellers and selling merchandise of which they understood nothing; Louis XIV. interfered, and separated the two communities. The binders then became the *relieurs-doreurs* of books; they had their own organisation, but remained subject to the university; the heads of the fraternity were called the "guards." The principal arrangements of the regulation of 1749 were: the members of the corporation had the sole right to bind books, from the elegant volume to registers of blank paper. Five years of apprenticeship and three of fellowship were necessary to obtain the freedom and the right to hold a shop. Moreover, no one could become a master-binder unless he could read and write. One regulation ordained that the workman should be "able to bind and ornament ordinary books or others, to return them in perfect order, to sew the sheets with thread on real bands, with joints of parchment, and not of paper; and in case of noncompliance, the said books were to be re-bound at the expense of the offender, who was besides condemned to a penalty of thirty livres for each volume." Their establishment was confined to the quarter from the Rue St. André des Arts to the Place Maubert; they regulated the sale of calfskin and of tools; in a word,

they were surrounded by precautions by which the production
remained always under the supervision of the masters and

Fig. 171.—Mosaic binding of the eighteenth century for the *Spaccio de
la Bestia Trionfante.*

completely satisfied the client. This exacting policy was, in
fact, a close imitation of the royal ordinance of 1686.

The mosaic bindings used from the end of the reign of

Louis XIV. were an application of pared leathers of colours different from the background, pasted on to the side. The binders of the regency executed a great number, now attributed to Pasdeloup, just as all the crayons of the sixteenth century are called Clouets, and the panels on wood, Holbeins. It is not that there was great originality or any particular art in these works ; more often the workman did no more than imitate Le Gascon or Eve or the older binders, and accommodated the processes of these artists to the fashion of his time. Of bindings in this style we may cite the *Spaccio de la Bestia Trionfante* (Fig. 171), printed at Paris in 1584, for which the binder designed a cover of doubtful taste and undeniably wanting in proportion. The tendency was then to flowers occupying three-fourths of the page, to compartments too large, to seeded pomegranates, as on the binding of the *Spaccio* here reproduced. Had Pasdeloup himself invented these mediocre combinations, he could not be proclaimed the regenerator of a fallen art. The bastard style of these works may be compared to their mosaics, constructed of pieces ; it is a little of everything, and as a whole it is nothing. However, in the midst of a vast amount of very inferior work, some pleasing decoration is from time to time met with ; the design of a volume with the arms of the Regent (Fig. 172), and his wife, Mademoiselle de Blois, is neither wanting in elegance nor in taste ; though far from perfection, it has better proportion and balance.

We should, however, hesitate to give names to all these works. Besides the Pasdeloups, there were the Deromes, partly abandoning the mosaics, devising flowers and *dentelles* in combination, and no longer the simple products of the fillet. They formed quite a dynasty ; and if there were at least twelve

Pasdeloups, there were not less than fourteen Deromes all booksellers and binders from the reign of Louis XIV. The most celebrated was Jacques Antoine, who died in 1761.

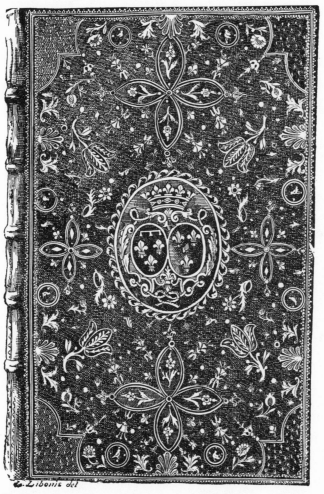

Fig. 172.—Mosaic binding of the eighteenth century, with the arms of the Regent. M. Morgand's collection.

Pierre Paul Dubuisson was not only a binder; he was also a draughtsman. He designed heraldic ornaments, and models for gilding tools, in which his contemporaries emulated him. He

was intimate with the delicate vignettist Eisen, and the counsels
of an artist of his merit could not but be useful to him. It is
an extraordinary thing that in this world of celebrated printers,
amateur financiers, and notable painters and engravers, not a
single man should have been found to give a real impulse to
the art of which we speak, and to prevent the dull continuance
of experiments on the whole so poor. Doubtless the *dentelles*
of Derome had a certain air of gaiety, to which the books of
the eighteenth century accommodated themselves perfectly; the
tools of Dubuisson produce most pleasing designs; but the old,
the great binders, had altogether disappeared.

Besides, Derome massacred without pity the rarest works.
He loved edges very regularly cut, and he did not fail to hew
down margins opposed to his taste. He sawed books as well;
that is to say, in place of sewing the sheets on to projecting
bands, he made a groove in the back, in which the cord was
embedded. The books bound by him have no wear.

To these celebrated names of French binders of the eighteenth century we may add Le Monnier, who worked for the
Orleans princes; Tessier, his successor; Laferté, who decorated
the small volumes of the Duc de la Vallière as Chamot covered
the large ones; in 1766 Chamot was royal binder. There was
also Pierre Engerrand, then Biziaux, an original, who worked
for Madame de Pompadour and Beaumarchais. Boyet, or
Boyer, worked (1670-80) in the style of Le Gascon, with the
same minute tooling, but simpler in character. Duseuil put very
elaborate and delicate tooling on his covers from about 1710
to 1720.

The Revolution destroyed many of the fine works which
displayed the symbols of royalty or nobility, and Mercier wrote
certain wicked little poems against binding. Lesné was the

poet of bookbinding, and he invented the process of bare limp calf without boards. Certainly from Grolier to Lesné there were numerous changes, so numerous that, in spite of the bare calf, it may be said that the art was nearly dead. In our days it has a little recovered. Amateurs have found new names, and often artists, to patronise : Trautz-Bauzonnet, Capé, Duru, Lortic, Marius-Michel, in France ; Bedford, Rivière (whose tree-calf bindings deserve to be mentioned), Zaehnsdorf (who is justly renowned for his excellent workmanship, and has himself written a work on the Art of Bookbinding), Pratt, etc., in England ; Matthews, Bradstreet, Smith, in the United States ; and many others. Unhappily, fortune does not permit everyone to furnish his library luxuriously ; the true connoisseur searches rather for Groliers, Eves, and Le Gascons, than concerns himself about modern workmanship. Whatever may be its value, it is only fit to clothe the works of the present time. A book published by Lemerre and bound by Petit is in true character, but a fifteenth or sixteenth century book that has passed under the hands of Trautz-Bauzonnet, or Lortic, will be very much like an ancient enamel in a modern frame newly gilt. An old book in its original binding, even if shabby, has a certain charm and character of its own, which is quite wanting when presented in a modern dress.

Bookbinding in England has, with very few exceptions, never attained the artistic excellence reached in France. From the fifteenth century to the end of the sixteenth all the best work was executed by foreigners ; amongst the most noteworthy of these were Thomas Berthelet, printer and binder to Henry VIII. and Edward VI., and the unknown binder employed by Robert Dudley, Earl of Leicester. John Gibson of Edinburgh, who was appointed bookbinder to James VI., King of Scotland, in 1581 ; Robert Barker and John Norton, binders to James after his accession to the English throne ; Samuel Mearne, binder to Charles II. ; and Zuckerman, were all good binders, but most of their work is a mere imitation of foreign designs. The one purely original English binder is Roger Payne, who learnt his craft from Mr. Pote, bookseller to Eton College, and from about 1767 worked for thirty years in London, performing with his own hands every stage of the work, even to cutting his own tools. The result was good, solid work, with perfectly original and often beautiful decoration, appropriate to the character of the work itself. His favourite style was drooping lines of leaf ornaments in the borders and geometrical patterns produced by small tools. After him came C. Kalthoeber, a German, who worked much in the same style ; Charles Lewis, who was an artist in the true sense of the word, and, coming down to our own time, Francis Bedford, who, never pretending to originality, copied the best designs of the French and Italian binders of the Renascence and later periods. His full calf books, with handsomely tooled backs, are models of solidity and taste ; and his decorations on the sides of morocco-bound books are always in good taste, and often of great elegance.

Parallel with the luxurious bindings with which we have been exclusively occupied, there has always been the commercial work, prepared in numbers for the trade. In the fourteenth, fifteenth and sixteenth centuries, panel stamps were much used for this class of work. Later on plates were engraved with imitations of tooled work, and applied to the sides by a press, parts being sometimes afterwards finished by hand to make the work appear to have been executed by the skill of the craftsman. The interlacings of Grolier and the delicate work of the Eves and the Parisian binders of the seventeenth century were imitated in this manner. If bindings adorned with panel stamps can hardly be considered works of art, they were at least honest work, and when the stamps were well designed and engraved and skilfully applied, the effect was often excellent; but the blocking of later times is hateful. Liturgical books, on which in old times so much loving care was expended, are now almost always bound in this manner, their purchasers apparently being satisfied so long as the covers are gorgeously gilt.

The interest in Fine Bindings seems, however, to be reviving, if we may judge from the number of the following important works which have lately appeared on this fascinating subject, viz. :—

Remarkable Bindings in the British Museum, with 60 monotint plates, described by H. B. Wheatley. 4to. London, 1889.

Manuel Historique et Bibliographique de l'Amateur de Reliures, par Léon Gruel. With 66 plates, 4to. Paris, 1887.

Facsimiles of Choice Examples of Historical and Artistic Bookbinding, by B. Quaritch. In parts of ten coloured plates each. Royal 8vo. London, 1889.

La Reliure Française depuis l'Invention de l'Imprimerie jusqu'à la Fin du 18ᵉ *Siècle,* par Marius-Michel. With 22 plates. 4to. Paris, 1880.

Les Reliures de l'Art à la Bibliothèque Nationale, par H. Bouchot. With 80 plates. Royal 8vo. Paris, 1888.

Album de Reliures Artistiques et Historiques, par le Bibliophile Julien. With plates. 4to. Paris, 1869-72.

La Reliure de Luxe, par L. Derome. With 63 plates. Royal 8vo. Paris.

La Reliure Moderne Artistique et Fantaisiste, par Octave Uzanne. With 72 plates. Royal 8vo. Paris.

La Reliure Ancienne, par Gustave Brunet. With 113 plates. Royal 8vo. Paris.

The Art of Bookbinding, by J. W. Zaehnsdorf.   8vo.   London, 1879.

On Bookbindings Ancient and Modern, by J. Cundall.   With 28 facs.-plates of bookbinding.   4to.   London, 1881.

Facsimiles of Old Bookbinding in the Collection of James Gibson Craig.   With 27 beautiful plates in chromolith.   Folio.   Edinburgh, 1882.

L'Ornamentation des Reliures Modernes, by Marius Michel.   With numerous illustrations and 16 plates of reproductions.   8vo.   Paris, 1889.

Armorial du Bibliophile, by Joannis Guigard.   2 vols. 4to.   Paris, 1873.

Nouvel Armorial du Bibliophile, by Joannis Guigard.   2 vols. 8vo.   With 2,500 Armoiries.   Paris, 1889.

LIBRARIES.

RT, science and literature took re-
fuge in convents in the Middle
Ages, before the invention of printing, and libraries
did not count many books. According to daily wants, the monastery
scribes copied the treatises lent by
neighbouring houses, and the collection was thus painfully made
during many centuries. Two or

three hundred works constituted ordinary collections ; the powerful abbeys found in their staff the means of enriching their libraries, and the products of the skill of the scribe and the illuminator were objects of commerce. Some of the MSS. were magnificent in their costly beauty.

Excepting kings and some princes, few people possessed a library. The great expense of transcription, the want of facility for procuring originals, and the enormous price of manuscripts left no hope to bibliophiles of moderate fortune. Typography, on the contrary, having multiplied books and put at relatively modest prices reproductions formerly inaccessible, private collections commenced. We have had occasion to speak before of Grolier and Maioli ; they were the most illustrious, but not the only ones.

At first a public library was an unknown thing. There was a greater dearth of readers than of books, and yet the needs of students and scholars led to devices in which the principle of the modern library is involved. Perhaps the richest library of the Middle Ages and the Renaissance was that of the King of France, but it was a private and not a public library. Since the time of Jean le Bon the acquisitions had been numerous, and Gutenberg's invention contributed to augment the stock of volumes everywhere. Charles VIII. and Louis XII. found or "conveyed" in their expeditions in Italy, and were able to add to the original nucleus, many rare editions, especially from the Sforzas at Pavia, who had in their collections marvels without number. Brought together at Blois, under the care of Jean de Labarre, the royal library did not yet occupy a very large space, in spite of its increase. Under Charles V. the number of books was about a thousand ; about 1500 or 1510 they were nearly doubled, but the printed books did not number more than two hundred.

So restricted, the royal library travelled with the other treasures of the Crown ; Francis I. transported it from Blois to Fontainebleau, and parts of it even went with the King to the Italian wars, as related above. In its new quarters the royal collection, in spite of the successive accessions of the books of Jean d'Angoulême, grandfather of the King, and of those of the dukes of Orleans, counted but 1,781 manuscripts and a hundred and nine printed books on the shelves. The King, ambitious in literature no less than in arts, nominated an illustrious *savant*, Guillaume Budé, to the office of keeper of his library ; and this office was maintained by his successors until the fall of the royal power.

With Budé commenced the system of continuous acquisitions. The treasury was liberally opened to vendors of rarities. At this time the books, placed upon their sides, one upon another, gave no idea of a modern library, with its volumes ranged on end, having their titles between the bands of the back. In speaking of Grolier, we remarked that the sides of a binding alone had importance on account of their place on the shelves ; it was the same with Francis I.

Under Henry II. the Fontainebleau collection was somewhat pillaged for Diana of Poitiers, but, as a corrective for this dilapidation, the King adopted a measure, since preserved, which substituted for acquisitions a regular and uninterrupted supply ; this was the contribution by publishers to the library of one bound copy on vellum of all the works printed under privilege. The ordinance was made in 1556 ; the successors of Henry II. had only this means of increasing the number of their volumes, with the exception that Charles IX. expended a large sum in the purchase of Grolier's collection of medals.

Such was the working of the royal library for about a half-century, but the idea of making it public had not come. Diffused as was then the passion for books, it had not yet been popularized to the point of being understood by the public at large. Amateurs and lovers of reading formed special collections in their houses, at times rivalling that of the King. Then the fashion was no more to lay the books on their sides, but they were now ranged to allow room for new acquisitions. Henry IV., who had not his great-uncle's predilection for Fontainebleau, commanded the removal to Paris of the books buried in the castle. He added to them those of Catherine de Medici coming from Marshal Strozzi ; and as the college of Clermont had become vacant by the dispersion of the Jesuits, he lodged the library in 1599 in one of the rooms of that establishment, under the care of Jacques Auguste de Thou, keeper of the library.

We now see the royal collection brought to Paris, which it has never quitted ; but before its definitive installation, before it was made public, it passed through a century, during which additions were made, purchases increased, and the number of manuscripts and printed books augmented in enormous proportions. Henry IV. desired to place it near the court, to avoid pillage and to have the chief librarian near to him. The return of the Jesuits in 1604 upset the first establishment a little ; the college of Clermont was evacuated ; the books were transported to the Cordeliers and distributed in rooms on the ground and first floors, whence the names of upper and lower libraries. There was a mass of volumes very little used, for the public did not enjoy them, and the King held them as his own ; but the time was near when the collection was to take a very serious step under the influence of the brothers Dupuy in 1645, and afterwards of Jerome Bignon. Always shut up in the incommodious chambers of the Cordeliers, the library contained 5,259 volumes, manuscript and printed, perhaps less than some private libraries ; after the Dupuys it had at least 10,329 printed books.

Mazarin was the first to comprehend the natural use of collections of books : publicity. His private library, placed before 1651 in his magnificent house in the Rue Richelieu, where later the royal library was definitively lodged, was opened to readers every Tuesday, from eight to eleven and two to five. Dispersed in 1651, at the fall of the Cardinal, it was later reconstituted, and in less than ten years afterwards the former minister was able to open it in its new quarters, the College of the Four Nations, where it is still.

While the Mazarine library was administering liberally to the wants of the public, that of the King remained closely shut up in the rooms of the Cordeliers. To remedy this state of things, Colbert offered two houses in the Rue Vivienne to the King, where the books could find a more convenient lodging, and allow room for increase. The removal was made in 1666. The royal collection for fifty-five years was lodged only a few steps from its final resting-place, the Hôtel de Nevers. So was called at the end of the seventeenth century the splendid mansion of Mazarin, situated near the Porte de Richelieu, in the street of the same name, whence his books had been previously torn and sold to all the dealers. Divided into two parts at the death of the Cardinal in 1661, the palace fell to his nephews, one part to the Duc de Mazarin, the other to the Duc de Nevers. At first the King dreamed, under the advice of Louvois, of acquiring the land in the neighbourhood of the Rue Vivienne and of elevating a monument for his library, for the thought of putting the Hotel de Nevers to this use had not then occurred to him; but the Duc de Mazarin having alienated his part of the palace in favour of the Company of the Indies, Abbé Bignon, then royal librarian, understood the advantage he could derive from the acquisition.

Thanks to the administration of Colbert and the liberalities of the King, the collection had been augmented threefold. At the time of the removal to the Rue Vivenne, Nicolas Clément worked at the classifying and cataloguing of 35,000 volumes. He distributed them into methodical classes, and devoted nine years—1675 to 1684—to his work. But this first arrangement was soon insufficient. Less than four years after, he commenced a new inventory in twenty-one volumes, which occupied thirty years, having been finished in the course of March, 1714. This time the numbers amounted to 43,000 printed volumes; his twenty-three principal divisions, containing all the letters of the alphabet, are very nearly preserved up to our day. In 1697 the question of publishing this enormous work was agitated, and on this point Clément had a curious correspondence with a learned Dane named Frederick Bostgaard; he also, in a celebrated pamphlet, *Idée d'une Nouvelle Manière de dresser le Catalogue d'une Bibliothèque*, made some practical observations. He resolved this arduous question in favour of arrangement of important collections by difference of sizes; but his project was not executed, although favoured from the first by Abbé Bignon.

As the collection was not available for workers, the work of Clément had only a relative importance. A councillor of the Prince of Waldeck, a German of the name of Nemeitz, who travelled in France in the beginning of the eighteenth century, having seen it in the houses of the Rue Vivienne, says that the library occupied then twenty-six rooms and contained 75,000 volumes in all; it was shown readily to visitors, but not to the general public. Nemeitz gives some other curious particulars as to the libraries of Paris (*Séjour à Paris:* Leyde, 1727, 8vo).

The bank of Law, that had been lodged for some time in the Hotel de Nevers, alienated by the heirs of Mazarin, soon disappeared with the ruin of his system. As we have said above, Bignon appreciated the importance of the neglected palace for commodiously lodging the royal collections. This was in 1721. The collection was about to be subdivided into four sections, or, as they were then called in the administrative style, four distinct departments: manuscripts, printed books, titles, and engraved plates. The keeper of the library pressed the Regent to profit by the occasion, to which he agreed. In the month of September the removal commenced, and from the Rue Vivienne, the royal library, the first in the world and the most valuable, as Naudé says, entered the former palace of the Cardinal, which it was never to quit again.

We approach the epoch when the private character of this great scientific establishment was definitely to cease, and it was to open its doors to the learned of all countries. In 1735 it was decided to print the catalogue of some divisions only: theology, canonical law, public law, and *belles lettres.* This resolution coincided precisely with the opening of the doors which took place in 1737, in which year appeared the first volume of the catalogue comprising the sacred Scriptures. At the end of the eighteenth century the royal library was finally established; the printed books then comprised about 200,000 volumes, and access was had by a staircase leading to six grand saloons, which were surrounded by galleries. From this moment the rooms became too small. At the Revolution the number of books had increased to 300,000, and projects of enlargement commenced and have continued to our time; but, in spite of these proposals, the surface occupied by the library has remained the same since the time of Louis XV. Enlargements and alterations have been made year after year on the same ground without much new construction. But how the treasures have been augmented to this time! If the printed books at the Revolution represented a little more than 300,000 volumes, to-day they exceed two millions; the prints number two and a half millions; the medals 100,000; the manuscripts, something over 90,000.

If we have thus brought the summary history of the National Library of Paris to our days, it was to avoid mixing it with other matters. We have entered into such detail regarding it as is fitting to an institution which is, next to the British Museum, the most important library in the world. We now return to the seventeenth century.

At the time when Henry IV. carried from Fontainebleau to Paris the nucleus of volumes that was to have so brilliant a destiny, the passion for books had singularly spread itself in France. We have already spoken of Mazarin ; after him Cardinal Richelieu designed to open his private collection to the public, and in his will he manifested his clearly held intention. He went further in his last wishes : he pre-scribed the daily sweeping and dusting of the precious collection, and its augmentation by a thousand livres tournois each year. The great personages of the time were not behind ; and Sauval says that in the seventeenth century there were 1,000 or 1,200 private libraries in Paris, numbering 1,700,000 volumes.

In the provinces there were few public libraries. The communities and learned Societies, the Jesuits and other religious houses, and the universities had collections. At Orleans a library was opened for Germans, and the students of that country were able to work at their ease under the supervision of two librarians.

At the end of the eighteenth century the number of libraries had increased in large proportions; the amateurs had made their influence felt. The Book was not sought only for what it contained, but also for its exterior clothing. Only the great libraries open to everybody remained eclectic, and provided a little of everything. Besides the royal library, there were in Paris a great number of other collections, many of which the revolutionary storm upset or destroyed. That of St. Germain des Près was burnt in 1794. That of St. Geneviève, founded in 1625, had benefited by celebrated donations, among others those of the cardinals De Berulle and de la Rochefoucauld; the Arsenal, created by the Marquis de Paulmy, was successively enriched by important acquisitions, among which was the collection of the Duc de la Vallière. These collections still exist, and are open to the public, as also are the National Library, the Mazarine, the Sorbonne, the Museum, the School of Fine Arts, the City of Paris, the Institute, the Louvre, and the several scientific faculties.

The provinces have not been behind in the movement. Many of the great cities contain a considerable number of books easily accessible, among them the libraries of Bordeaux and Rouen, amounting to 150,000 volumes; Troyes and Besançon, 100,000, etc. Few important centres have less than

20,000. These collections have been generally founded by the acquisition of the books of those of the religious establishments closed by the Revolution.

In our time public libraries are augmented by the legal deposit, gifts of the State, legacies of private persons, and purchases. The legal deposit in France relates almost exclusively to the National Library, and proceeds from the measures taken by Henry II. in 1556. Each French printer has now to deposit a certain number of copies of the works that he issues, and these volumes go to swell the number of books in the Rue de Richelieu. At the rate of 30,000 a year, the time is easily anticipated and very near when the space will be found insufficient. Some measures will have to be taken.

Germany, the cradle of printing, was not favoured in the beginning. There was, however, at the close of the sixteenth century, in Wolfenbüttel, a little town in the duchy of Brunswick, a curious collection of books, in a detached building. The engraver Merian has preserved for us the physiognomy of this library, which in his time contained nearly 200,000 volumes. The rather low rooms were shelved all round; in the middle were cases of the height of a man, also filled with books; the readers helped themselves, and were seated for working. The exterior of the building, without being sumptuous, was isolated and detached. This collection now possesses the Bible, glass, and inkstand of Luther and his portrait by Lucas Cranach.

Another curious library, dating from 1575, is that of the university of Leyden. An engraving by Woudan shows its state in 1610, with its classifications and divisions. The books were ranged in cases provided with breast-high desks. The books were placed with the edges in front, and not as now, and were so attached that they could only be consulted in their place. Each body of shelving contained a series of authors : Theology, philosophy, mathematics, history, medicine, law, and literature. The room, of square shape, was lighted by windows right and left. Between the bays were portraits, views of cities, and maps. On the right, in a shrine, was enclosed the legacy of Joseph Scaliger. Communication was less liberal than at Wolfenbüttel ; the readers were obliged to take the books from the shelves themselves and read them standing before the desks.

In England the opportunity of forming a great national collection at the period of the dissolution of the monasteries was neglected. Even later, when much literary treasure might easily have been secured, the suggestions of Dee were unheeded, and it was not until the closing years of Elizabeth that the first great English library arose through the generosity of Sir Thomas Bodley, who in 1597 offered to the library of the university the volumes collected by him during his travels on the Continent, whose value exceeded £10,000. The first stone of a new building was laid in 1610, but from 1602 the collection was open to readers in a provisional locality. David Loggan, the engraver, has preserved for us interior views of the Bodleian of the seventeenth century. The rooms are disposed in the form of the letter H, with pavilions to east and west, united by a gallery. The books were and are still in the body of the library, placed against the walls, with tables and immovable seats. The volumes were not displaced ; they were consulted in their own place. Each room had two floors, with access to the second by stairs.

In London it was Sir Hans Sloane who had the idea of founding a great collection by offering to the State for £20,0ⁿ his collection of books, which was valued at £50,000. Created in 1753 by an Act of Parliament, the British Museum, as it was named, was quickly augmented by many private libraries, among which was the library of printed books and manuscripts collected by the kings of England from Henry VII. to William III., which was added in the reign of George II. The very extensive and valuable library formed by George III., and amounting to 250,000 volumes, was added by George IV. The Harleian collection added 7,500 volumes, and Sir Robert Cotton's manuscripts, which had been purchased by the nation in 1700, served to add to the importance of the new institution. To-day the printed books amount to 1,300,000, and are only surpassed by the National Library of France as well in number of books as in number of readers. This immense collection increases at a great rate, one source being the compulsory deposit of a copy of every new book in order to secure copyright. Donations and legacies are constantly being made, and an annual sum for purchases is voted by Parliament. The arrangements of the British Museum are on a most liberal scale for the convenience of the readers. The general catalogue, extending to more than 7,000 MS. volumes, is now in process of printing. The British Museum is the only one of the libraries of the first class that has undertaken such a gigantic task.

Besides the copy deposited by publishers in the British Museum, the law of copyright compels the deposit of four other copies, which go to augment the collections of the Bodleian Library of Oxford, the University Library of Cambridge, and the libraries of Edinburgh and Dublin.

For the Fine Arts the National Art Library, founded in 1852 at the South Kensington Museum, ought to be mentioned, which contains now the most important collection of Fine Art books in the world.

If we search among the cities of Europe where establishments of this kind are most honoured, Berlin will take the third place with 900,000 printed books and 20,000 manuscripts, preserved in the Royal Library. The building, constructed between 1775 and 1780, owes its special form to Frederick II., who desired that it should take the form of a chest of drawers. On the façade an inscription in the Latin tongue, suggested to the king from the Abbé Terrasson's Romance *Séthos* (1731), indicates that here is a spiritual refectory—*nutrimentum spiritus*. Following come Munich, with 800,000 printed books; Vienna, 400,000; Dresden, 300,000; then the universities: Leipzig, whose library, founded in 1409 and reorganised in 1830, contains 150,000 books and 2,000 manuscripts; Heidelberg; Göttingen, etc.

In Italy, Florence has, in the National Library, 400,000 volumes, which was formed in 1861 by the union of the famous Magliabecchi and the equally celebrated Laurentian, created by Cosmo de' Medici in the middle of the fifteenth century, and containing more than 8,000 manuscripts of an incalculable value. Milan has at the Brera a collection of 162,000 books and 50,000 medals, and at the Ambrosian, due to Cardinal Frederick Borromeo, 164,000 printed books and 8,000 manuscripts.

Rome possesses a dozen collections and celebrated deposits. The Vatican, not numerous, is most choice ; the importance of its manuscripts is known to the entire world, but only a pàrt of the 220,000 printed books are catalogued. The Library of Victor Emmanuel, formerly of the Jesuits, amounts to about 360,000 volumes. At Venice the Biblioteca Marciana has 260,000 volumes of printed books and some thousands of MSS. and documents.

The magnificent educational establishments in the form of public libraries provided in the United States deserve special mention. Nearly every city has its public library, supported by a small tax ; and many large libraries are wholly supported by private munificence. The first to be established was founded in 1732 by Benjamin Franklin in Philadelphia, and still exists as the Library Company ; many important bequests have been made to it, the latest being £200,000 by Dr. Richard Rush. The library now numbers 150,000 volumes. The Congressional Library of Washington, besides its annual income from Government, receives by deposit for copyright a copy of every work published in the United States ; it now has 565,000 volumes. There are next in importance the Boston Library with 450,000 and the Boston Athenæum with 220,000 volumes.

The Astor Library and the Lenox Library of New York were both founded and endowed by the families whose name they bear ; the former has 223,284 volumes, the latter 25,000. The city of Chicago recently fell heir to the magnificent sum of over one million sterling, bequeathed by Mr. Newberry for the establishment of a library of reference, and New York was benefited by the late Mr. Tilden to the extent of £800,000 for a public library.

When we have named the libraries of St. Petersburg and Moscow for Russia, Stockholm for Sweden, and the Escurial for Spain, we shall have mentioned very hastily the most important establishments in the world. For more than four centuries the love of books has preserved and fortified itself, and increases each day. If we were to endeavour to approximately imagine the number of printed books diffused, we should be frightened at it. It is by miles that to-day are counted the shelves of the National Library or of the British Museum ; and each year the production is accelerated, as is also the number of readers.

In conclusion we ought to mention the modern development of Free Public Libraries in England, and the popularisation of learning resulting from the introduction of the Public Libraries Act. The Free Libraries generally consist of a lending department with a reference library, which latter, in the case of the wealthier institutions, such as those in the great towns of Liverpool, Manchester and Birmingham, is very important indeed, and lends a special interest to the collection.

There are also Subscription, Collegiate and Learned Society Libraries, all of which, in addition to those which we have mentioned, have made the treasures of literature accessible to the many, which formerly were reserved for the few.

THE ART OF DESCRIBING AND CATALOGUING IN-CUNABULA, AND THE METHOD OF COLLECTING THEM.

O F all bibliographical inquiries none presents such formidable difficulties as that dealing with the art of printing during the fifteenth century. A well-drawn-up catalogue of "Incunabula," or works printed in the fifteenth century, is in itself a scientific achievement requiring as a preliminary condition not only an extensive knowledge of such first impressions, but also a thorough acquaintance with the history of mediæval printing in general. Doubtless this latter branch already forms the subject of a comprehensive literature; but it is precisely this very literature, teeming as it does with all kinds of errors, that causes the greatest embarrassment to the bibliographer, not unfrequently leading to absolutely false conclusions. An experience spread over many years is a fundamental condition of any really solid performance in this department.

Antiquarian lore of a scientific character and instinct must of course work in all directions, and can only incidentally expect to light upon incunabula, if only because of their greater rarity. Still certain definite rules and principles should be observed in the bibliographical descriptions which have to be made in trade or library catalogues of such first impressions as may occasionally come to light.

The object of the present chapter is to establish some norma or standard, which may be capable of general application, and of throwing as full a light even on apparently minute points, as is required for really important features in the description of incunabula. The whole subject is here treated entirely from the practical standpoint, and in such a way as to prove a welcome aid both to librarian and collector.

In descriptive catalogues of early books two points above all others should be attended to and kept carefully distinct. These are the statements that will have to be made :—

(*a*) Regarding the printed work as such, that is, as representing its class, as a copy of the edition; and

(*b*) Regarding the book in question specially and individually.

It is evident that the properties characteristic of the *printed work* as such, (*a*), will be equally characteristic of each and every copy of the same work. These are the points more fully detailed in the following enumeration.

·On the other hand, the special qualities possessed by the particular copy of the work to be catalogued, are peculiar to the *said copy alone*, occurring in no other, or only in a very few still extant specimens of the same issue.

Before proceeding to describe an early impression, it will be well under all circumstances to consult the subjoined bibliographical works, and first ascertain whether the work in question has been previously described. Nor should a mere casual agreement of authorities be always accepted as conclusive, unless they are found to be *fully* applicable to the copy in question. Slight differences may of course occur, but only such as regard the number of sheets, or trifling variations in the text. Should all statements accord, we may then rest satisfied with a brief summary, of which more further on.

The most valuable bibliographical aids for preparing catalogues of incunabula are the following :—

Hain, L., Repertorium Bibliographicum, in quo libri omnes ab arte typographica inventa usque ad annum MD. typis expressi . . . recensentur. 2 vols. in 4 tom., 8vo. Stuttgartiæ, 1826-38.

Panzer, G. W., Annales Typographici ab artis inventæ origine ad annum MD. Vols. i.-v., 4to. (Vols. vi.-xi. only contain works printed since 1501, hence need not here be considered.) Nurembergæ 1793-97.

Panzer, G. W., Annalen der älteren deutschen Literatur. With supplts. Nürnberg and Leipzig, 1788—1802

Campbell, F. A. G., Annales de la typographie néerlandaise au xvᵉ siècle With 2 suppls. 8vo. The Hague, 1874-84.

Brunet, J. Ch., Manuel du libraire et de l'amateur de livres. 6 vols., 8vo. Paris, 1860-65.

Graesse, J. G. Th., Trésor de livres rares et précieux ou nouveau dictionnaire bibliographique. 6 vols. and suppl., 4to. Dresden, 1859-69.

Holtrop, Joh. Gust. Monuments typogr. des Pays-Bas au XVᵐᵉ siècle. Collection de facsimile d'après les originaux conservés à la Bibl. Roy.

de la Haye et ailleurs. Avec 130 planches et 1 carte. XIII et 138 pp. Fol. La Haye, 1868.

Ebert, F. A. Allgem. bibliograph. Lexikon. 2 vols., 4to. Lpz., 1821-30.

Lowndes, W. Th. The Bibliographer's Manual of English Literature, containing an account of books published in Great Britain and Ireland since the invention of printing, with notes and prices. New edition, revised and enlarged by H. G. Bohn. 4 vols., 8vo. London, 1864.

And numerous special Bibliographies, which need not here be mentioned.

Foremost stands Hain's *Repertorium*, but for which, all bibliographical research in this domain would be seriously hampered. Those articles which in this work are marked by an * preceding the consecutive numbers, were seen and described by Hain himself. With extremely few exceptions these descriptions are made with minute accuracy, and may be regarded as the most trustworthy of their kind. The other articles are quotations from other sources, which however are not mentioned. The work itself, however, is no library catalogue, but should rather be described as a *theoretical* catalogue ; hence all particulars bearing on other copies than those under examination are omitted.

Next in importance comes Panzer's *Annales*, which also offers valuable and welcome aids, but which should be consulted with some caution. It is especially defective in not giving perfectly accurate copies of titles, the linear divisions not being retained, and the abbreviations being given in full. On the other hand, the alphabetical arrangement according to the place of printing presents many advantages.

Brunet's and Graesse's large bibliographical works are very incomplete as regards early books, although still valuable as supplements to Hain and Panzer.

Campbell's *Annales* comprises Netherlandish works alone, but for this group it may be described as an excellent work of reference, fulfilling all reasonable requirements.

The present essay is intended not only to guide professional librarians and booksellers in preparing systematic catalogues of incunabula on a uniform plan, but also to indicate the right road to tyros in this field. Hence divers matters will have to be touched upon with which many must be familiar, while other points will be dealt with in detail which may in themselves seem trivial. In studies needing minute accuracy, things apparently insignificant are often of great importance.

We will now discuss more fully each separate point in those researches which have to be made with a view to correct and complete descriptions of incunabula. Here the student will find many practical hints which will enable him the more easily to grapple with certain technical and other difficulties.

1. The Author's Name.

Titles, or title pages as now understood, do not, strictly speaking, occur in early printed books, although there are some fifteenth-century books with title pages, but they are the minority. The typographers of the fifteenth century began their works just as in mediæval manuscripts, which start at once with the text proper, the *first words* alone indicating the contents of the book. We often meet with such expressions as " *Incipit liber* . . . " or " Here begins . . . ." A preface, an epistle, a register, or the like, very frequently precedes the text itself, and here as a rule will be found the name of the author. Frequently it is to be found in the summary at the beginning of the text.

But should the beginning of the book be searched in vain, then the concluding page must be consulted for title and author. It was in fact a universal practice to introduce at the end title, author, printing place, printer, and date; and such concluding paragraphs were known by the name of "Colophon" or "Rubrum." The latter term was due to the fact that in manuscripts such endings were sometimes written in red ink. They were also, especially during the first period, impressed in red in printed works, after the work was finished. These concluding paragraphs, however, are frequently absent, or else are limited to a few words, such as "*Finis*," "*Explicit liber*," "*Hic est Finis*," "Here ends," and so on.

When a name has at last been discovered, no time should be lost in consulting Hain's *Repertorium*. Then the title of the work will soon be found, even though the *same* incunabulum may not be indicated. The name of the author (always in the nominative case and independently of the form in the text) must then be entered in such a way that the by-name or surname, by which the author is actually known, shall always stand first. Then should follow the Christian name, which it will be best to give in full, without abbreviation. Owing to the numerous homonymous names current in mediæval times, it will be further necessary to add in brackets the author's position or distinctive title. For instance : Antoninus [Archiep. Florent.] ; Antonio S. de Padova ; Antonio Bettini de Siena [Vescovo di Fuligno], etc.

2. TITLE OF THE WORK.

The title of the work will also for the most part be found simultaneously with the name of the author.

Where any of the above-mentioned bibliographical works, and especially Hain and Panzer, give a full description of the incunabulum, including an accurate reproduction of the initial and final lines with all abbreviations and linear divisions, it will suffice to give in full those words alone that constitute

the title of the work, according to modern usage and orthography. For instance : Augustinus, S. Aurel., De Civitate
Dei libri xxii. ; or, Breydenbach, Bern. de, Heilige Reisen,
etc. In this case we may dispense with a complete copy of
the initial and final lines, and for all the rest refer the reader
to Hain or Panzer.

But where the work has not yet been accurately described,
it must here be at once dealt with more fully, without
prejudice to the reproduction of the title, which has to be
given later on. For instance : Ailliaco, Petrus de, Tractatus
de anima. editus a dño petro de Ailliaco.

3. The Dating.

By the dating of an incunabulum is understood the indication,
mostly contained in the colophon, of the place, printer and
year of issue. The dating may be :

(*a*) Complete, when all three of these points are in
evidence ; or,

(*b*) Incomplete, when one or two of these statements are
missing ; or,

(*c*) The dating may be absent altogether.

In the first case these data (place, printer, and year) must
be briefly mentioned. Thus : Breydenbach, Bern. de, Heilige
Reisen. Augsburg, Anton Sorg, 1488. In the second case
the absence of one or other of these particulars must be
specified, for which purpose the following abbreviations are
employed :—

1. If the place alone be missing, *s. l.* (sine loco).
2. If the printer alone be missing, *s. t.* (sine typographo).
3. If the year alone be missing, *s. a.* (sine anno).
4. If both place and printer, *s. a. et t.* (sine anno et typographo).

5. If both place and year, *s. l. et. a.* (sine loco et anno).

6. If printer and year, *s. t. et a.* (sine typographo et anno).

7. If all, *s. n.* (sine nota, or absque ulla nota).

Now it is the business of bibliographers to supply these missing data. In many cases the bibliographical works of reference give the required information ; but in many cases they fail to do so.

When the data in question have been determined, the names of place, printer and year are to be added in brackets. For more easy reference round brackets ( ) are recommended to be used in the first instance, square [ ] in the second. Thus : Biblia latina (   ) [Strassburg, Joh. Mentel, circa 1463].

4. THE SIZE.

The determination of the size may present difficulties, inasmuch as small folio and quarto, or small quarto and octavo, may be confounded. But a sure means of distinguishing between these several forms is afforded by the position of the wire-lines of the paper. When held to the light the paper shows the thin narrow laid wires which are divided by a number of straight lines standing wider apart, called *chain wires ;* when the chain wires run horizontally the book is a quarto, vertically a folio or an octavo. This principle is simply explained from the fact that the mould used by the old paper makers was a wire sieve, in which the vertical and thicker chain wires reappear in the paper. The chain wires always running from top to bottom, the sheet when folded makes a folio with straight lines, and when the folio is folded again it makes a quarto with horizontal lines.

5. Detailed Reproduction of Title.

Should the particulars given in Hain or Panzer not fully accord with the printed work in hand, or should the said work not be mentioned at all, then, besides the above-described short statement of the title to be always given for the synoptic arrangement, a complete copy must be made both of the initial lines and of the colophon. Attention must be paid to the orthography, the abbreviations, the disposition of the lines (these being indicated by a vertical stroke |), the over and under-lined letters, the marks of abbreviation (for instance a reversed *c ɔ* for *con*, a *9* for *us*, the sign ꝝ, resembling the figure 4, for *rum*, *ʟ* for *et*, *ȝ* for *ue*, and so on), and all must be faithfully copied. When the catalogue has to be printed, these signs must be specially cast, as they are not often found in our modern printing offices.

To spell out the abbreviations, as French bibliographers are especially fond of doing, is the one sure means of making "confusion worse confounded." Let this practice be therefore carefully avoided. Those who have much to do with early books will soon learn to decipher the abbreviations, which in fact present not the slightest difficulty. On the other hand, the restoration of the abbreviations from the reduced texts is often impossible, because they are frequently used in a perfectly arbitrary way. For instance, *domini* may be shortened *dñi*, or *dōini*, or *domīi*, and such trivial discrepancies may easily lead to mistakes.

Obvious misprints in the text as well as in the date must of course be also accurately reproduced ; attention however may as a rule be drawn to such errors by appending a (*sic !*), or at least (!). The misprints are often so incredibly naïve, that one feels inclined to suspect a mistake in the rendering rather than in the original. Here it will suffice to mention the glaring instance of the colophon in the Mayence Breviary of 1457, where "spalmorum (!) codex" occurs instead of "psalmorum codex."

Between initial lines and colophon should be inserted : *At the end*, which in manuscript are underlined, and in print italicised. When title and final paragraph are very lengthy, words or clauses not needed for the understanding of the context may be omitted and indicated by dots, without however changing aught in the construction. It is also well to avoid substituting dots for the last words of lines, so that the linear division may remain perfectly clear.

To illustrate the foregoing with an example, we give here the description of *Schedel's Nuremberg Chronicle*. This well-known and widely-dispersed early book, which still frequently turns up, at once presents certain difficulties to the tyro. No author's name is to be found either at the beginning or in the colophon, and this is true both of the Latin and the German edition. The original Latin edition, printed in 1493 by Koberger in Nuremberg, begins with an alphabetical register; but no author's name can be discovered either in it or in the initial lines of the *Chronicle* itself, while the concluding paragraph is also silent on the point. Nevertheless the author gives his name, which occurs on p. 266*v*. Now the description of the work is to be made as follows :—

Schedel, Dr. Hartman, Liber chronicarum. Nuremberg, Ant. Koberger, 1493. Large Fol.

Leaf 1*r*. (woodcut title) (R)Egiſtrum | huius ope- | ris libri cro- | nicarum | cū figuris et ymagi- | bus ab inicio mundi : | L. 1—20, *Register :* L. 21*r* (with *Nr. I*) : Epitoma operū ſex dierū de mūdi fabrica Prologus | L. 266*v*, line 23 :

Completo in famofiffima Nurembergenfi vrbe Operi | de hyftorijs etatum mundi.
ac defcriptione vrbium fe- | lix imponitur finis.   Collectum breui tempore Auxilio
docto | ris hartmäni Schedel. qua fieri potuit diligentia.   Anno xp̄i | Millefimo
quadringentefimo nonagefimotercio. die quarto | menfis Iunij. | *At the end,* L. *320v*:
(A) Deft nunc ftudiofe lector finis libri Cronicarum per | viam epithomatis ꝛ bre-
viarij compilati opus q̄dem | preclarum ꝛ a doctiffimo quoqꝛ comparandum.
Continet | . . . Ad in | tuitū autem ꝛ preces prouidorū ciuiū Sebaldi Schreyer | ꝛ
Sebaftiani kamermaifter hunc librum dominus Antho | nius koberger Nuremberge
impreffit.   Adhibitis tamē vi | ris. . . . Michaele | wolgemut et wilhelmo Pleyden-
wurff. quarū folerti acu- | ratiffimaqꝛ animadverfione tum ciuitatum tum illuftrium
| virorum figure inferte funt.   Confummatū autem duodeci | ma menfis Iulij.
Anno falutis nr̄e. 1493. | L. *321r*: De Sarmacia regione Europe. L. *325v*, last
line : Laus deo.

6. The Collation and the Number of Leaves.

It will not suffice simply to count the leaves of the book
as it stands, which would in fact be quite useless. We must
also ascertain whether the work is complete. For this purpose
a careful examination must be made of the collation of the
sheets. Even in the case of bound books this can be quite
easily done by slightly bending them somewhat further back
at the places corresponding with the several sections ; it can
then be quite clearly seen at the upper or lower edge of
the back whether all the leaves of each sheet are perfect.
These sheets naturally consist always of a number of leaves
divisible by two.   There are sections of three, four, five or
six sheets, making six, eight, ten or twelve leaves ; but less
than three or more than six sheets very seldom occur in a
section.   In one and the same book, the number of sheets to
the section is usually the same.   Very frequently there occurs
at the beginning or end a blank leaf, which when forming
part of the section is reckoned in, but must be indicated as

such. Thus : 316 leaves [of which one blank]. If the number
of leaves in the collation is odd, we may be sure that a leaf
is missing.

But to ascertain whether any leaf is missing it will
be necessary to see that the text is consecutive at the end
of one and the beginning of the next page. This plan
is available in the case of incunabula which bear neither
signatures, catch-words nor pagination. After ascertaining that
the sheets are complete, the leaves must be separately counted,
in doing which the pages must always be completely turned
over. This will also afford an opportunity of noticing whether
any leaves happen to be torn, soiled or imperfect. It will
be well to number each leaf with a pencil in one corner, by
which it will also be possible in the description to refer to any
particular leaf or leaves. The front is indicated with *r* (*recto*),
the reverse with *v* (*verso*), as for instance on L. 176*r* woodcut.

If the book is perfect it will suffice to give the number
of leaves ; thus, (128 Ll., the last blank). If any leaves
be missing, the fact should be indicated in this same place ;
thus, 125 instead of 127 Ll., of which 11 and the last
[blank] L. missing. Should the number of leaves not correspond with that given for instance by Hain, this fact must
also be stated. Thus : 130 [not 128] Ll. ; or 174 [not 175
as stated by Hain], and so on. Here also a fixed form of
expression should be adhered to throughout.

The test of completeness will be greatly facilitated when the
work has

7. SIGNATURES, CATCH-WORDS, AND PAGINATION.

The sheets are signed, that is to say, below the text at
the foot of the page there occurs a letter which is repeated

on each consecutive sheet with a continuously increasing index number : A_1, A_2, A_3, and so on. Should a section consist, for instance, of three sheets, the signature on the first half of the first sheet will be A ; on the first half of the second sheet, A_2 ; on the first half of the third sheet, A_3 ; on the second half of the third sheet, A_4 ; on the second half of the second and first sheet there will be no signature. With sections consisting of four sheets the signatures run to A_5; of five sheets to A_6 ; of six sheets to A_7. But it should be noticed at once that the signature is not always present on the second half of sheets 3, 4, 5, or 6, but that the sheets are frequently signed on their first half alone. Many incunabula give at the end (often on a separate leaf) a register containing the first words of each page (of the first halves of the sections), as well as their signatures.

From the foregoing it will be easy to collate a book with signed sheets. The signatures run through the alphabet, U and W always omitted, and begin again with A (usually Aa or AA). Even should the leaves be numbered, it is still desirable to verify the signatures, as the numbering is very often wrong, whereas in the signatures misprints are scarcely ever found. It may happen, however, that the signatures are placed so far below the text that they have been cut away by the binder, in which case the book may appear to be without signatures. We may give as a case in point DUNS JOH. SCOTUS, *Quotlibeta quæstionum :* Venice, Alb. de Stendal, 1474. Hain, 6,433, says expressly without signatures ; Panzer, III., p. 104, cum sign.

In some incunabula we also occasionally come upon an apparently different kind of signature. Instead of letters numbers are used, so that, for instance, the first half of the section is numbered with 1, 2, 3, 4 ; the first half of the second, with 5, 6, 7, 8, etc. Or else instead of the ciphers

continuous letters, as, for instance, on the first section A, B, C, D ;
on the second, E, F, G, H, etc. ; and at times other combinations. As an interesting example, we may mention the following
Viennese work :—

GERSON, JOH., De confessione et absolutione. *At the end :*
Impressum wienne anno domini Mcccc lxxxii. 4to. This
work consists altogether of fourteen sheets, of which the first
eight form a section. Leaves 1, 2, 3, and 4 bear the signatures
A, B, C, D ; the second section consists of six sheets, of which
the first halves are signed E, F, G. All such deviations from
the usual system of signing must be expressly specified.

When pagination occurs, it must of course be verified ; when
folio numbers are partly present, partly absent, both must be
accurately stated, as must also be the presence or absence of
catch-words, that is, the first word of the next page below the
text. Thus : 212 Ll. sigt. without catch-word and pagination ;
or, 172 Ll. without sigt. catch-word and pagination ; or, when
pagination alone is given, 112 nos. Ll. no sigt. and catch-
word, etc.

8. THE SPACING.

By spacing is understood the manner of dividing the composition. The lines may run across the whole page (continuous
lines), or they may be disposed in 2, 3 or 4 columns. In theological and legal works it very frequently happens that the
matter is so arranged that the text proper appears enclosed by
the commentary, the latter in smaller type, but both arranged
in columns. Thus : 315 Ls. sigt. no catch-word and pagination
2 col. text enclosed by the comment. Moreover there not
seldom occur side-notes, which run down the outer edge of

the leaf, and which indicate the substance of the text. The presence of these marginal notes, as they are called, must be indicated in all cases.

Lastly, it must be ascertained whether the width of the columns (length of the lines) is uniform on all the pages. Here also there often occur remarkable discrepancies. The above-mentioned Gerson, *De Confessione*, presents an interesting example of this point also. On the first sheet the width of the composition is 91 *mm* ; on sheets 2 to 7 from 101 to 102 *mm* ; on sheet 8 again 91 *mm* ; on sheet 9, 107 ; sheet 10, 112 ; sheets 11 and 12, 121 ; sheet 13, 112 ; and sheet 14, 106 *mm*.

9. The Number of Lines.

Special importance attaches to the number of lines in a full page of text. We start from the assumption that the lines are not interrupted by the heading of chapters, sections or remarks (commentaries, interlinear versions, etc.). In the case of type varying in size, that of the text proper, and not that of the commentary is alone considered. Turn over the pages until you have found a full clear page of text, and then count the lines. It may happen that a work with running commentary may present not a single page of uninterrupted text. In this case the lines of the commentary running down the edge (not the marginal notes) are to be counted, and then it must be expressly stated that the given number is that of the commentary, not of the text. Thus : 315 Ls. sigt. no catch-word and pagination ; 2 cols. 54 lines [of the commentary]. Nor should you rest satisfied with counting one page, but test several in different parts of the book. The number of lines even in one and the same work is not always alike, and many discrepancies occur, especially in the earlier issues. The number of lines as determined must be recorded. Thus: 315 Ls. no sigt. catch-word and pagination; 2 cols. 27 and 28 lines. The larger or smaller number of lines on a full page of type often deter-mines the age of a printed work. It is a curious fact, highly interesting in the history of printing, that the number of lines increases with the development of the typographic art. It will suffice here to refer, for instance, to the first Bibles. Pfister's Bible has 36 lines; the Gutenberg Bible 42 ; that of Fust and Schoeffer (1462) 48 lines. This remark applies also to the number of lines in the old Donatus editions. Altogether it is evident that the number of lines plays an important part in determining or identifying imperfect incunabula.

10. THE FORMS OF TYPE.

The types of incunabula have either a Gothic or a Roman form, or else are a combination of both ; in which case they are called half or semi-Gothic. From the form of the Black-letter or Gothic has been derived the later "Swabian," and the modern German character, the "Fracturschrift," as it is called from its angular, jagged, pointed, broken forms. The semi-Gothic consists of Roman capitals and small letters of Gothic shape. The type used by Peter Schoeffer in his *Cronik der Sassen*, *Cuba*, *Hortus sanitatis*, Breydenbach's *Reisen*, has lost the black-letter or Gothic character, and should be called "Swabian."

11. MAJUSCULES, MINUSCULES, ABBREVIATIONS, PUNCTUATION.

Connected with the form of the types are the questions, whether different kinds of type are used, and if so how many kinds ; whether the initial letters (at the beginning of the sentence) appear printed off with the rest, or whether the space was reserved to be afterwards filled in by the " rubric-writer ; " to what extent abbreviations are employed ; whether several kinds of orthographic stops occur ; whether the spacing or general arrangement of the composition presents any peculiar features.

Should a printed work begin with a wood-cut initial, or with any ornamental majuscule distinct from the type in the text, but printed with the rest, and not painted or sketched in afterwards, in the copy of the title the fact must be at once recorded by bracketing all such initials. Thus, as already indicated in *Schedel's Chronicle :* (R)Egistrum . . . or (A)D est . . .). But when the space has been left free for the initial to be afterwards painted in, in the place of this initial we simply put an empty bracket, for instance, ( )Egistrum ; ( )Dest ; and this is done even when the initial in question has been *de facto* painted in the copy of the work to be catalogued.

Instead of the full stop Linhard Holl of Ulm, for instance, used little crosses, as did also Joh. Medemblick of Cologne and the Brothers of Common Life in Bruxelles ; and Goetz of Cologne substituted for the dot a letter z, taken from a smaller fount, while John Zainer of Ulm used in his first issues a full stop in the form of a little star, introducing it according to his own "sweet will."

Frequently the punctuation is omitted altogether, as in the first Viennese work : Meyger, *Tractatus distinctionum* 1482. Frequently also the lines are not quite straight, but uneven, and of unequal length, or else the register is crooked, the first and second forms do not coincide, and so on. Features such as these often give a clue to the age of the printed work.

Many letters have unusual forms, which point to particular printing offices. We may refer to John Mentelin of Strasburg with his "eccentric R;" to Nic. Goetz of Cologne with his Gothic V always set up awry; to Peter Friedberg of Mayence with his thick antique S introduced into the Gothic text; to George Huszner of Strasburg, who used a Roman H with a boss on the [lower side of the cross stroke; to Michael Reyser of Eichstädt and later of Würzburg, who used an identical H, but with the boss on the upper side of the cross-stroke; lastly to Günther Zainer of Augsburg, who applied similar bosses to his Roman H, I, L, M, N, and T. A remarkable Gothic S with two oblique cross-strokes distinguishes the types of the Strasburg printer, Joh. Prys, while Johann Schaffler of Ulm employs a reversed Gothic S when he runs short of D. Heinr. Quentel of Cologne scatters a *thick half-Roman* D over his Gothic printed matter. In the Latin and Greek works printed by Ch. Beyamus and J. Glim of Savigliano, the *d* has invariably a Gothic character. The dotted *i* is absent in Gering, Krantz and Freyburger's first Paris issues, as well as in those printed by Berth. Guldinbeck in Rome. We find this dot replaced by a half-crescent like a hood in the works issued by Alb. Pfister of Bamberg, and B. Gothan of Lübeck, as well as in the first Mayence publications. John of Spire, the first Venetian printer, uses the stroke for the hyphen and =, & for the final syllable *et*, as in *tac&, lic&,* for *tacet, licet.*

In many printed works we are struck by the variety of forms for one and the same letter, which would seem to point to a limited stock of type. Many offices, such as those of Conr. Zeninger of Nürnberg and Joh. Grüninger of Strasburg, were noted for the exceptional number of misprints in the works issued by them. All this makes it abundantly evident how important is the accurate observation of seemingly trivial points in identifying incunabula.

12. THE PRINTER'S INKS AND PRINTER'S MARKS.

Fust and Schoeffer already began to print in two colours, using even four in the *Psalterium* of 1457. The device was employed for emphasizing certain passages of the text, chapter headings, initial and final paragraphs and the like. As has already been explained, a large number of scribes and manuscript writers were thrown out of employment by the discovery of typography, and it may well be imagined that those early printers were exposed to serious agitation on the part of the writers' guilds. It is highly probable that some kind of compromise was arranged, the typographers, for instance, consenting to secure the writers some source of income by leaving the rubrics to be filled in by them; still we can readily understand that not all printers would be induced to yield even this point. Hence many printed works are found provided by the rubric writers with initial and final paragraphs, chapter headings, initial letters and stops, while others were simply printed off in red and black.

In others again there occur at the end, after the colophon, emblematic or symbolic representations, which were chosen by the respective offices as trade or printers' marks. The booksellers or publishers on their part adopted certain corresponding marks. Even so early as the fifteenth century the printer of a work was not always, as we mentioned before, its publisher. We often meet with the intimation that such-and-such a work has been printed by So-and-so at the charge of So-and-so. These circumstances may be mentioned in the general remarks whenever they are not implied in the detailed copy of the title-page. But from our standpoint the first consideration must always be for the printer. The points in question may be specified in the following way : 127 Ls. sigt. no catch-word and pagination, 2 cols. 30 lines Goth., with woodcut initials, red and black print; on L. 127*v* the printer's mark.

A special embellishment much affected by the Italian printers were the so-called " literæ florentes " ("flourishes"), which were first employed by the Augsburg typographer Erhard Ratdolt (at work in Venice from 1476 till 1486). These are initial letters elegantly formed of floral scrolls and ornaments, which Ratdolt borrowed from the Italian manuscripts and had carved in wood. They appear both in red and black print. As many incunabula owe their value to these "literæ florentes," prominence should be given to them in descriptive catalogues.

13. THE ARTISTIC GET-UP.

Pictorial decoration still plays the same part as in mediæval times. Illustrated works always found more admirers and purchasers than others, apart even from those for the under-standing of which illustrations were absolutely indispensable. Hence it is incumbent on the compiler of catalogues not only to indicate the kind of artistic embellishment, but also the number of woodcuts, initials (printed), borderings, etc. Where the re-spective wood engravers or draughtsmen are known, their names and monograms must of course also be mentioned. Should the work present no special interest as regards its general get-up (initials, borderings, etc.), it will be unnecessary to enumerate all the ornamental letters occurring in the text, the mere mention of the fact being in this case quite sufficient.

With many incunabula ornamented with woodcuts the interest

in the printed text falls into the background, the essential value of the work consisting in the illustrations. In this department protracted experience alone, combined with a taste for such things and a natural appreciation of the beautiful, can develop the genuine connoisseur. Hence special attention must be given to those incunabula which are adorned with wood or metal engravings. Let monograms and other marks be studied, the literature of the subject explored, or more experienced persons consulted. R. Muther's *Deutsche Bücherillustration der Gothik und Frührenaissance,* 1460 to 1530, fol. (Leipzig, 1884), may be recommended as a very valuable recent publication calculated to afford useful aid, especially to the young student. Care, however, should be taken to avoid basing on mere conjectures and the like, positive statements or conclusions, which may afterwards prove to be groundless.

14. BIBLIOGRAPHICAL DIRECTIONS.

The beginner would create many difficulties for himself by seeking for incunabula in the bibliographical works of reference above mentioned. In these works the arrangement of the title shows great diversity, and each system has its own justification. Thus Hain and Campbell give the authors in alphabetical order; Panzer in the *Annales* the arrangement according to localities, but in the German *Annalen* the chronological order; while some catalogues of antiquarians adopt that of the typographers and the period of their activity. Research would be greatly facilitated by a work comprising all four of these systems.

When the title in question has been determined and found to be in complete agreement with the work to be catalogued, the reference is made in the following way. In the case of Hain and Campbell, quote the number, taking care not to omit the above-mentioned *.   Thus : Hain 3756; or, Hain *5370.   In the case of Panzer quote the number of volume and page, thus: Panzer, iii., p. 560 ; or, Panzer, *Deutsche Ann.*, p. 73 ; Panzer, *Supplement*, p. 15, etc., etc.   But references will also have to be made to other bibliographical works, Hain and Panzer being in many respects defective.   Recent investigation has given rise to numerous monographs on particular printing places, printers, etc. These monographs contain much useful material, and consequently should be consulted in descriptions of incunabula laying claim to scientific value.

15. QUALITY OF THE PAPER—EDITIONS ON VELLUM.

At all times the bitterest enemies, while on the other hand the greatest embellishers, of the book have been the binders! They must be reproached with incredible sins against good taste, as well as pitiless inroads on the artistic equipment. With Vandalic barbarism they have cut away the most lovely miniatures, initials, borders, woodcuts, and not seldom even a slice of the text itself.   But they were not the only criminals, and many "collectors" of the choicest typographical treasures have also deserved to be impaled.   Who has not heard of the abbot with "symmetry" on the brain, who ruthlessly caused the incunabula of the convent library to be all bound of one size, so that the book-shelves might present a symmetrical appearance ?   Those that were found to be too big had to be cut down !   Next to these foes the greatest havoc has been made by "the tooth of time."   Hence it is always to be regarded as a rare chance when an otherwise well-preserved incunabulum has also retained its wide paper margin and rough edges, and this point should always be mentioned.   But most precious of all are those incunabula that have remained uncut, though such cases are doubtless excessively rare. The sheets seldom preserve their natural edge, which, in the case of hand-made paper, is of course never a straight line, and which, owing to its scrubby appearance, is said to be with rough edges or "bearded" (*cum barbis*). All such specimens are highly prized.

Besides the paper edition, at most a few copies were struck off on vellum, and these, owing to the small number printed and the high price of the material, were always very costly.

In this connection a few words may be devoted to the watermarks, which have also not unfrequently considerable weight in determining a printed work of the fifteenth century. The paper mills made use of certain signs as marks for the various descriptions of paper produced by them, and these marks were impressed on each sheet while being manufactured. The number of such marks is legion. Unfortunately no systematic work has yet appeared on the water-marks ("filigree") peculiar to German papers. For France, an excellent work is the *Etude sur les Filigrans des Papiers Employés en France aux* 14ᵉ *et* 15ᵉ *Siècles*, by Midou and Matton (Paris: 1868), and *La Legende Paléographique du Papier de Coton*, par C. M. Briquet (Genève: 1884). The subject of watermarks has, however, been incidentally discussed by B. Hausmann (*Albert Dürer's Copperplates*); by Dr. Fr. Wibiral (*Anthony van Dyck*); by Weigel and Zestermann (*Anfänge der Druckerkunst*); by C. M. Briquet (*Papiers et Filigranes des Archives de Gènes* 1154—1700. Basle: 1888); and in many earlier works, such as B. G. Fischer's *Versuch die Papierzeichen als Kennzeichen der Alterthumskunde anzuwenden* (Nürnberg: 1084), as well as sporadically in monographs and periodicals (*Gazette des Beaux Arts*, vols. ii.-iv., viii. and ix.), and in cyclopedias, as, for instance, the article on *Wassermarke* in *Ebert's Bibliograph. Lexicon.*

Meanwhile it will be advisable to specify the kind of watermark or watermarks in the case of all undated and hitherto undescribed incunabula. There is, however, amongst bibliographers a temptation to exaggerate the use and importance of watermarks as evidence of the date of undated documents, as the manufacture of paper was sometimes post-dated or represents the makes of many mills through many years.

16. RUBRICS, COLOURING, MINIATURES.

As already stated, the printer often left a part of his work to be completed by the scribe. In the first years of the new invention, the typographers were fain to make their products resemble as closely as possible the manuscripts hitherto in vogue. Every invention has always been and is still looked upon with a certain degree of suspicion ; so difficult is it to break with long-standing usages to which people have become endeared. With all the more hostility must an invention have been regarded, which was calculated to direct intellectual life and work into new channels. The view, as mentioned before, that the first typographers issued their printed works as manuscripts, although questioned by many, may nevertheless be accepted as prevalent. The *Psalterium* of 1457, one of the masterpieces of the Fust-Schoeffer press, can in fact at the first glance scarcely be distinguished from a manuscript.

Hence before being exposed for sale, the first books were handed over to the scribe (Clericus, Rubricator), who filled in the spaces reserved in the printing with the required letters, sentences, headings, signatures, etc., in coloured ink. This work we call rubricking, because usually executed in a red (*ruber*) colour. Many printing offices kept their own rubricators, and the work was also carried on in the monasteries. But it absorbed much time, and could not always be got through rapidly enough to meet the demand for the new work, and thus it happened that non-rubricated copies got into circulation. Nor is it improbable that the price of rubricated and non-rubricated books varied; many buyers, especially monasteries which possessed every facility for supplying the rubrics themselves, would in fact prefer the non-rubricated copies, owing to their lower price. At the end of many rubricated incunabula, we often find notices introduced by the scribe giving information on the date, the owner, the place, the price, and so on. Such notes are also called hand rubrics; nor is it necessary specially to dwell on the great value these notes must often have had, and still have, in determining or identifying undated incunabula.

The process was executed in divers ways. Doubtless as a rule the scribe was satisfied with filling in the missing initial letters, stops, beginning of chapter, sentence or verse, after numbering of the pages and so on. But we frequently come upon old printed works with initials, borderings, and lastly, whole pictures, in fact MINIATURES, all beautifully ornamented in gold and various colours. In these incunabula veritable works of art have often been preserved, which, thanks to their execution and state of preservation, represent a considerable value. It will be the duty of the compiler of the catalogue to describe the manner and style of these artistic embellishments, to determine the school of art to which the painting belongs, and where needed to explain the composition.

In the case of incunabula ornamented with woodcuts, it should be specified whether the woodcuts are coloured, and if so, to what period the colouring should be assigned.

17. THE HAND RUBRICS.

It has already been stated in dealing with the rubrics, that the notices made by the rubricators are deserving of attention. But we occasionally meet with notes by another contemporary or later hand, the intrinsic value of which as bearing on the subject under discussion will have to be tested. Hand rubrics of this class often give useful information regarding the former owner of the work, its price, date and place.

18. DETAILED DESCRIPTION OF THE BINDING.

Bindings remarkable for their artistic execution, or otherwise presenting features of historical interest, will require a more detailed description. Many bear, as we have seen in the chapter on Bindings, on the outside fine impressions of family arms, portraits, dates, mottoes, etc., all of which are to be mentioned according to their importance. Extant book plates (*ex libris*), occurring mostly on the inside of the front cover, library stamps and similar indications, should be noted. For bindings of French origin, most valuable information is given in J. Guigard's excellent work, *Armorial du Bibliophile*, 2 tom. (Paris : 1870-73).

But our attention should not be exclusively devoted to the beauty of the binding, for there are other standpoints from which old bindings have to be considered. And first and foremost there is the age, the approximate determination of which is, however, a question of experience. In the case of undated works, the source and origin of the binding often present numerous clues for their identification. In general it must be assumed that during the fifteenth century scarcely any except bound books were exposed for sale. The modern intermediate process of stitching in wrappers was scarcely convenient, if only because of the very bulk of the incunabula. Smaller issues alone in 4to or 8vo, and then only when limited in size to a single sheet, can have been disposed of in the stitched form, and even these were doubtless protected by stout wrappers. But here also the monastic establishments may have made an exception to the general rule. To these places the books were presumably consigned *in crudo*, that is, in the rough state, or in sheets, for one or more of the inmates would doubtless be skilled in the bookbinder's art.

It may accordingly be assumed that the original bindings of incunabula date from the time of their issue. In the case of collective volumes whose contents date from the period, we may without risk of error take it for granted that the dated and undated printed works forming part of the volume all belong to about the same period. In such cases we have often at hand the means of forming an estimate of the date of a work. In the same way the character (style) of the binding will often afford a clue to the country, and even to the very town, where the work has been printed.

Besides its age, we are also interested in the material of the binding. Incunabula were mostly bound in wood, which was entirely or half covered with leather, hogskin, or parchment. To attach the cover to the book itself, strips of parchment were used, and for this purpose were generally utilized useless or superfluous manuscripts, Donatus, Almanacks, letters of indulgence, stock inventories, etc. This explains how it happens that in taking old bindings to pieces, many a valuable find has been and may still be made. But in saying this, we do not of course recommend the wholesale destruction of old bindings with the probable result of finding nothing after all.

But on this point a few remarks may be found useful. Slips pasted to the insides of the covers, or even used as fly-leaves, have already yielded many treasures, such as leaflets, woodcuts, enamels, presentations, almanacks, playing-cards. We may refer to the first dated woodcut, " The St. Christopher" of 1423, mentioned in the first part of this work, which was discovered by the bibliographer Heinecken on the inside of a cover (the *Laus Virginis*, a manuscript of 1417) in the library of the Carthusian monastery at Buxheim. Unfortunately the days of such discoveries are well-nigh over; there are already too many vigilant eyes about. Still we would recommend bindings in boards to be always carefully examined, even when more recent than the fifteenth century. The old boards were mostly prepared by pasting together damaged sheets, many materials being thus used up which would at present possess some historic value.

Lastly, attention should be directed to the clasps, corner-pieces, hasps, fragments of chains, etc., as valuable specimens of the mediæval mechanical arts have often been preserved in such objects. It may be mentioned that in many libraries of the Middle Ages the books were secured with chains, a practice which naturally disappeared with the spread of typography and the consequent increased facilities for procuring books.

19. Condition and State of the Copy.

What is understood by the good condition of an early printed work will scarcely need any detailed explanation. In the preparation especially of sale catalogues it should be conscientiously stated whether and to what extent there may be damp or water stains; how far the state of the book may have been affected by any other outward influences; whether there are any leaves either torn or partly or altogether abstracted, or whether the book has suffered injury of any other kind. In the case of incunabula with woodcuts, the condition of the impression should be stated,—whether, for instance, any colouring has been attempted by an unskilled hand, etc.

20. RARE COPIES; EDITIO PRINCEPS; PRICE.

The rareness or frequent occurrence of an incunabulum will naturally depend in general on its actual supply and demand. Statements of this sort should be made with caution. In many countries certain incunabula are frequent, which elsewhere are considered rare. Here, again, long years of experience, with an accurate knowledge of the markets of the world, can alone secure correct information.

The case is somewhat different when we have to ascertain whether a given incunabulum is the *first edition* or not of the work in question. This is a fact which must be decided by consulting the literature bearing on the subject.

Regarding the price which the bookseller expects for his copies of incunabula, no definite rules can be laid down. Here it is impossible to give trade prices in the modern sense of the term, nor even approximate current prices. Apparently the only course open to the beginner is to glean all the information he can by sedulous consultation of English and Foreign sale catalogues, the catalogues of the leading dealers, or by referring to the *Book Prices Current*, published by Elliot Stock. One and the same book may bring totally different prices according to the general appearance and condition of the copies offered for sale, and the library it comes from. In Brunet's and Graesse's large bibliographical works the prices realized at famous sales or demanded by antiquarians of repute are quoted ; but such figures are nowadays quite illusory.

21. HISTORICAL AND LITERARY NOTICES.

A catalogue of incunabula, whether prepared by antiquarians or for sale purposes, will acquire the greater permanent value the richer it is on the one hand in descriptions of the printed works, on the other in notices bearing on such works. We will here refer only to the catalogues of Bernhard Quaritch, London, and Albert Cohn, Berlin, which are at present eagerly collected by all book-lovers and librarians, precisely because they present such varied bibliographical explanations.

Everything known to the compiler himself of the catalogue regarding the contents, the author, the printer, the work, or the given specimen, should be faithfully recorded. The cultured antiquarian should not shirk the slight extra expense which may be entailed by the somewhat richer contents of the catalogue, for which a permanent value may be thus secured even long after the stock has been disposed of. But in all cases let the fundamental principle be scrupulously adhered to of stating only what is certainly known and true, and can at any time be verified. Let all vagueness and ambiguity be avoided, and let TRUTH alone be still your watchword.

THE METHOD OF COLLECTING.

O early as the seventeenth century the posses-
sion of incunabula, that is, of works dating
from the decades immediately following the
invention of the typographic art, was highly
valued by all important libraries and amateurs.
The fact is explained on the one hand by the comparative
scarcity of such works, by far the greater portion of which have
perished during the wars and civil strife ; on the other by
the consideration that these venerable monuments from the
first years of an invention affecting the whole world possess
a high historical and antiquarian interest and fascination which
cannot but be more and more recognised with the increasing
importance of the art itself.

Nevertheless it was long before any steps were taken to
systematically arrange these treasures, to determine undated
issues by all the resources of comparative bibliography,—in a
word, to critically study the still extant incunabula.

At first sight it might seem incumbent on us first of all
to come to a clear understanding on the temporal limitation
of this term " incunabulum." But the following inquiry appears
so intimately bound up with the essence of the subject, that
for the present purpose it becomes a matter of indifference
whether we regard as incunabula the works of the fifteenth
century alone, or with former bibliographers include those

issued before 1520, or even before 1535. But in any case both extrinsic and intrinsic reasons suggest that the term be limited to the year 1500, with which both the century of the invention and the infancy of the art itself were brought to a close.

The collecting of incunabula may from the very nature of the case be viewed from the most diverse standpoints.

But even an absolutely unsystematic collection, that is, the acquisition of the greatest possible number of incunabula, without regard to all the other points to be mentioned further on, need by no means exclude a systematic arrangement and cataloguing of all the works thus brought together. At the same time, such a method of collecting cannot be recommended even in the case of the exceptional pecuniary resources at the command of the great public libraries and amateur millionaires. For with such a method it becomes a pure matter of chance whether the collection acquire any considerable completeness in any given direction, or whether the whole shall ever possess any great bibliographical value. It cannot however be denied that this plan, however irrational it ·may otherwise appear, is so far the most economical that by its means a large collection of incunabula may be most rapidly and cheaply brought together.

But this method, if it at all deserves to be so described, must be absolutely set aside in the case of *small* and *average* collections. Whoever with rather limited means sets about scraping together the largest possible number of incunabula at random, without troubling himself about their origin, rarity, contents and so forth, will not acquire a real library of early works, but merely a wilderness of musty old scholastic books mainly of no bibliographical value. This at least will be the

23.

result, unless he should happen to be favoured by such a run of lucky hits as are daily becoming more improbable. The reason is because by pursuing such a course pretty well every-thing turns on the question of *cheapness*, which by no means excludes relative excessive prices.

As in other domains, here also is applicable the maxim : *Quality, not quantity.*

It follows that a certain limit must be absolutely assigned to the extent of the collection.

In connection with such a limitation there must at the same time be adopted for the several cases a corresponding system of *fitting up, arranging, enlarging*, and *cataloguing* a really genuine library of incunabula.

In the following remarks it will be our endeavour to establish the principles which seem to us applicable in all such cases. Our treatise naturally makes no claim to completeness, as here the broad features of the subject can alone be touched upon, without however excluding the subdivisions of particular classes, which may form the material of numerous special collections. Nor do we pretend to give any opinion as to the most desirable standpoints to be kept in view in making collections. This must depend on the one hand on the preferences and previous culture of the individual collector, on the other on the extent of his available means, points on which it would be absurd to lay down any general laws. In these things there can be no common standard applicable to all ! Only we would venture to point out that the various methods of collecting give occasion to all sorts of *combinations*, and that in fact for many of these methods it seems scarcely advisable absolutely to exclude some such combination.

It might also be pointed out that the features to be

developed in special cases should also be kept in view in the arrangement, cataloguing and completing of general libraries of incunabula, nay, that some of these principles cannot be at all overlooked in any rational method of cataloguing.

The collection of incunabula may be divided into the following classes, and based upon the collection of :

1. DATED OR UNDATED WORKS.

Till about the year 1480 works either not at all or only imperfectly dated were far more numerous than those which gave the printing-place, printer and year of issue. Especially during the first years after the invention the names of place and printer were frequently omitted.

Absolutely undated works we call those which give neither place, printer nor year ; imperfectly dated, those which give at least one of these particulars. Here occur the most diverse combinations, as mentioned in the previous chapter, some very frequently. Such are : (*a*) works giving printer and year, but no place ; (*b*) works with printer's name, but without place or year ; (*c*) works without year, but with place and printer ; (*d*) works with place alone ; (*e*) printer alone ; (*f*) year alone. Of most frequent occurrence are the forms under *b*, *c*, and *f*.

Works fully dated so far as in general to leave no doubt regarding their origin (exceptions however occur even here, as in pirated editions) take on the whole a higher place as bibliographical documents than those altogether or partly undated. But here if anywhere is applicable the saying, " No rule without an exception." The very finest treasures of this sort are undated, whereas hundreds of very inferior worth display a full date.

Of many printers we possess scarcely any dated, or at

least any fully dated works. Hence a library excluding undated, or at all events incompletely dated works, easily acquires a certain one-sided character, without thereby necessarily gaining in material value.

Apart from this point, modern science presents so many aids for the absolute identification of undated or imperfectly dated works, that there is no intrinsic justification for a systematic under-estimation of such works.

The further question arises, how should the collector act in the case of such undated works as cannot be identified, or identified beyond all doubt? In principle such works should be excluded by those bibliophiles who from the character of their collection must attach importance to the undoubted determination of the origin of each printed work, and who have neither time nor means themselves to remove all doubts on these heads. But for large libraries such a limitation would be altogether misplaced; for the accurate investigation of undated incunabula has already led to the most unexpected results.

2. Works in Particular Languages.

By far the greater number of all incunabula are in the Latin language. From this fact alone it at once follows that early printed works in all modern languages must be more or less rare. Hence collectors excluding Latin incunabula will obviously be restricted to those in their own mother-tongue, or else in such other modern languages as take a prominent position in a geographical, historical or linguistic sense. As a rule English, French, German, Italian, or Spanish incunabula are only to be procured with such difficulty, and on such unfavourable conditions, that with relatively limited means it would be beside the purpose to think of acquiring them.

3. WORKS FROM PARTICULAR COUNTRIES.

As already pointed out, in all civilised lands far more was printed in Latin than in the vernacular, a fact that can cause no surprise considering the state of science and letters, as well as the slight development of the modern European languages at that time. Thus German, for instance, is represented by scarcely one-eighth of the books printed in Germany before 1500. On the other hand it not unfrequently happened that German books were printed abroad by German printers, by whom the young art was rapidly spread throughout other lands.

Hence collections of incunabula from any particular countries can by no means consist exclusively of works in the respective languages. They should in fact rather exclude such works, as even so the restriction to the Latin language will still leave a very wide field to the collector's activity.

By far the relatively largest portion of all incunabula belong to ITALY, where the art was early developed, and more particularly to ROME and VENICE, whose incunabula alone would form a large library. The result is a comparative cheapness of most incunabula printed in Italy, and especially in Venice, the more so that during the last twenty years many of them have been thrown on the market by the sequestration of the Italian monastic estates and the dispersion of private collections.

Hence those who may not have previously limited their operations to some other particular region, will as a rule find themselves the owners of a preponderating number of Italian incunabula.

But rational collectors, especially when not guided by the question of quality as is usually the case in this domain, will probably soon discover that it is better to secure a relatively rich collection from a more or less restricted field, than to possess a correspondingly smaller number of specimens from several different countries. All alike aim at the greatest possible completeness within the region to which they have chosen to confine themselves.

In the case of such restricted collections the first consideration will naturally be for the collector's native land, whether this expression be taken in a narrower or a wider sense, as for instance according to the political frontiers of the fifteenth century, or of the present time. For such lands however as can show but few incunabula, such a voluntary limitation will not always be found convenient. In this case specimens from richer fields will doubtless be also admitted. For the rest incunabula from Germany, as the home of the invention of printing, will always possess a paramount interest even for foreigners, especially if they are anxious to secure copies from the oldest places where the art was practised.

4. Works from Particular Periods.

We have already pointed out that from the material standpoint it is difficult to assign definite temporal limits to the term "incunabula." Hence it must be left to each individual collector to decide on the period to which he will extend its use, and also whether he will limit his collection to any and what particular year within that period. There is undoubtedly a certain justification for including on principle those works alone that fall within a given period not far removed from the date of the invention.

Other temporal limitations might also be suggested; these however would presuppose an arrangement of the collection according to place. Such a combination of territorial and temporal standpoints leads, for instance, to a collection limited to places where the art was introduced before a given year, or, say, to the ten, fifteen, twenty, etc., earliest places, or else to the oldest places of a given country, but within each of these places down to the year 1500. Such combinations are historically so far justified that those places form in a measure the landmarks in the victorious career of this far-reaching invention.

Considerations of space and economy may under certain circumstances render it advisable to restrict the collection from more important places to works comprised within a certain date.

5. WORKS BELONGING TO A PARTICULAR BRANCH OF LITERATURE.

The great majority of all incunabula are devoted to theology, and all other branches of letters taken together are not half so numerously represented as this one subject. Hence, owing to their relative rareness, incunabula dealing with worldly matters possess a certain outward interest, apart altogether from the contents of each individual work.

But on the other hand, within this general category every branch is more or less fully represented according to the standard of contemporary knowledge. Classical subjects naturally take the foremost position. But we also meet with numerous chronicles, fugitive pieces, polemical writings, popular treatises on natural history, descriptions of travels, almanacks, occasional verses and other poetical effusions of later mediæval times, grammars, dictionaries, encyclopædias, musical works, etc. In short, for the history of every science, as well as of literature in its narrower sense, the printed works of the fifteenth century present rich stores of information that have hitherto been little utilized.

It is obvious that the use of such treasures would be immensely facilitated by bringing together special collections of incunabula for the several branches, or at least by thoroughly cataloguing from this standpoint the already existing general libraries of early printed works.

6. WORKS WHOSE CONTENTS PRESENT SPECIAL CURIOUS INTEREST.

Besides these special libraries, for which the greatest possible completeness will naturally be aimed at within the respective branches, others might be suggested, which, whether limited or not to special branches, would consist only of those incunabula whose contents are specially remarkable on account of their curious contents, in fact "curios" of literary or historic interest.

Such early works which apart from their age and scarcity as early issues, are in themselves of peculiar interest, and would accordingly deserve to be re-issued either wholly or in part do occur sometimes. The acquisition, however, of these works, being for the most part very scarce, would involve a considerable outlay.

7. WORKS OF SPECIAL IMPORTANCE FOR THE HISTORY OF TYPOGRAPHY.

Apart from the "incunabula" there are here to be considered:

(*a*) Works in which, absolutely or within a given region, there occur for the first time *place, printer and year*, or one alone or any two of these data; works in which catch-words, pagination, title page occur for the first time; works which are the oldest specimens of a particular form of type; works in which initial letters or marginal embellishments were printed for the first time.

(*b*) Works which are of importance for the development of contractions or abbreviations.

(*c*) Works containing particular flaws calculated to throw light on the contemporary technical processes.

(*d*) Works in which are for the first time noticed certain technical improvements, etc., etc.

8. WORKS ILLUSTRATED WITH WOODCUTS.

A few years after the issue of the first book printed with movable types, we meet the first rude beginnings of book illustration by means of woodcuts, an art which later acquired such importance. Gradually the draughtsmanship becomes more artistic, the technique freer and surer, until towards the close of the fifteenth century we find in the Italian School and in Schedel's *Chronik* woodcuts which recall the first masters of the following century.

Hence a special collection of incunabula with woodcuts presents great interest for the history of art, and to a less extent for the æsthetic side of art. At the same time such illustrated incunabula are very numerous, some seven hundred being known from Germany alone. In recent years, however, these, like all other wood-engravings, have risen in price to such an extent that a special collection of this sort is about one of the most costly things in the world.

9. PERFECTLY PRESERVED COPIES.

Such specimens naturally command all the higher price, inasmuch as the condition of most extant incunabula leaves much to be desired. Besides the frequent absence of particular leaves, they are largely damaged by worms, or disfigured by the gnawings of mice, by damp stains, reckless cutting down in binding, etc.

Each collector will best know how far he should go in respect of the condition of a given incunabulum. Anyhow, wealthy bibliophiles are perfectly justified in seeing on principle that the book is as flawless as possible.

It would be a mistake, however, to ride this hobby too far. An imperfect and worm-eaten *unicum* is far more valuable than a spotless perfect specimen of an issue, of which some sixty copies are known to exist. Hence, when it is a question of securing specially rare copies, we cannot always insist upon their perfect and flawless state.

The foregoing remark leads to the consideration of

10. EXTREMELY RARE WORKS.

Certainly the terms *rare* or *scarce* are somewhat vague. There are incunabula of which formerly only a few copies were known, but of which in recent years several others were offered for sale in rapid succession. Has the book on that account ceased to be rare? Anyhow there are several degrees of rareness to be distinguished. Apart from other considerations, it will be judicious to include in the collection only such incunabula as are at least to a certain extent scarce, even though it be impracticable to confine ourselves to rarities of the *first order*, all of these being, of course, already bought up.

11. IMPRESSIONS ON VELLUM—WORKS EXCEPTIONALLY RICH IN ARTISTIC EMBELLISHMENTS, INITIAL LETTERS AND THE LIKE.

What has been said respecting scarce specimens in general, naturally applies also to particular groups of the same category consequently also for works with an unusual wealth of artistic ornamentation in initials, borderings, miniature painting, etc. But it applies still more especially to works printed on vellum, all the more that but few of these are extant, while some are absolutely unique. In fact, works on vellum were issued only by a very small number of early printing offices.

12. COLLECTIONS ACCORDING TO PLACE, PRINTER AND VARIETIES OF TYPES.

Those confining their purchases to incunabula of some particular country, but who are at the same time anxious to have as complete a representation as possible of the earliest development of the typographic art in that region, should make every effort to secure incunabula from all the printing establishments of the countries in question. Among the productions issued by each of these places such a collection will pay attention to the several printers, as well as to the varieties of types employed by each of them. Owing to the extreme scarcity of the specimens from certain offices absolute completeness in this respect is of course practically out of the question. But it may not be so difficult to form a *relatively* complete collection, that is, one in which shall be represented the majority of the printing places and printers of a given country. At least this may be possible, provided other considerations be kept mainly in abeyance, and the collector be satisfied with one specimen of each printer, as well as of each kind of type. For collectors of limited means this method is perhaps to be preferred before all others. In this way each distinct book becomes in fact an illustration in the history of the development of the typographic art.

At the same time this method is also the best for every

collection that has to be made from the typographical stand-point, whether such a collection is to embrace the productions of one country only, or those of all the regions with which we are here concerned. The same method also facilitates more than any other the identification of undated works.

Collecting according to *typographical specialities*, as this method might be called, may of course be brought into harmony with all others hitherto touched upon, although in such cases the fundamental principle cannot always be strictly adhered to. It would lead us too far to enter in detail on all the combinations that are here possible.

It will suffice to state that a collection made from this point of view will acquire a fair completeness all the more easily the less it aims at securing dated works, and especially such as bear the printer's mark. The creation of an ideal library of incunabula, in which every place, printer and form of type shall be represented by both dated and undated copies, will always present extreme difficulties. Still more difficult must be a collection of "incunabula" of every place and every printer, especially as these belong for the most part to the category of rarities. As a rule it will be found impossible to procure the first issue of each particular form of type.

13. CONCLUDING REMARKS.

The foregoing remarks may suffice to give the reader some idea of the numerous points to be considered in making collections of incunabula. Much that has here been stated may look like so many truisms. Nevertheless the points touched upon may not seem quite superfluous in the absence of a thoroughly systematic bibliographical treatment of the subject.   Nor can this essay pretend to supply the place of such a work, especially when we consider how often both public libraries and private collectors have gone blindly to work in forming their collections.

We have already mentioned that the principles or guiding rules here severally developed are also applicable for the systematic cataloguing of already existing general libraries of incunabula.

LATIN-ENGLISH

AND

ENGLISH-LATIN

TOPOGRAPHICAL INDEX

OF THE

PRINCIPAL TOWNS

WHERE EARLY PRINTING PRESSES WERE ESTABLISHED.

LATIN-ENGLISH.

Aarhusum, *Aarhus* 1519.
Abbatis Villa, *Abbeville* 1486.
Abredonia, *Aberdeen* 1519.
Alatum Castrum, *Edinburgh* 1509.
Alba Bulgarica, *Belgrade* 1552.
Aldenarda, *Audenarde* 1480.
Aldenburgum, *Altenburg* 1523.
Alepum, *Aleppo* 1706.
Alostum (**Alost**), *Aalst* 1473.
Alta Villa, *Eltwyl* 1462.
Aquæ Bonæ, *Bonn* 1543.
Aquincum, *Buda (Ofen)* 1472.
Araugia, *Aarau* 1511.
Argentoratum, *Strasburg* 1466.
Arosia, *Westerås* 1621.
Asculum Picenum, *Ascoli* 1477.
Augusta Bracara, *Braga* 1494.
Augusta Nemetum, *Spire (Speier)* 1477.
Augusta Tiberii, *Ratisbon (Regensburg)* 1490.
Augusta Vindelicorum, *Augsburg* 1472.
Aurelia, *Orléans* 1490.
Avenio, *Avignon* 1497.

Bacodurum, *Passau* 1482.
Bamberga, *Bamberg* 1450.
Bancona, *Oppenheim* 1494.
Barcino, *Barcelona* 1478.
Basilea, *Bâle* or *Basle* 1470.
Batavia, *Batavia* 1668.
Berna, *Berne* 1525.
Berolinum, *Berlin* 1540.
Berona (in Ergovia), *Beromünster* 1470.
Bonna, *Bonn* 1543.
Bononia, *Bologna* 1471.

Brangonia, *Worcester* 1548.
Brixia, *Brescia* 1473.
Brugæ Bearniæ, *Bruges (Brügge)* 1475.
Bruna, *Brünn* 1491.
Brunsviga, *Brunswick* 1509.
Bruxella, *Brussels (Bruxelles)* 1476.
Burdigala, *Bordeaux* 1486.
Burgdorfium, *Burgdorf* 1475.
Burgi, *Burgos* 1485.
Buscoduca, *Bois-le-Duc (Hertogenbusch)* 1484.

Cabelia, *Chablis* 1478.
Cadomum, *Caen* 1480.
Cæsaraugusta, *Saragossa (Zaragoza)* 1475
Cale, *Oporto* 1622.
Calium (**ad Calem**), *Cagli* 1475.
Camboricum, *Cambridge* 1556; *United States* 1638.
Cantuaria, *Canterbury* 1549.
Capitabriga, *Cambridge* 1556; *United States* 1638.
Caroli Hesychium, *Karlsruhe* 1545.
Cassella (or **Casseletum**), *Cassel* 1611.
Casulæ, *Casole* 1475.
Chalybon, *Aleppo* 1706.
Christiania, *Christiania* 1643.
Chrysii Auraria, *Altenburg* (Hungary) 1558.
Cibinium, *Hermannstadt* 1575.
Clinfacum, *Cluny* 1493.
Colonia, *Cologne* 1470.
Complutum, *Alcalá de Henares*, 1499.
Comum, *Como* 1474.

Conimbrica, *Coimbra* 1536.
Corduba, *Cordova* 1495.
Cracovia, *Cracow* 1491.
Cremona, *Cremona* 1473.
Culemburgum, *Culemborg* 1483.
Cutna, *Kuttenberg* 1489.

Damascus, *Damascus* 1605.
Darmstadium, *Darmstadt* 1611.
Daventria, *Deventer* 1477.
Debrecinum, *Debreczin* 1565.
Delfi, *Delft* 1477.
Derbatum, *Dorpat* 1642.
Divio, *Dijon* 1491.
Dresda, *Dresden* 1524.
Dublinum, *Dublin* 1551.

Eboracum, *York* 1509.
Edinum, *Edinburgh* 1509.
Einsilda, *Einsiedeln* 1664.
Emmerani Cœnob., *Ratisbon (Regensburg)* 1490.
Engolisma, *Angoulême* 1491.
Erfordia, *Erfurt* 1494.
Ezelinga, *Esslingen* 1473.

Fanum Fortunæ, *Fano* 1475
Fanum St. Galli, *St. Gall* 1577
Ferrara, *Ferrara* 1471
Fivizanum, *Fivizzano* 1472
Formosa, *Formosa* 1661.
Francofurtum ad Mænum, *Frankfort-on-the-Main* 1531.
Francofurtum ad Oderam, *Frankfort-on-the-Oder* 1567.
Freiberga in Misnia, *Freiberg (Freyberg)*, 1495.
Friburgum, *Freiburg i. Br.* 1493.
Friburgum Helv., *Fribourg (Freiburg) in Switzerland* 1585.
Frisinga, *Freysingen* 1494.

Galgocinum, *Galgocz* 1584.
Galli Fanum, *St. Gall* 1577.

Ganda, *Ghent* 1483.
Geneva, *Geneva* 1478.
Genua, *Genoa* 1472.
Gerunda, *Gerona* 1483.
Gippesvicum, *Ipswich* 1538.
Goslaria, *Goslar* 1604.
Gothoburgum, *Gothenburg* 1650.
Gouda, *Gouda* 1477.
Gronaicum, *Greenwich* 1564.

Hadrianopolis, *Adrianople* 1554.
Hafnia, *Copenhagen* 1490.
Haga Comitis, *The Hague* 1516.
Hagenoa, *Hagenau* 1500.
Halebum, *Aleppo* 1706.
Hamburgum, *Hamburg* 1491.
Hasseletum, *Hasselt* 1480.
Heidelberga, *Heidelberg* 1485.
Herbipolis, *Würzburg* 1479.
Hesychia Carolina, *Karlsruhe* 1545.
Hispalis, *Seville* 1480.
Holmia, *Stockholm* 1474.
Hyctopolis ad Istrum, *Ratisbon (Regensburg)* 1490.

Ilerda, *Lerida* 1479.
Ingolstadium, *Ingolstadt* 1490.

Kralia, *Kralitz* (Moravia) 1579.
Kuttenberga, *Kuttenberg* 1489.

Lauginga, *Laugingen* 1473.
Lausanna, *Lausanne* 1556.
Leiria, *Leiria* 1484.
Lemovicum, *Limoges* 1495.
Leopolis, *Lemberg* 1593.
Leovardia, *Leuwarden* 1485.
Lethes fl., *Lima* 1585.
Leuphana, *Luneburg* 1493.
Limonum, *Poitiers* 1479.
Lipsia, *Leipzig* 1479.
Lobavia, *Löbau* 1718.
Londinium, *London* 1477.
Londinium Gothorum, *Lund* 1663.

24

Loudeacum, *Loudéac* 1484.
Lovania, *Louvain* (*Lœwen*) 1473.
Lubeca, *Lübeck* 1498.
Lucerna Helvetiorum, *Lucerne* 1524.
Lugdunum, *Lyons* (*Lyon*) 1473.
Lugdunum Batavorum, *Leyden* 1483.
Luneburgum, *Luneburg* 1493.

Madritum, *Madrid* 1500.
Magdeburgum, *Magdeburg* 1488.
Manilla, *Manila* 1590.
Mantua, *Mantua* 1472.
Marionis, *Hamburg* 1491.
Marionis Altera, *Lübeck* 1498.
Marsiburgum, *Merseburg* 1473.
Mediolanum, *Milan* 1469.
Memminga, *Memmingen* 1482.
Messina, *Messina* 1473.
Mesuium, *Brunswick* 1509.
Misna, *Meissen* 1508.
Mogontiacum, *Mayence* (*Mainz*) 1448.
Mohilavia, *Mohileff* 1617.
Monachium, *Munich* 1482.
Monasterium, *Münster* 1485.
Monasterium B. Mariæ de Monserrato,
    Nuestra Señora de Monserrate 1499.
Monasterium Tavistock, *Tavistock* 1525.
Monasterium Wadstenense, *Wadstenia*
    1495.
Mons Regalis, *Monte Reale* 1472.
Mons Regalis, *Monterey* 1494.
Mons Serratus, *Monserrate* 1499.
Monyorokerekinum, *Eberau* (Hungary)
    1589.
Moscovia, *Moscow* 1553.
Murcia, *Murcia* 1487.
Mutina, *Modena* 1480.

Namnetus Portus, *Nantes* 1493.
Neapolis, *Naples* 1472.
Neoburgum, *Neufchâtel* 1530.
Norimberga, *Nurenberg* 1470.
Noviomagus, *Nimeguen* 1470.
Novum Eboracum, *New York* 1693.

Novum Londinium, *New London* 1709.

Ocellodurum, *Zamora* 1482.
Offenburgum, *Offenburg* 1494.
Olisipo, *Lisboa* 1495.
Othania, *Odense* 1482.

Pampalona, *Pampelona* 1489.
Panormus, *Palermo* 1477.
Parisius, *Paris* 1470.
Parma, *Parma* 1473.
Perusia, *Perugia* 1475.
Petropolis, *St. Petersburg* 1710.
Philadelphia, *Philadelphia* 1686.
Piacentia, *Piacenza* 1475.
Pintia, *Valladolid* 1493.
Pons Neviæ, *Puebla de Navia* 1612.
Posnania, *Posen* 1577.
Prætorium, *Kingston* 1720.
Probatopolis, *Schaffhausen* 1577.
Provinum, *Provins* 1496.

Redones, *Rennes* 1484.
Regiomontium Borussiæ, *Königsberg i.*
    Pr. 1523.
Regiopolis, *Kingston* 1720.
Rhegium, *Reggio* 1498.
Ripa, *Ribe* 1508.
Roe Fontes, *Röskyld* 1534.
Roma, *Rome* 1467-68.
Romanovia, *Romanoff* 1619.
Rostochium, *Rostock* 1496.
Rotomagus, *Rouen* 1487.
Ruotlinga, *Reutlingen* 1500.

Salmantica, *Salamanca* 1485.
Sarvarinum, *Uj-Szigeth-Sárvár* 1539.
Schiedamum, *Schiedam* 1483.
Schoonhovia, *Schoenhooven* 1495.
Sedinum, *Stettin* 1577.
Sentice, *Zamora* 1482.
Singidunum, *Belgrade* 1552.
Slesvicum, *Schleswig* 1485.
Smyrna, *Smyrna* 1658,
Stutgardia, *Stuttgart* 1486.

Sublacense Cœnob., *Subiaco* 1464.

Szegedinum, *Szegedin* 1567.

Ternobum, *Tyrnau* 1578.

Ticinum, *Pavia* 1476.

Tigurum, *Zürich* 1504.

Timalinum, *Puebla de Navia* 1612.

Toletum, *Toledo* 1486.

Tolosa, *Tolosa* 1480.

Tolosa Tectosagum, *Toulouse* 1479.

Trajectum Inferius, *Utrecht* 1473.

Trecæ, *Troy (Troyes)* 1483.

Tridentum, *Trent (Trient)* 1475.

Tubinga, *Tübingen* 1498.

Tzernigovia, *Tschernigow* (*Czernigow*), 193.

Ulma, *Ulm* 1470.

Upsalia, *Upsala* 1510.

Valentia, *Valencia* 1474.

Varadinum, *Grosswardein* 1585.

Varsavia, *Warsaw* 1580.

Venetia, *Venice* 1469.

Venta, *Winchester* 1545.

Verona, *Verona* 1470.

Vesontio, *Besançon* 1487.

Viburgus, *Viborg* 1528.

Vigornia, *Worcester* 1548.

Vilna, *Wilna* 1525.

Vindabona, *Vienna (Wien)* 1482.

Vinterberga, *Winterberg* 1484.

Vratislavia, *Breslau* 1538.

Zamoscium, *Zamosc* 1557.

Zwolla, *Zwolle* 1479.

ENGLISH-LATIN.

Aalst, *Alostum* 1473.

Aarau, *Araugia* 1511.

Aarhus, *Aarhusum* 1519.

Abbeville, *Abbatis Villa* 1486.

Aberdeen, *Abredonia* 1519.

Adrianople, *Hadrianopolis* 1554.

Alcalá de Henares, *Complutum* 1499.

Aleppo, *Alepum, Chalybon, Halebum* 1706.

Alost, *Alostum* 1473.

Altenburg (Germany), *Aldenburgum* 1523.

Altenburg (Hungary), *Chrysii Auraria* 1558.

Angoulême, *Engolisma* 1491.

Ascoli, *Asculum Picenum* 1477.

Audenarde, *Aldenarda* 1480.

Augsburg, *Augusta Vindelicorum* 1472.

Avignon, *Avenio* 1497.

Bâle (Basle), *Basilea* 1470.

Bamberg, *Bamberga* 1450.

Barcelona, *Barcino* 1478.

Batavia, *Batavia* 1668.

Belgrade, *Alba Bulgarica, Singidunum* 1552.

Berlin, *Berolinum* 1540.

Berne, *Berna* 1525.

Beromunster, *Berona* 1470.

Bois-le-Duc, *Buscoduca* 1484.

Bologna, *Bononia* 1471.

Bonn, *Aquæ Bonæ, Bonna* 1543.

Bordeaux, *Burdigala* 1486.

Braga, *Augusta Bracara* 1494.

Brescia, *Brixia* 1473.

Breslau *Vatrislavia* 1538.

Bruges (Brügge), *Brugæ Bearniæ* 1475

Brünn, *Bruna* 1491.

Brunswick, *Brunsviga, Mesnium* 1509.

Brussels, *Bruxella* 1476.

Buda (Ofen), *Aquincum* 1472.

Burgdorf, *Burgdorfium* 1475.

Burgos, *Burgi* 1485.

Caen, *Cadomum* 1480.

Cagli, *Calium (ad Calem)* 1475.
Cambridge, *Camboricum, Capitabriga* 1556.
Canterbury, *Cantuaria* 1549.
Casole, *Casulæ* 1475.
Cassel, *Cassella, Casseletum* 1611.
Chablis, *Cabelia* 1478.
Christiana, *Christiana* 1643.
Cluny, *Cliniacum* 1493.
Coimbra, *Conimbrica* 1536.
Cologne, *Colonia* 1470.
Como, *Comum* 1474.
Copenhagen, *Hafnia* 1490.
Cordova, *Corduba* 1495.
Cracow, *Cracovia* 1491.
Cremona, *Cremona* 1473.
Culemborg, *Culenburgum* 1483.
Czernigow, *Tzernogavia* 1493.

Damascus, *Damascus* 1605.
Darmstadt, *Darmstadium* 1611.
Debreczin, *Debrecinum* 1565.
Delft, *Delfi* 1477.
Deventer, *Daventria* 1477.
Dijon, *Divio* 1491.
Dorpat, *Derbatum* 1642.
Dresden, *Dresda* 1524.
Dublin, *Dublinum* 1551.

Eberau (Hungary), *Monyorokerekinum* 1589.
Edinburgh, *Alatum Castrum, Edinum* 1509.
Einsiedeln, *Einsilda* 1664.
Eltwyl, *Alta Villa* 1462.
Erfurt, *Erfordia* 1494.
Esslingen, *Ezelinga* 1473.

Fano, *Fanum Fortunæ* 1475.
Ferrara, *Ferrara* 1471.
Fivizzano, *Fivizanum* 1472.
Formosa, *Formosa* 1661.
Frankfort-on-the-Main, *Francofurtum ad Mænum* 1531.

Frankfort-on-the-Oder, *Francofurtum ad Oderam* 1567.
Freiberg (Freyburg), *Freiberga in Misnia* 1495.
Freiburg i. Br., *Friburgum* 1493.
Freysingen, *Frisinga* 1494.
Fribourg (Freiburg) in Switzerland, *Friburgum Helv.* 1585.

Galgocz, *Galgocinum* 1584.
Geneva, *Geneva* 1478.
Genoa, *Genua* 1472.
Gerona, *Gerunda* 1483.
Ghent, *Ganda* 1483.
Goslar, *Goslaria* 1604.
Gothenburg, *Gothoburgum* 1650.
Gouda, *Gouda* 1477.
Greenwich, *Gronaicum* 1564.
Grosswardein, *Varadinum* 1585.

Hagenau, *Hagenoa* 1500.
Hague, The, *Haga Comitis* 1516.
Hamburg, *Hamburgum, Marionis* 1491.
Hasselt, *Hasseletum* 1480.
Hermannstadt, *Cibinium* 1575.

Ingolstadt, *Ingolstadium* 1490.
Ipswich, *Gippesvicum* 1538.

Karlsruhe, *Caroli Hesychium, Hesychia Carolina* 1545.
Kingston, *Prætorium, Regiopolis* 1720.
Königsberg i. Pr., *Regiomontium Borussiæ* 1523.
Kralitz (Moravia), *Kralia* 1579.
Kuttenberg, *Cutna, Kuttenberga* 1489.

Laugingen, *Lauginga* 1473.
Lausanne, *Lausanna* 1556.
Leipzig, *Lipsia* 1479.
Leiria, *Leiria* 1484.
Lemberg, *Leopolis* 1593.
Lerida, *Ilerda* 1479.
Leuwarden, *Leovardia* 1485.

Leyden, *Lugdunum Batavorum* 1483.
Lima, *Lethes fl.* 1585.
Limoges, *Lemovicum* 1495.
Lisboa, *Olisipo* 1495.
Löbau, *Lobavia* 1718.
Lœwen (Louvain), *Lovania* 1473.
London, *Londinium* 1477.
Loudéac, *Loudeacum* 1484.
Louvain, *Lovania* 1473.
Lübeck, *Lubeca, Marionis Altera* 1498.
Lund, *Londinium Gothorum* 1663.
Luneburg, *Luneburgum* 1493.
Lyons (Lyon), *Lugdunum* 1473.

Madrid, *Madritum* 1500.
Magdeburg, *Magdeburgum* 1488.
Mainz. See *Mayence.*
Manila, *Manilla* 1590.
Mayence, *Mogontiacum* 1448.
Meissen, *Misna* 1508.
Memmingen, *Memminga* 1482.
Merseburg, *Marsiburgum* 1473.
Messina, *Messina* 1473.
Milan, *Mediolanum* 1469.
Modena, *Mutina* 1480.
Mohileff, *Mohilavia* 1617.
Monserrate (Nuestra Señora de), *Monasterium B. Mariæ de Monserrato, Mons Serratus* 1499.
Monte Reale, *Mons Regalis* 1472
Monterey, *Mons Regalis* 1494.
Moscow, *Moscovia* 1553.
München. See *Munich.*
Munich (München), *Monachium* 1482.
Münster, *Monasterium* 1485.
Murcia, *Murcia* 1487.

Nantes, *Namnetus Portus* 1493.
Naples, *Neapolis* 1472.
Neufchâtel, *Neoburgum* 1530.
New London, *Novum Londinium* 1709.
New York, *Novum Eboracum* 1693.
Nimeguen, *Noviomagus* 1479.
Nurenberg (Nürnberg), *Norimberga* 1470.

Odense, *Othania* 1482.
Offenburg, *Offenburgum* 1494.
Oppenheim, *Bancona* 1494.
Orléans, *Aurelia* 1490.

Palermo, *Panormu* 1477.
Pampelona, *Pampalona* 1489.
Paris, *Parisius* 1470.
Parma, *Parma* 1473.
Passau, *Bacodurum* 1482.
Pavia, *Ticinum* 1476.
Perugia, *Perusia* 1475.
Philadelphia, *Philadelphia* 1686.
Piacenza, *Piacentia* 1475.
Poitiers, *Limonum* 1479.
Posen, *Posnania* 1577.
Provins, *Pruvinum* 1496.
Puebla de Navia, *Pons Neviæ, Timalinum* 1612.

Ratisbon, *Augusta Tiberii, Emmerani Cœnob., Hyctopolis ad Istrum* 1490.
Regensburg. See *Ratisbon.*
Reggio, *Rhegium* 1498.
Rennes, *Redones* 1484.
Reutlingen, *Ruotlinga* 1500.
Ribe, *Ripa* 1508.
Romanoff, *Romanovia* 1619.
Rome, *Roma* 1467-8.
Röskyld, *Roe Fontes* 1534.
Rostock, *Rostochium* 1496.
Rouen, *Rotomagus* 1487.

Salamanca, *Salmantica* 1485.
Saragossa (Zaragoza), *Cæsaraugusta* 1475.
Schaffhausen, *Probatopolis* 1577.
Schiedam, *Schiedamum* 1483.
Schleswig, *Slesvicum* 1485.
Schoenhooven, *Schoonhovia* 1495.
Seville, *Hispalis* 1480.
Smyrna, *Smyrna* 1658.
Speier. See *Spire.*
Spire, *Augusta Nemetum* 1477.

St. Gall, *Fanum St. Galli, Galli Fanum* 1577.

St. Petersburg, *Petropolis* 1710.

Stockholm, *Holmia* 1474.

Strasburg, *Argentoratum* 1466.

Stuttgart, *Stutgardia* 1486.

Subiaco, *Sublacense Cœnob.* 1464.

Szegedin, *Szegedinum* 1567.

Szigeth (Uj-Szigeth-Sárvár), *Sarvarinum* 1539.

Tavistock, *Monasterium Tavistock* 1525.

Toledo, *Toletum* 1486.

Tolosa, *Tolosa* 1480.

Toulouse, *Tolosa Tectosagum* 1479.

Trent (Trient), *Tridentum* 1475.

Troy (Troyes), *Trecæ* 1483.

Tschernigow, *Tzernigovia* 1493.

Tübingen, *Tubinga* 1498.

Tyrnau, *Ternobum* 1578.

Ulm, *Ulma* 1470.

Upsala, *Upsalia* 1510.

Utrecht, *Trajectum Inferius* 1473.

Valencia, *Valentia* 1474.

Valladolid, *Pintia* 1493

Venice, *Venetia* 1469.

Verona, *Verona* 1470.

Viborg, *Viburgus* 1528.

Vienna, *Vindabona* 1482.

Wadstenia, *Monasterium Wadstenense* 1495.

Warsaw, *Varsavia* 1580.

Westerås, *Arosia* 1621.

Wilna, *Vilna* 1525.

Winchester, *Venta* 1545.

Winterberg, *Vinterberga* 1484.

Worcester, *Brangonia, Vigornia* 1548.

Würzburg, *Herbipolis* 1479.

York, *Eboracum.*

Zamora, *Ocellodurum, Sentice* 1482.

Zamose, *Zamoscium* 1557.

Zürich, *Tigurum* 1504.

Zwolle, *Zwolla* 1479.

GENERAL INDEX.

Abbreviations, 330, 337.

Adolph of Nassau, 36.

Ælius Donatus, 8.

Æsop's *Fables*, first Dutch translation, 1485, 82.

Alciati's *Emblems*, 143.

Alding, Henry, printer in Sicily, 44.

Aldus Manutius, 66, 108, 113, 252, 271.

America, North, printing in, 228.

Ames' *Typograph. Antiquities*, 50.

Amman, Jost, 251.

Andrea, John, 112, 113.

Angoulême, Jean d', 309.

Anne de Bretagne, 268.

Anopistographs, printed on one side only, 18.

Antwerp, early printing at, 155.

Apuleius' *L'Amour de Cupidon et de Psyche*, 140.

Ars Memorandi, block book, 13.

Ars Moriendi, block book, 10.

Art au Morier, block book, 12.

Artistic get-up, 341.

Asola, Andrew (A. Torresani), 66.

Astor Library, 320.

Audran, C., engraver, 166.

Author's name, 326.

Bacon's *Advancement of Learning*, 153.

Badier, Florimond, binder, 295.

Badius, Josse, of Asch, printer in Paris, 138, 257.

Balbus', John, *Catholicon*, printed by Gutenberg, 33.

Baldini, Baccio, designs for early Italian books, 67.

Ballard, Robert, printer for music, 152, 196.

Barbier, Jean, printer, 53.

Barbin, Claude, publisher, 187.

Barbou, bookseller of Paris, 196, 208.

Barker, Robert, binder, 304.

  ,,   Robert, first authorized version of the Bible, 192.

Barnes, Dame Juliana, *Treatyses perteynynge to Fyshing*, 52.

Bartolozzi, engraver, 219.

Baskerville, John, printer of Birmingham, 218, 254.

Batarde la Grosse, 47.

Bechtermunze, Henry, pupil of Gutenberg, 34; his *Vocabularium*, 44.

Bedford, Francis, binder, 303.

Belfort, Andrew, 44.

Bergman de Olpe, printer of Seb. Brandt's *Ship of Fools*, 79.

Bernard, Le Petit, or Bernard Solomon, designer, 145.

Berthelet, Thomas, binder, 303.

Bewick, Thomas, engraver, 224.

Beyamus, C., of Savigliano, 339.

Beza, Theodore, 136.

Bible, the first English in Roman type, 117.

  ,,   the Gutenberg, 23.

  ,,   the Mayence of 1462, 35.

  ,,   the thirty-six line, by A. Pfister, 34.

Biblia Pauperum, block book, 10.

Bibliographical directions, 342.

Biblioteca Marciana, Venice, 319.

Bignon, Abbé, 312.

Bill of type, 255.

Bindings, descriptions of, 262, 347.

Biziaux, binder, 302.

Blades, W., 48.

Blake, William, 221.

Blanc, Charles, 241.

Block books, the, 10.

Boccaccio's *Decameron*, fol., 1620, 191.

Bodley, Sir Thomas, 317.
Bodoni, printer, 254.
Boner's, Ulrich, *Fables*, by A. Pfister, 1461,62.
Bonhomme, printer at Lyons, 145.
Book trade of the fifteenth century, 42.
Books of Hours, 85.
Bookworms, 268.
Borel, Petrus, 238.
Borromeo, Cardinal, 319.
Bosse, Abraham, engraver, 177.
Bostgaard, Fred, 312.
Boston Library, 320.
Botticelli, Sandro, plates to Dante, 67.
Boucher, François, designer, 198.
Bourdichon, Jean, designer, 83.
Boydell's, Alderman, Shakespeare, 219.
Boyet, binder, 302.
Bradstreet, binder, 303.
Brandt's, Seb., *Shyp of Folys*, by Pynson,118.
Brandt's, Sebastian, *Ship of Fools*, by Bergman de Olpe, 79.
Breydenbach's *Pérégrinations en Terre Sainte*, printed by Topie de Pymont, 150.
British Museum, 314, 317.
Brocard, Andrew, bookseller, 103.
Brothers, The, of Common Life, 45, 338.
Brown, H. K., designer, 245.
Brunet's Manual, 325.
Bucking, Arnold, printer at Rome, 70.
Budé, Guillaume, 309.
Buon, Nicholas, bookseller, 165, 169.
Butler's *Hudibras*, 1663, 193.

Cæsaris, Peter, Paris printer, 82.
Caldecott, Randolph, designer, 246.
Callot, Jacques, engraver, 175.
Campbell's *Annales*, 325.
Capé, binder, 303.
Cardon, Horace, publisher, 166.
Caron, Antoine, engraver, 164.
Cars, Laurent, engraver, 198.
Caslon, William, type-founder, 218, 254.
Catch-words, 333.
Catherine de Medici, 286.
Catholicon, The, printed by Gutenberg, 33.
Cawood, John, printer, 118.
Caxton, William, first English printer, 47-50, 253.
Cazin, publisher, 209.

Chaillot, Robin, publisher, 99.
Chamfleury, by G. Tory, 131.
Chamot, binder, 302.
Champavert, Contes Immoreaux, 238.
Chapman's *Homer*, 1611, 191.
Chappuis, Claude, bookseller to Francis I., 136.
Charles V., 308.
Charles VII., 53.
Charles VIII., 123, 308.
Charles IX., 288, 310.
Chaucer, printed by T. Godfray, 1532, 118.
Chauveau, François, engraver, 188.
Chevalier, Peter, publisher of the *Métanéalogie*, 164.
Chicago Library, 320.
Chodowiecki, D. N., designer, 216.
Choffard, engraver, 190, 207.
Chronicle of Aragon, The, 1523, 116.
Cicero, *De Officiis*, 4to, by Fust and Schoeffer, 1465, 38.
Claude's *Liber Veritatis*, 1777, 219.
Clement, Nicolas, 312.
Clennell, Luke, engraver, 224, 244.
Clouet, François, 147, 153.
Clousier, royal printer, 227.
Cochin, vignettist, 200.
Cohn, Albert, bookseller of Berlin, 29, 351.
Coignard, bookseller, 196.
Colard Mansion, printer at Bruges, 46, 81.
Colbert, 288, 312.
Colines, Simon de, printer at Paris, 1527, 129, 131.
Cologne Chronicle, The, 1499, 24, 26, 73.
Common Prayer Book (the first), known as Edward VI.'s, 119.
Colonna's, Francesco, Poliphili's *Hypnerotomachia*, 70.
Colophon, the, 327.
Collation, the, 332.
Collections according to place and printer, 363.
Combe's *Dr. Syntax's Three Tours*, 245.
Commin, Vincent, bookseller in Paris, 98.
Condition of the copy, 349.
Congress Library of Washington, 320.
Constitutiones of Pope Clement V., 35.
Cornelis de la Haye, 147.
Coster, Laurent, 9.

Cotton, Sir Robert, 318.
Cousin, Jean, designer, 145, 148, 151.
Coverdale's English Bible, 118.
Cramoisy, Sébastien, printer of Paris, 164, 174, 296.
Cranach, Lucas, 116, 316.
Cranmer's Bible, 119.
„ Catechism, 119.
Cruikshank, George, 245.
Curmer, publisher of Paris, 240.

Dances of Death, The, 73, 100.
Dante, by Bonino de Boni. i, 1487, 71.
Dated and Undated Works, 355.
Dating, the, 328.
Daumier, designer, 242.
David, J. L., designer, 212, 214.
Day, John, printer, 116, 253.
De Bry, 192.
De Lormel, 211.
De Norvins, *Hist. de Napoléon,* illustrated by Raffet, 242.
Decameron, illustrated by Gravelot, 204.
Del'a Bella, engraver, 177.
De la Marche, Olivier, 82.
Denis de la Noue, 166.
Derome, binder, 301.
Desarques, *La Manière Universelle,* 177.
Desenne, 230.
Desportes, Philippe, 287.
Devéria, designer, 237.
D'Houry, 196.
Diana of Poitiers, 286, 309.
Dickens, Charles, 245.
Didot, Ambroise Firmin, 233.
„ family, the, 231, 254.
„ François, 202.
„ Pierre François, 227.
Diodorus Siculus, by Geoffroy Tory, 134.
Dolet, Etienne, 159.
Donatus, the, 8, 10.
Dorat, *Les Baisers,* 1770, 207.
Doré, Gustave, designer, 243.
Doyle, Richard, 246.
Dritzehen, Andrew, 16.
„ Nicolas, 17.
Dubochet, publisher of Paris, 239.
Du Cerceau, *Les Plus Beaux Bastiments de France,* 151.

Dubois, Gilles, binder, 296.
Dubuisson, Pierre Paul, binder, 301.
Duc d'Orleans, 195.
Duchesne, 236.
Dumesnil, Robert, 148.
Dünne, goldsmith, 17.
Duplat's relief engraving on stone, 223.
Duplessi-Bertaux, 214.
Duplessis, George, 141.
Du Pré, Galliot, 142.
„ „ Jean, printer, 96, 105.
Dupuy Brothers, librarians, 311.
Durandus' *Rationale,* 34.
Dürer's, Albert, *Apocalypse,* 75, 77, 113.
„ „ *Life of the Virgin,* 78.
„ „ *Passion,* 78.
Duru, binder, 303.
Duseuil, binder, 302.
Dutuit, E., *Manuel de Estampes,* 39.

Earlom, Richard, 219.
East India Company, 120.
Eisen, 204, 302.
Elizabeth's, Queen, Prayer Book, 116.
Elzevir, Abraham, 170.
„ Bonaventure, 170.
„ Daniel, 172.
„ Louis, 170.
Engerrand, Pierre, binder, 302.
Enschedé family, the, 173.
Entrée, l', du Roi Henri II. à Lyon, 146.
Erasmus' *Eloge de la Folie,* 142.
Etienne, Robert, 134, 137, 138, 253.
Euclid, Elements of, 1482, 65.
Eustace, Guillaume, 97, 125.
Eve, Clovis, 293.
„ Nicholas, 290.
Eyck, Van, 9.

Faithorne, W., 192.
Fanti's, Sigismond, *Trionfo di Fortuna,* 112.
Fasciculus Temporum, by John Veldener, 81.
Fasciculus Temporum, printed by Arnold Ther Hoernen, 72.
Fermiers Généraux, Les, 207, 209.
Fichet, Guillaume, 39, 56, 58, 61.
„ Pierre, 25.
Finiguerra, Maso, 66.
Flaxman, 230.

Formschneiders, the, 142.
Fornazeris, J de, 166.
Foster, Birket, 246.
Foucquet, Jean, 83, 288.
Fouet, Robert, 170.
Foulis Press, Glasgow, the, 218.
Fount of type, 255.
Fournier, 254.
Fra Angelico, 64.
Francesco da Bologna, 108.
Francis I., 123, 136, 268, 281, 283, 309.
Franklin, Benjamin, 228, 320.
Frederick II., 319.
Free Public Libraries, 321.
Frelon, 141.
Freyburger, Michael, 57, 59.
Friedberg, Peter, Mayence, 339.
Froben, Johannes, 74, 140, 253.
Froissart's *Chronicles*, 118.
Fuller's *Worthies of England*, 193.
Furne, publisher of Paris, 241.
Fuseli, 230.
Fust, John, 15, 18, 39, 260.

Gaguin, Robert, 39.
Gaguin's *Compendium*, 122.
Galen's *De Temperamentis*, 1521, 120.
Galliot du Pré, 142.
Garamond, Claude, 137, 173, 253.
Gasparin of Bergamo, *Letters*, 59.
Gaston de Foix, 2.
Gaultier, Léonard, 157, 164.
Gavarni, designer, 243.
Gensfleisch, John, 15.
Gérard, 230.
Gérard de Leeu, 82.
Gering, Krantz, and Freyburger, 339.
Gering, Ulrich, printer in Paris, 57, 59, 62.
Gesù, Nicholas and Dominic Dal, 112.
Gibson, John, binder, 303.
Gigoux, Jean, the younger, 238, 239.
Gilbert, Sir John, 246.
Gilles Remacle, 97.
Gillot, Claude, 190, 196, 198.
Girodet, 230, 234.
Giunta, Lucantonio, 111, 113.
Glim, J., of Savigliano, 339.
Goetz, Nicholas, of Cologne, 338.
Gombauld, 169.

Gothan, B., of Lubeck, 339.
Gourmont, Gilles de, 127.
   ,,   Jean de, 153.
Graesse's *Trésor*, 325.
Grafton, Richard, 119.
Grandes Chroniques, Les, 96.
Grandes Heures, Les, by Vérard, 95.
Grandjean, 254.
Grand Navire Publishing Company, the, 174.
Grandville, designer, 243.
Gravelot, H. F., engraver, 203, 219.
Greuter, Fred, 169.
Grolier, Jehan, 131, 271, 276, 308.
Grosse la Batarde, 47.
Grünenberg, John, 116.
Gruninger, John, of Strasburg, 339.
Gruuthuise, Louis de la, 283.
Guadagnino, John Andrea, 112.
Guiffrey, J. J., 296.
Guise, Henri de, 288.
Guldinbeck, Berth., of Rome, 339.
Gutenberg, John, 2, 15, 17, 54, 255.
Gutenberg's Bible, 22, 23.
Guy Jouvenal, 106.

Hachette, L., publisher at Paris, 243.
Hagenbach, Peter, 44.
Hahn, Ulrich, 44, 63.
Hain's *Repertorium*, 325.
Hakluyt's *Principall Navigations*, 120.
Halle's *Chronicle*, 119.
Harding, S. and E., 220.
Hardouin, Gilles, 97.
Harleian Collection, 318.
Heilmann, Andrew, 16.
Heinecken, bibliographer, 349.
Heinlein, John, 56, 58, 61.
Henri II., 280, 286, 309.
Henri III., 158, 288, 290.
Henri IV., 162, 163, 292, 310, 314.
Heures à l'Usage de Rome, 8vo, 1488, 86.
Hiérat, Antoine, 168.
Higden's *Polychronicon*, 1527, 121.
Histoire du Costume, by Moreau, 211.
Historical notices, 351.
Hoernen, Arnold Ther, 44, 73.
Hogarth, William, 219.
Holbein's *Dance of Death*, 140.

Holbein, Hans, 75, 100.
Holinshed's Chronicles, 118.
Holl, Linhard, of Ulm, 338.
Hollar, W., 192.
Hortus Deliciarum, 169.
Houbraken, 219.
Houdard de la Motte, 196.
Hulsius, 192.
Hussner, George, of Strasburg, 339.
Hyginus' Poeticon Astronomicum, 65.

Iamblichus, the, of the Libri collection, 276.
Illustrated London News, 236.
Image makers, 5.
Imposition of pages, 255.
Imprimerie Nationale, 138.
Incunabula, 8, 321.
Isaac, Jasper, 164, 166.
Isenburg, Diether von, 36.

Jackson, J., engraver, 244.
Jacob, bibliophile, 238.
Jenson, Nicolas, 54, 65, 66, 113, 252, 261.
Johannot, the brothers, 237.
Johannot, Tony, 225.
Joly, Marc Antoine, 199.
Jombert, printer, 201.
Juda, Leon de, 139.
Juif, Gerard, 150.
Junius, Hadrian, 8, 9, 15.
Juste, François, 125.

Kalthœber, C., binder, 304.
Kaulbach, W. von, 248.
Kempis, Thomas à, De Imitatione, by J. and
    D. Elzevir, 172.
Kerver, Jacques, 139.
    „   Thielman, 96, 122.
Koberger, Antony, 44, 74.
Koelhof, first printer to use signatures, 44.
Koenig, Fr., inventor of steam press, 257.
Krantz, Martin, 57, 60.
Kyngston, John, 119.

Labarre, Jean de, 308.
Lacroix, Paul, 238.
Laferté, binder, 302.
Lafontaine, Les Contes, 207.
Lahure, printer, Paris, 244.

Lallemant, Jean, 272, 280.
Langland's Pierce Plowman, 1550, 118.
Langlois, François, 176.
Lanweryn, Mark, 273.
Lascaris' Greek Grammar, 1494, 109.
La Tour, binder, 296.
Le Bon, Jean, 308.
Le Brun, painter, 184.
Le Challeux, Jacques, 153.
Le Fevre, Malheurs de Troye, 81.
Le Gascon, binder, 292, 294.
Le Maire's, Jean, Illustrations de la Gaule,
    122.
Le Rouge's La Mer des Histoires, 84.
Le Roy, Adrien, 152.
Le Royer, Jean, 149.
Lebé, Guillaume, 156, 254.
Leclerc, Sebastien, 185.
Leech, John, 246.
Lemonnier, binder, 302.
Lenoir, Philippe, 284.
Lenox Library, 320.
Léonardo da Vinci, 113.
Léonord, 196.
Lepautre, engraver, 187.
Leroy, Guillaume, 106.
Lesné, binder, 303.
Letters of indulgence, 20.
Lettou, John, 51.
Levasseur, binder, 296.
Leu, Thomas de, 157, 163.
Lewis, Charles, binder, 304.
Leyden Library, 316.
Libraries, 307.
Linschoten, 192.
Lipsius, Justus, 155.
Livre de Perspective, by Jean Cousin, 148.
Livre de Portraiture, by Jean Cousin, 149,
    151.
Loggan, David, 317.
Lorenzo, Nicholas di, 67.
Lorris, Guillaume de, 106.
Lortic, binder, 303.
Loslein, Peter, 44.
Louis XI., 54, 123.
Louis XII., 108, 123, 268, 282.
Louis XIII., 169, 175, 163, 165, 292.
Louis XIV., 162, 182, 296, 298.
Louis XV., 209, 226, 314.

Louis XVI., 209, 227.
Louis XVIII., 227.
Louisa of Lorraine, 290.
Louvre editions, 231.
Luther, Martin, 21.
Lutzelburger, Hans, 141.

Macault, Antoine, 134.
Macé at Caen, 155.
Machlinia, William, 51.
Magasin Pittoresque, 236.
Mainyal, George, 62.
Maioli, Thomas, 272, 308.
Majuscules, 337.
Manipulus Curatorum, 61.
Mansfeldt, Count, 288.
Mansion, Colard, printer at Bruges, 46, 81, 253.
Manutius, Aldus, 66, 108, 113, 252, 271.
Marchant's, Guyot, *Dance of Death*, 1485, 101, 284.
Marius-Michell, binder, 303.
Marnef, Geoffroy de, 122.
    „   Jeanne de, 140.
Martyr's, Peter, *Decades of the New World*, 120.
Master, the, *à la Navette*, 81.
Matthews, binder, 303.
Matthias van der Goes, 82.
Mayer, Henry, 62.
Mazarin, Duc de, 311.
Mazarine Library, 311.
Mearne, Samuel, binder, 304.
Medemblick, John, of Cologne, 338.
Medici, Marie de, 162.
    „   Catherine de, 310.
    „   Cosmo de, 319.
Meissonier, 240.
Mellan, Claude, 166.
Mentelin, John, of Strasburg, 339.
Menzel, Adolph, 248.
Mer, la, des Histoires, 1488, 84, 122.
Merian, engraver, 316.
Merius, binder, 296.
Meslier, Denis, 98.
Meteren, Van, 118.
Method of collecting books, the, 352.
Metlinger at Dijon, 62.
Miegen, 168.

Milton, *Paradise Lost*, 193.
Miniatures, 345.
Minuscules, 337.
Mirror makers, 16.
Misprints, 330.
Missale Herbipolense, 1479, 81
Molière Œuvres, by Prault, 199.
Montenay's, Georgette de, *Emblèmes*, 151.
Monteregio, John de, *Calendario*, 65.
Montmorency, Anne de, 287.
More, Sir Thomas, 118.
Moreau, the younger, 204, 209.
Moretus, Jean, 157.
Mosaic binding, 299.
Mospach, Josse Ott von, 20.
Movable type, 9.
Moxon, publisher, 254.
Musæus' *Hero and Leander*, 1494, 108.
Muther's *Deutsche Bücherillustration*, 342.
Mystère de la Passion, 96.

Napoleonic era, 234.
National Library, Florence, 319.
    „   „   Paris, 316.
Nautonnier, Guillaume de, 167.
Necker, Jost, 114.
Nemeitz, 312.
Nesle, Marquis de, 288.
Neumeister, John, 44, 62.
Nevers, Duc de, 153, 311.
Nicholas V., Pope, 20.
Nivelle, Michel, 169, 174.
Norton, John, binder, 304.
Notary, Julian, 53.
Number of lines in a page, 336.
Nuremberg Chronicle, 77, 331.

Olivier de la Marche, 82.
Os, Peter van, 81.
Oswen, John, 121.
Ovid's *Métamorphoses*, by Sebastien Leclerc, 187.

Pacioli, Fra Luca, *De Divina Proportione*, 113.
Pagination, 333.
Palmart, Lambert, 46.
Panel-stamps, 265.

Pannartz and Sweynheim, printers at Rome, 44.
Panzer, *Annalen*, 325.
Paper-making, 259.
Papillon, Jean, 222.
  ,, Jean Baptiste, 222.
Paris, Jean de, 83.
  ,, Libraries, 315.
  ,, Missal, the, 97.
Pasdeloup, binder, 300.
Pasquier-Bonhomme, 83.
Pass, Crispin, 169.
Passe-Partout, the, 158.
Passionale Christi, of Lucas Cranach, 115.
Pasti, Matteo, 64.
Pastissier François, by the Elzevirs, 172.
Patisson, Mamert, 151.
Paulin, publisher, 238.
Payne, Roger, binder, 304.
Perréal, Jean, 83, 133.
Perrissin, Jean, 152.
Peter of Cremona's *Dante*, 1491, 70.
Peter van Os, 81.
Petit, Jean, 122, 127.
Petrarch's *Works*, 1501, 109.
Pfennigthurm, the, of Strasburg, 16.
Pfinzing, Melchior, 114.
Pfister, Albert, 34, 37, 62, 339.
Philippe II., 155.
Philippe, Laurent, 99.
Philippe le Noir, 122.
" Phiz " (H. K. Browne), 245.
Photography as means of illustration, 243.
Picart, Bernard, 190.
  ,, Jean, 168.
Piccini, J., 168.
Pico de la Mirandola, 108.
Pictor, Bernard, 44.
  ,, Loslein and Ratdolt, 65.
Pigorreau, gilder, 292.
Pigouchet, Philippe, 83, 85.
Plantin, Christopher, 116, 154, 253.
Platen, the, of the press, 257.
Playing cards, 5.
Pleydenwurff, William, 75.
Pluvinel's *Manège Royal*, 169.
Poliphili's *Hypnerotomachia*, 70.
Pollajuolo, 68.

Polyglot Bible by C. Plantin, 156.
  ,,   ,, by Vitré, 181.
Pompadour, M. de, 202, 288.
Ponte, Gotardo de, 113.
Portese, Agostino da, 112.
Portrait, the, in the book, 104.
Powell, Humphrey, 119.
Pratt, binder, 303.
Preller, Fried, 246, 248.
Price of rare books, 350.
Primaticcio, 143.
Printer's ink, 340.
  ,, marks, 103, 340.
Promptuaire des Médailles, 146.
Prud'hon, 230.
Prynne, William, 192.
Prys, John, of Strasburg, 339.
Psalter, second edition of 1459, 31.
  ,, the, of 1457, 340, 345.
Ptolemy's *Cosmographia*, 1478, 70.
Punctuation, 337.
Purchas: his Pilgrimes, 192.
Pymont, Topie de, 150.
Pynson, Richard, 52, 116, 118, 253.

Quaritch, Bernard, bookseller of London, 24, 351.
Quentel, Henry, of Cologne, 339.

Racine, Louvre edition, 231.
Raffet, designer, 241.
Rahmenschneiders, the, 82.
Raoul le Fevre, *Histoires de Troyes*, 56.
Rare books, 362.
Ratdolt, Erhard, 44, 65, 113, 341.
Rationarium Evangelistarum, 14.
Ravenna, Peter of, 112.
Remacle, Gilles, 97.
Rembold, Berthold, 62.
Renée of Ferrara, 137.
Retzsch, Moritz, designer, 246.
Reyser, Michael, of Eichstädt, 339.
Richter, Ludwig, designer, 247.
Riviere, binder, 303.
Roffet, Pierre, 284.
Rogers' *Poems*, 244.
Roman, Le, de la Rose, 105.
Rood, Theodoricus, first printer at Oxford, 52.

Rossi, Lorenzo, St. Jerome, 1497, 102.
Rosso, 143.
Roville, printer at Lyons, 145, 146.
Rowlandson, Thomas, 244.
Royal Library, Berlin, 319.
    „   „   Paris, 309.
Royal Printing House, Paris, 165, 175, 225.
Rubens, Peter Paul, 158.
Rubrics, 345, 347.
Ruette, binder, 297.
Rüppel, Berthold, 44.

Sadeler, Jean, 158.
Saint-Aubin, designer, 200, 209.
Saint-Pierre, Bernardin de, 234.
St. Albans, Boke of, 52.
St. Christopher, 1423, xylographic block, 4, 349.
St.Gelais,Octavian de,*Le Vergier d'Honneur*, 121.
St. Jerome, *Letters*, 1488, 66.
Salisbury Primer, 119.
Salomon, Bernard, 145.
Sanlecques, Jacques, 173, 254.
Sauval, 294.
Savary de Breves, 181.
Saxton's Atlas, 1579, 121.
Scaliger, Joseph, 317.
Scarron's *Works*, 177.
Schaffler, John, of Ulm, 339.
Schatzbehalter, the, 1491, 75.
Schäufelin, Hans Leonard, 114.
Schedel's, Dr. Hartmann, *Nuremberg Chronicle*, 77.
Schnorr von Carolsfeld, designer, 247.
Schoeffer, Peter, 19, 39, 56.
    „   Ivo, 168.
Schoepflin, 16.
Schongauer, Martin, 14.
Schönsperger, Hans, 114.
Schwind, Moritz von, designer, 246.
Séguier, Chancellor, 297.
Semblancay, 272, 280.
Seneca of Toledo, 15, 10, 116.
Servetus, 160.
Sessa, Melchior, 112.
Seyssel, Claude de, 122.
Sforza, 144, 308.
Shakespeare, Boydell's edition, 1791, 219.

Shakespeare, quarto edition, 119.
Shakespeare's *Works*, by Jaggard and Blount, 1623, 191.
Ship of Fools, 79.
Siberch, John, printer at Cambridge, 121.
Sidney's *Arcadia*, 1590, 118.
Signatures, 333.
Signs-manual, 3.
Singleton, Hugh, 119.
Size, the, 329.
Sloane, Sir Hans,founder of British Museum, 50.
Smirke, Robert, 220, 317.
Songe de Poliphile, Le, 140.
South Kensington Museum Art Library, 318.
Spacing, the, 335.
Speculum Hum. Salvationis, 7, 9.
Spenser's *Faerie Queene*, 1590, 118.
Spiegelmachers, 16.
Spiess, Weigand, 34.
Spindeler, Nicolas, 44.
Spira, Johannes de, 44, 339.
    „   Vendelin de, 44.
Stanhope Press, the, 257.
Stationers' Company, the, 119.
Stol, John, 82.
Stothard, Thomas, 220, 244.
Strange, Sir Robert, 219.
Sturt's Common Prayer Book, 219.
Sublet des Noyers, 175.
Sutton, Henry, 119.
Sweynheim, Conrad, printer at Rome, 44.

Tailleurs d'images, 4.
Tallemant des Reaux, 294.
Tessier, binder, 302.
Ther Hoernen, Arnold, first printer using Arabic numerals, 103.
Theuerdanck, The, 114, 115.
Thevet, *Cosmographie Universelle*, 151.
Thompson, John, engraver, 235, 244.
Thou, Christophe de, 281.
    „   Jacques de, 289, 310.
Times, The, 227.
Title, the, 327, 330.
Todtentantz, The, 73.
Tooling, gold, 270.
Topographical index, 366.
Tornes, Hans de, 145.

Torquemada, Cardinal, 42, 63.
Torresani, Andrea, 66, 108.
Tortorel, Jacques, 152.
Tory, Geoffroy, 126, 253, 276, 278, 282.
Trautz-Bauzonnet, binder, 303.
Traviès, designer, 242.
Treschel, Jean, 103, 140.
Treves, Peter of, 121.
Tritenheim, John of, 19.
Tyndall's English New Testament, 118.
Type casting, 251.
Type, forms of, 337.
Types, presses, paper, 250.

University Library, Cambridge, 318.

Valadel's editions, *Petits Formats*, 209.
Valdarfer, Christopher, 44.
Valla, *Elegantia Latinæ Linguæ*, 61.
Valladier, André, 164.
Valturius, *De Re Militari*, 64.
Van der Goes, Matthias, 82.
Van Dyck, Christopher, 254.
Van Meteren, 118.
Vatican Library, 319.
Veldener, John, 81.
Vellum, editions on, 343, 362.
Vérard, Antoine, 82, 92, 284.
Vergèce, Ange, 137.
Verona, John of, 64.
Viator, *Perspective*, 284.
Virgil's *Works*, by Aldus Manutius, 1501, 109.
Vitré, Antoine, 166, 180.
Vitruvius, by Cesariano, 113.
Vocabularium ex quo, the, 32.
Vollehoe, John of, 82.
Voragine's *Golden Legend*, 96, 112.
Vos, Martin de, 158.
Vostre, Simon, 82, 85, 86, 87, 284.
Vriedman, John, 150.
Vyel, Andrew, 44.

Walchius' *Decas Fabularum Generis Humani*, 36.

Walter, John, 227.
Walton's *Complete Angler*, 193.
Water-marks, 259, 344.
Watteau, 196.
Wechel, printer at Paris, 145.
Wencker, 16.
Wensler, Michael, printer, 62.
Werner, Anton von, designer, 246.
West, Benjamin, designer, 236.
Westall, Richard, designer, 220.
Westphalia, Conrad of, 46.
  „   John of, printer at Louvain, 46, 81.
Whitchurche, Edward, 119.
Wierix, engraver, 157, 164.
Winterberger, J., printer of Vienna, 63.
Woeriot, P., engraver, 128, 151.
Wohlgemuth, Michael, 75, 76.
Wolfenbüllel Library, 316.
Works belonging to a particular branch of literature, 359.
Works illustrated with wood-cuts, 361.
Works in particular languages, 356.
Works of importance for the history of printing, 360.
Works of particular countries, 357.
Works of particular periods, 358.
Works whose contents present special interest, 360.
Wynkyn de Worde, 51, 52, 119.

Xylographs, 4, 10.

Zaehnsdorf, J., binder, 303.
Zainer, Günther, of Augsburg, 72, 339.
  „   's *Book on Chess* by Jacopo da Cessole, 72.
  „   , John, of Ulm, 338.
Zell, Ulrich, 25, 34, 44.
Zeninger, Conr., of Nurnberg, 339.
Zenoi, Domenic, 168.
Zonta, L. (Giunta), 111.
Zuckermann, binder, 304.
Zum Jungen at Mayence, 18.